Dying The RIGHT Way

A System of Caregiving and Planning for Families

Dying The
RIGHT Way

A System of Caregiving and Planning for Families

Janice Louise Long

New York

Dying the RIGHT Way
A System of Caregiving and Planning For Families

ISBN 978-1-60037-700-6

Library of Congress Control Number: 2009935321

Cover Design by: Johnson2design
www.johnson2design.com
megan@johnson2design.com

MORGAN · JAMES
THE ENTREPRENEURIAL PUBLISHER

Morgan James Publishing
1225 Franklin Ave., STE 325
Garden City, NY 11530-1693
Toll Free 800-485-4943
www.MorganJamesPublishing.com

In an effort to support local communities, raise awareness and funds, Morgan James Publishing donates one percent of all book sales for the life of each book to Habitat for Humanity. Get involved today, visit **www.HelpHabitatForHumanity.org**.

DEDICATION

Dying the RIGHT Way

is dedicated with much love to my parents,

Joseph D. and Elizabeth M. Long

Table of Contents

List of Figures

List of Caregiving Forms

List of Tables

LIST OF ABBREVIATIONS

ACEP	American College of Emergency Physicians
AD	Alzheimer's Disease
AL	Assisted Living
APS	Adult Protective Services
CD	Compact diskette
CDC	Centers for Disease Control and Prevention
COPD	Chronic Obstructive Pulmonary Disease
CPR	Cardio Pulmonary Resuscitation
DMV	Department of Motor Vehicles
DNR	Do Not Resuscitate
DPOA	Durable Power of Attorney
EMR	Emergency Medical Response
GST	Generation-skipping transfer
HCPOA	Health Care Power of Attorney
HMO	Health Maintenance Organization
ICU	Intensive Care Unit
IIAM	International Institute for the Advancement of Medicine
IL	Independent Living
IRS	Internal Revenue Service
IV	Intravenous
Lt	Lieutenant
MD	Medical Doctor
MID	Multi-infarct dementia
MMSE	Mini-Mental State Examination
MOM	Milk of Magnesia
MPOA	Medical Power of Attorney
MRI	Magnetic Resonance Image
OMI	Office of the Medical Investigator
Rehab	Rehabilitative Care
SSA	Social Security Agency
TIA	Transient Ischemic Attack
TIN	Tax Identification Number
VasD	Vascular Dementia

ACKNOWLEDGEMENTS

First and foremost, I thank my parents for asking and trusting me to come and care for them during their final years. I am grateful that my life circumstances worked out so that I could do so. I love you both and miss you very much.

I thank my family – my brothers and my daughters for their support during the four year caregiving period. I know I was tired and grouchy sometimes, but I knew what the goal was and even through some tough times, we met the goal.

I thank Arizona (our caregiving supervisor) for helping me through the caregiving process. The caregiving maxims at the end of the Introduction are her daily mantra. I learned them as well and they do help. The maxims help one to take a deep breath, to rethink what is going on, and to regather the right perspective. "The patient is always 100% forgiven" and "Your Dad is still your Dad, he is just a different Dad" are my two favorite maxims.

I am so appreciative of those who reviewed my book and wrote endorsements for it. Michelle Tatlock, D.Min, BCC provided input relating to her experiences as a pastoral care gerontologist, from the perspectives of the patient, the family, and the health care team. Her input led to the research for a larger chapter relating to life support. I thank Dr. Effie Medford, Dr. Mary Harris, and Barbara Karnes, R.N. for the time they spent reading my book and offering suggestions for its improvement.

I thank my friends, of whom there are many, for their invaluable support and encouragement during the time I was writing, editing, and formatting this book. I treasure you always through the years and the travails of life.

Lastly, I thank my writing mentor, Tom Bird, and the Mastermind Writing Group for their support and love. Tom taught me the process to write this story, and the Mastermind Writing Group encouraged me throughout the process of finishing the details and getting the book to publication. I also thank Morgan James Publishing for being so wonderful, so understanding, and for making the publication process so enjoyable.

INTRODUCTION

This book was conceived during the four year period in which I took care of my parents in their final years of life. My desire is to help other families who might be experiencing caregiving or for those who anticipate performing caregiving duties. The four years were extremely rewarding to me, as I was able to spend that time with my parents and knew that I was contributing to their well being and health. Having a direct hands-on approach enabled them to live longer than they might have otherwise. I estimate that both of them lived <u>at least</u> a year longer and experienced an improved life style throughout the entire caregiving period, over what they had been managing on their own.

What did caregiving at home bring to our family? It kept Mom and Dad comfortable in their familiar surroundings (very important for Dad), they had one-on-one care, everything related to their care was monitored, and in reality – they were much happier being at home. Their most important concern was that we were able to honor their most implicit wish – to stay at home.

A Stitch in Time, Saves Nine

The concept behind "Dying the RIGHT Way" is to provide a guide for keeping your elders (or other family members requiring long term care) healthy as long as possible, providing one-on-one hands-on care, keeping their nutritional levels as high as possible, and planning for the time when their health declines to the point of death. The phrase "a stitch in time, saves nine" accurately describes this book. This guide includes caregiving tips, forms, legal concerns, what to plan for end-of-life care, questions to ask throughout the phases of planning, what questions to ask if a loved one is on life support or when hiring caregivers or interviewing residential facilities, how to plan for the funeral, and what needs to be done to settle the estate.

Please note that although this book is primarily focused on caring for the elderly, my thoughts are also meant for the parent who is approaching the time when they will need help, the adult children who want to help, but don't know how, and any family who is involved in caregiving. The caregiving information contained in this book will also be invaluable to caregivers.

My Mom and Dad did as much as they could to prepare their legal and funeral arrangements, based upon their own experiences with their parents and relatives. But several issues were not resolved during this time, e.g., what happens if they go on life support, will Mom be in pain when she dies, will she struggle for breath, how do I hire caregivers, how much do I pay them, what is Hospice, what happens after cremation.

During my caregiving experience, I learned many lessons and developed a caregiving system that may easily be implemented for any family. I am going to share these four years with you, my readers – the happiness, the worry, the heartbreaks, and the peace of knowing our family did the right thing to the best of our abilities.

Home Sweet Home

My parents were always insistent that they wanted to remain at "Home, Sweet Home" and did not want to go to a nursing home. In fact, Dad was adamant about this point. Fortunately, my Dad had the resources for us to hire private caregivers when the time came to do so. Certainly, in today's world, independent, assisted living, and nursing home facilities have evolved to allow cleaner, healthier facilities, with the inclusion of socialization and activities for the people that live there. My parents were not familiar with this new world of elder care. Like my parents, negative views of senior care residences still seem to be prevalent among many seniors.

> "Clarity, a division of Plantronics and the leading innovator and supplier of creative solutions to people with hearing loss, released the results to a research study conducted in late 2007 that took a closer look at aging in place. The study examined the attitudes and anxieties of the nation's aging population. Clarity interviewed senior citizens and baby boomer children to understand the perspectives of both older Americans and their caretakers. The study found the vast majority of seniors (89%) want to age in place-or grow older without having to move from their homes-but more than half (53%) were concerned about their ability to do so. Seniors cited health and memory problems and the inability to drive as reasons they may have to move from home."
>
> Retrieved August 2009, from http://www.journeytowellness.com/elder-care-article/aging-in-place-aging-with-grace.html

Taking care of unresolved issues took time away from not only my caregiving duties, but also, my family. Some of the issues that arose were surprises, as well. Having all possible details taken care of prior to the need for caregiving will make everything run more smoothly, especially during a crisis. We do not function at our best in the midst of a crisis. Perhaps sections of this book will enable your family to find aspects of your family life that can be taken care of sooner rather than later. Please be as open as possible with yourselves and your family during these arrangements to avoid future problems that might be unsettling. This book covers many aspects of caregiving and afterward.

Follow the Yellow Brick Road

I will briefly explain legal and financial concerns, what forms to prepare, and questions to think about. I am certainly not an expert in legal and accounting matters, but hopefully this information will guide your family in their decision making. I am also including a section on dying, what to watch for, what to expect, and how to deal with life support (should that circumstance occur). These sections may be read at appropriate times during the caregiving cycle, but try to read them before a crisis occurs. An important concept here is for the one being cared for to express any concerns or wishes that he/she may have about dying (see chapters on life support and dying). The non-profit organization Aging with Dignity (http://www.agingwithdignity.org) has been successful in getting 43 states to adopt the "Five Wishes™" document, in lieu of a living will. This document may be ordered from the internet, outlining the wishes of each person being cared for to outline their desires during any critical care period. A proprietary copy of the Five Wishes is included in Appendix III – this copy lists 40 states that have adopted the Five Wishes™, but three more states have been added recently.

Many more resources are available on the Internet now than there were at the time I was performing caregiving duties. New information appears daily. If I had had even 1/10th of the resources that are available now, my job would have been much easier. However, I had many questions that I could not get answers to, even from our Hospice staff. I hope to answer some of these questions in this book. Our story is written as a guide to follow and to be added to as each circumstance allows. Hopefully, our story and the accommodations we made may be worked into each personal situation. Please note that some stories and forms are repeated for emphasis in a particular section.

During this time, I developed a system of forms, tips and hints for caregiving that I wish to share with others. My express hope is that this book will enable others to travel through this time passage more easily, with better family relationships. Communication is THE key, both to honor your parent(s) wishes, to find out how they want to be cared for, what their final wishes are, and to communicate these wishes to the family. The family caregiver may also wish to search within himself/herself to develop where the caregiving lines need to be drawn and professional caregiving personnel brought in, e.g., maintaining personal dignity of the parent, bathing, toileting, changing diapers, etc.

As my Mom had emphysema with dementia, and my Dad had Alzheimer's Disease, I am including information on dementia and Alzheimer's. The Centers for Disease Control and Prevention (CDC) website reports that the incidence of Alzheimer's doubles every five years beyond the age of 65 and may be as high as 50% after the age of 85.

Retrieved August 2009, from: http://www.cdc.gov/Features/Alzheimers/

There appears to be a racial component as well, especially with those who have both hypertension and high cholesterol. Current research has been done on African-Americans, but not on other racial groups.

> "Aggressive research is underway to identify the cause of Alzheimer's and links have been drawn to heredity, genetics and environmental factors. African–Americans seem more susceptible to the disease than other groups according to recent medical research. Because some research has shown Alzheimer's to be anywhere between 14 and 100% more prevalent among Blacks than whites, prevention and control of vascular risks like hypertension and high cholesterol is critically important. If there is a family history of the disease, early screening for Alzheimer's is also vital."

> Retrieved August 2009, from: http://www.journeytowellness.com/elder-care-article/the-long-goodbye-alzheimers-and-african-americans.html

Dementia is a debilitating disease which greatly affects the person who has it, the family members, and the primary caregivers. The health of the caregiver is especially important. Literature shows that the caregiver's health becomes affected as well, and can be debilitating enough that the caregiver becomes ill themselves. The effect on the caregiver's health is now termed "Caregiver Stress Syndrome" and has been studied for over 25 years.

"Research on caregivers has been ongoing for 25 years, and we have found repeatedly that many family caregivers suffer serious physical and mental symptoms as a result of the stresses of caregiving. Those symptoms include constant fatigue, sleeping difficulties, depression, anxiety, memory problems, high blood pressure, migraines, and lowered immune functioning resulting in higher susceptibility to infection. Caregivers are also more likely to neglect their health and mental health because of their caregiving responsibilities. Taken together, this cluster of symptoms and behaviors is sometimes referred to as "caregiver stress syndrome.""

Retrieved August 2009, from: http://www.journeytowellness.com/elder-care-article/responding-to-caregiver-stress-syndrome.html

Interestingly, a new study released in July 2009 on the caregiver relationship with the Alzheimer's patient shows that the closeness of this relationship (e.g., spouse, child) slows the progression of this disease.

"July 22, 2009-A study led by Johns Hopkins and Utah State University researchers suggests that a particularly close relationship with caregivers may give people with Alzheimer's disease a marked edge over those without one in retaining mind and brain function over time. The beneficial effect of emotional intimacy that the researchers saw among participants was on par with some drugs used to treat the disease.

A report on the study, believed to be the first to show that the patient-caregiver relationship may directly influence progression of Alzheimer's disease, is published in the September 2009 *The Journals of Gerontology Series B: Psychological Sciences and Social Sciences* and currently available online."

Retrieved October 2009, from: Press Release
http://www.hopkinsmedicine.org/Press_releases/2009/07_22a_09.html

The Alzheimer's Organization now distributes a brochure which lists the 10 symptoms of caregiver stress, and 10 steps to manage caregivers stress. The text for the 10 steps from this brochure appears on pages 137-138 in Chapter 6 under Stress, Caregiving.

I will share my Mom's and Dad's stories, explain what we did well, what we didn't do so well, the situations that came up, and will also include aspects of caregiving that I didn't have information about. This story is based upon my parent's health conditions, up to and including their deaths. Every patient is different and other's experiences will not be the same and may be much more difficult than I experienced. Remember that mistakes will be made, mishaps will occur, and allow for forgiveness when this happens. This is an important concept. It is next to impossible for mistakes not to happen occasionally. Condemning the caregiver will only cause further hardship and grief for everyone. The ultimate goal is for the loved one to have the best care possible.

Throughout my sadness and grief over losing my parents, I always had the desire to write this book to try and help other families. Writing this book created lots of tears, but became a healing process for me – remembering the four years I shared with Mom and Dad during their final years and illnesses. I had so many questions – from fear of the unknown and fear of their being in pain. I was always afraid my mother would suffocate during the dying process, but this did not happen. Throughout this story, I will be sharing our journey, personal thoughts, happy and sad occasions, how I lost my parents, and how we made this journey. As my career had revolved around health care and systems management, I became THE advocate for my parent's lives and their health, at their request.

Following the Introduction, the circumstances of how I came to caregive, what my Mom and Dad's situations were at that time, as well as a discussion of our caregiving continuum and the decline continuum are included in Chapter 1. Chapters 2 and 3 tell my Mom's and Dad's story, their individual health problems and what happened during their individual periods of caregiving. Chapters 4, 5, and 6 are all related to caregiving. Chapter 4 talks about how we tried to make living circumstances as easy as possible, how long it was until we needed outside caregiving personnel, how we went from part-time caregiving to full-time caregiving, and presents the concept of caregiving costs and Hospice. Chapter 5 introduces the levels and types of caregivers, offers a suggestion of a caregiver contract, discusses job responsibilities, and supplies. Chapter 6 contains the caregiving forms that were used in our caregiving continuum, and offers suggestions about daily caregiving. Chapter 7 discusses the types of residential facilities, questions to ask when looking for a facility, offers an idea of what costs could be, what rights your loved one has when in a residential setting, and an extensive discussion on Hospice: the team members, questions to ask when interviewing Hospice organizations, and the concept of a Health History Form. Chapter 8 talks about dying and life support, what to do when a loved one suddenly goes on life support, how the hospital and doctors might react, the Five Wishes document, what the dying person may be thinking, the dying process, and organ/tissue donation. Chapter 9 discusses the phases that the body goes through during the active dying process. Chapter 10 introduces the concept of grief and the stages of grief. Chapter 11 presents the legal forms such as: the Durable Power of Attorney (DPOA), the Healthcare Power of Attorney or Medical Power of Attorney (HCPOA, MPOA), the Do Not Resuscitate (DNR), and the Five Wishes, offers a Document Checklist, and information about finances and the estate rule. Chapter 12 lists steps for planning a funeral and offers suggestions by example. Chapter 13 lists the duties of the personal representative or executor for the settling of the estate. Six appendices follow the chapters. Appendix I includes a safety guide to prevent seniors from falling. Appendix II offers four actual questions from the Mini Mental State Exam (MMSE) and a simple interpretation of the test. The MMSE and any diagnosis resulting from the test should be performed by a medical doctor specializing in dementia. Appendix III offers a proprietary copy of the Five Wishes – a document that one may order and fill out to indicate wishes for sudden medical emergencies or for the end of life period: who is the designated person to make healthcare decisions, the types of medical treatment desired, comfort wishes, how family members or caregivers should treat the person, and what the person wants their family to know. Appendix IV offers information about massage oils as well as several recipes that we used for my parents. Appendix V offers several food recipes that I used with my parents. These recipes are delicious and easy for elders to eat. Appendix VI lists web resources by category of service.

If this book helps only one family, I will be happy. My heart goes out to all families that choose to caregive for their loved ones, and I wish all of you the best. I know everyone's caregiving journey is different, and some journeys will be more difficult than others.

Although this book primarily refers to my parents, all or part of this caregiving system could be adapted to any family member. Throughout the book, the person being cared for will be referred to as Mom, Dad, parent, loved one, and patient.

(Please note that the names in this book have been changed to protect the identities of those mentioned.)

Maxim's to Caregive By

Your Dad is still your Dad, he is just a different Dad

The patient is always 100% forgiven

Applaud and Praise

Always tell them they are beautiful

Give them a job and praise them for the job

Tell them: I really need your help -- can you help me?

Every day is an adventure - don't know who patient is going to be from day to day

Go into their world - don't bring them into your world

Don't take offense when they get angry, cuss you out, or accuse you of lying – they won't remember and don't mean it

Tell them: When you are ready, just let me know or come and get me

There's no crime in getting old - the patient may be a prisoner in his/her own mind, but not in reality. Don't treat them like they are a criminal

Their world is whatever age they are at

Every day is a new day - the patient/caregiver won't know what the day is like until it is experienced

Wait five minutes if patient doesn't want to do something -- their perspective will change and they won't remember what happened

Using the words "Do you remember" is a pitfall. The patient may not remember and may feel badly that they can't.

Try less – give in more

Accommodate, Accommodate, Accommodate

Create a loving and healthy environment

Use common sense, take deep breaths, and be cheerful

Change is constant

Don't take this path by yourself – support is absolutely crucial to your wellbeing now and afterwards

Note – these maxims may be used for caregiving or converted into maxims to live by, to keep marriages wholesome and healthy, to raise children by, and to keep friends by.

Courtesy of Arizona, our caregiving supervisor
© Copyright 2010, Janice Louise Long

Chapter 1:

My Dad Lost His Taxes – I didn't expect HIM to need help!

I flew home the first weekend of April in 2003, and for the first time, took a taxi to Mom and Dad's house. Dad had always picked me up at the airport, so this was a big change. To my surprise, Dad was waiting on the porch with the front door open. I surmised he had been watching for me. However, to see him on the porch was very unusual. Usually, Mom and Dad would just wait for me in the living room in their recliners and get up when I walked in the door. The first words Dad spoke to me were "We've got a problem!" Not "Hello" or "How was your flight?" My alarm sensors immediately went off – thinking something had happened to Mom. But no --- that wasn't it. I replied, "What's the problem, Dad?" His next statement was, "I can't find my taxes." That hit me right between the eyes! "What do you mean, Dad, you can't find your taxes?" His reply was, "I've lost them. I've driven all over town and I can't find them." I queried, "Do you know who you took them to?" "No," was the soft reply.

OK – just to backtrack the timing – it is now April 4th, 11 days before taxes are due. I was only going to be home 2-1/2 days. Needless to say, I was very busy that weekend. I had flown home to attend a funeral, but now had to deal with Dad's lawyer (to rewrite their Durable Power of Attorney and Healthcare Power of Attorney) and needed to find an accountant to extend Dad's taxes until we could figure out what to do. This short span of time was also spent assessing Mom and Dad's health.

Mom and Dad had four children, one girl and then, three boys. I was, therefore, the oldest and the only girl. Mom and Dad seemed to know that they were having trouble and asked me to move home to help out. They were excited that I thought I could arrange for this to work. I flew back to Virginia and told my boss that I would have to move home to care for my parents. Mom had been having problems, and I had been thinking that my trips back home would just become more frequent. I was not prepared for Dad to have a larger health problem than Mom.

Dad was Mom's caretaker, paid the bills, did the shopping and errands, and took care of the house. Now, he couldn't do those things. I telephoned my oldest brother in Texas, and he left immediately for Albuquerque, saying he could stay with Mom and Dad until I arrived. Back in Virginia, I prepared my house for sale and packed to move my children (just out of high school) and myself. We arrived in Albuquerque the 5th of July. An intervening trip found us a house to live in. My boss was very accommodating, even figuring out a way for me to telecommute from my Dad's house, so that I would have an income for my living expenses and my family. I was so fortunate!! My oldest brother also changed his life completely, moving back to Albuquerque and uprooting his career. We chose to make these changes for our parents. Our parents had given us a great upbringing and deserved our help.

I performed the role of caregiver for my parents for four years. My Mom lived for 2-1/2 years, and my Dad for four years. I learned how to keep their lives as healthy and independent as possible. They were able to stay in their home until they died – this was their PARAMOUNT WISH.

As a parent, it is vitally important to maintain independence and mobility for as long as possible. You, as a parent, and you, as a child, need to recognize this concept from both points of view. The parent needs to recognize when problems are occurring (if possible) and <u>be willing</u> to share these problems with the child(ren). You, the child, <u>need to watch for obstacles</u> that the parent is experiencing and ease them into another manner of handling the obstacle. Most of the time, this is just using common sense, seeing what is difficult, and figuring out another easier way to perform the task.

An example of this could be as simple as buying plastic quart jars to pour the gallon of milk or juice into. The gallon or even half-gallon size has become too cumbersome or too heavy for the parent to handle. Pouring the substance into smaller jars allows the parent to continue to serve their own needs in an easier manner. One quart plastic jars are available in most grocery stores. (The parent may be a frugal person and still wish for the gallon size to be purchased, as this size is generally less expensive.) Working on these types of situations together will create a common bond between the parent and the child, and perhaps, make future problems easier to deal with.

Extreme frustration exists on both sides. The parent does not want to admit they cannot do something. The child is extremely worried, but doesn't want to say anything until he/she has to. The parent doesn't want the child to worry or to be bothered with picky little details. I will tell you from my experience that the child is going to worry, no matter what. The child will actually be quite relieved to be asked to help and to be able to be of help.

Their Beginning

Mom and Dad were in the generation that participated in World War II. Both were in college at the beginning of the war, and Dad was a civil engineer in the Navy during the latter years of the war. They married in 1947 after Mom graduated from an internship in dietetics. During this time, smoking and drinking of alcohol were prevalent in their age groups. My Mom began smoking during her first year of college (away from home) and never stopped until she was diagnosed with emphysema at approximately age 69 – fifty years of cigarettes. Dad kept up with her, but would sometimes smoke cigars or pipes, instead of the cigarettes. For as long as I can remember, the kids would be shooed out of the living room when Dad came home from work. This was their time together to catch up on the day, to watch the news, and to relax with a couple of drinks, usually Martinis or Manhattans.

I was born as a premature infant ten months after their wedding, weighing in at 2-1/2 pounds. From that time forward, Mom stayed home to raise the children. Five years after they were married, they moved to Albuquerque to clear up my asthma and Dad really began his career as an architectural engineer at that point. He began his own business the year I graduated from high school, growing his company into one of the largest architectural firms in the state by the time he retired. Four children were born over 11 years. Mom and Dad's favorite hobbies were golf and reading. Dad also gardened and grew fruit and vegetables for our table. Dad was also an excellent water color artist.

The Care Beginning – Reality Set In

Mom and Dad really wanted to keep their independence, but knew they needed help. I stayed in my office for the entire day, with the exception of fixing their lunch or answering questions for them. I would arrive early in the morning and help Mom get dressed and do her hair. Grocery shopping or errands were performed even earlier in the morning or after work.

Finances, mail, and bills were worked on in the evenings at home. Even though I spent the majority of the day in the office and let them spend their time together in the living room, they insisted that I leave as soon as I could, giving them some alone time.

Medication management is especially crucial. When I arrived home to begin the caregiving for my parents, they had not taken their medications (meds) for three days. They were not even sure what meds to take when, as all the pill vials were stored in the refrigerator in one tray. The meds had been lumped into morning meds, whether or not that was the appropriate time to take them. The first thing we accomplished was to buy two color-coded (different colors for each person), seven day (Sunday through Saturday) pill boxes, one for Mom and one for Dad.

It was no problem for them to take their medications, once the boxes were in front of them by their placemats each day. They used the daily newspaper to tell which day it was, and took their meds every morning with their breakfast. Dad didn't like to swallow pills. He invariably left them to the end of the meal, and took them after Mom had left the table to get dressed. Sometimes, Mom would harass him to take them, which upset him. I just explained to her that it took him some time to get the pills down, and that I would check on him to make sure he took them. She knew he had trouble taking them and worried that he wouldn't take them if she wasn't in the room.

A calendar was also put on the kitchen counter, with each day crossed off as it occurred. This way, the date and day of the week could be easily found either from the calendar or from the newspaper. Doctor's and other appointments were written on this calendar, e.g., oxygen delivery, cleaning lady, birthdays, etc. Dad loved this calendar and checked it every morning. He was always ready early for any appointments or watching for the cleaning lady to arrive. If she was late, he was remarking on it. Eventually, the calendar was no longer used, as it just wasn't remembered by him. The newspaper still worked for some time. At any rate, having the calendar and the newspaper helped them to keep track of what day it was, which day to open on the pill box, and what was happening in their lives.

Mom and Dad always had their routines. Dad would make the coffee in the morning and get the newspaper from the driveway. Their regular breakfast was cereal, juice, and raisin toast. Occasionally, I bought them a granola type flake cereal that had extra nutrients and tasted better. They appreciated new tastes and changes from their routine, bland diet. I found that they loved bacon and bought microwaveable bacon that only took three minutes to fix – I gave them bacon every day. I was constantly on the search for new meal ideas to increase their nutritional intake. It was quite evident that, as many elderly do, that they were already eating foods that required minimum preparation and were not always nutritional.

It became important to watch and see what was difficult for them to do and adjust to help them stay independent. Thus, the plastic containers for milk and juice were the first adaptation we made. Dad would still occasionally spill some in the pouring process as he only had sight in one eye, but he could lift the containers much more easily. He would quickly wipe up any spills, so Mom wouldn't see them. (He usually poured the drinks at the higher countertop and we could quickly wipe up any spills.)

Funny how one remembers a particular day and time – like where I was when I heard that President John F. Kennedy had been shot. I was in high school and was leaving school early for a dermatology appoint to have some warts burned off my knee. Or, where one was on 9-11-2001 when New York City and the Pentagon were attacked (I lived in Fairfax, Virginia). The particular day I am thinking about was a sunny, warmer, spring day in late March. I was just beginning to leave my windows and doors open. I made my usual weekly (at least) telephone call home to my parents to see how they were doing. My time zone was two hours later than theirs, so it was usually possible to call before their 7 pm bedtime. During this conversation, Dad's words became unintelligible. I kept asking both of them if he was OK – they assured me that all was well. My first fear was that Dad had had a stroke. I called my oldest brother to talk to him. After our initial greeting, his first words to me were -- "Do you think Dad had a stroke?" – even before I said anything. We compared notes. An ensuing phone call to the two younger brothers sent them over to our parents' house to check on them. The report came back – all is well! I was glad there was no immediate problem, but I was still concerned. I was going to go home ten days later for a funeral, and would double-check the situation at that time. That's when Dad told me he lost his taxes!

Digressing to fill in some of Mom and Dad's prior health history – six months before, my Mom had fallen and cracked her hip. As she had previously been diagnosed with emphysema, her surgical repair was performed under local anesthesia (rather than general). Dad called me that night (a Wednesday) to let me know that she was in the hospital. I talked to her briefly and she seemed fine. The next day I went to work and told my boss that I might have to fly home, but that I would let her know – I just had a bad feeling. I left that evening to pick up my daughter from upstate New York. The next afternoon I called my Mom's hospital room to talk to her. The phone rang and rang – not normal for a bedridden patient. Finally, a nurse answered. Her questions to my queries were vague and she sounded concerned. I began to panic!! A phone call to my girlfriend, a doctor, elicited a visit by her to check on my Mom. Sure enough, my Mom had crashed -- she had been put on a respirator (automatic breathing device) and moved to the Intensive Care Unit (ICU).

The next morning (Friday), I flew home to Albuquerque, arriving at the hospital at midnight. Mom was under morphine sedation, but the nursing staff could adjust the sedation and allow her to wake up, so I could tell her I was there. The hardest thing I ever did that day was to go home and explain to Dad what was happening – that Mom's condition had become worse and that she might not live through this episode. Understandably, Dad couldn't fathom such an outcome. They would have been married for 55 years that month. Over the previous 10 years, Dad had taken care of Mother, as her breathing became shallower and her emphysema worsened. At the time of this incident, she stayed home most of the time and would only go out occasionally. She did some of the cooking, but none of the errands or shopping.

On the following Monday, the pulmonologist (lung doctor) woke Mom up from the sedation and explained to her that she had been on life support for five days, trying to allow her to heal from her surgery. He asked her for permission to remove the life support. She gave it. He explained that he was not sure how she would react and asked for permission to reinsert the life support (respirator) if she couldn't breathe. She was also able to give her permission for that to occur. Holding our breaths, the family went to the waiting room. All of the extended family was there. It took over thirty minutes to find out what happened.

Amazingly, Mom did very well, was breathing on her own, and an hour later was moved out of the ICU to a step-down unit (lower level of care). Evidently, the five days of sedation had allowed enough healing to occur that she could now breathe on her own. Two days after that, she moved to the Rehabilitation (Rehab) Unit for about three weeks until she could go home. We don't know why Mom "crashed" following this surgery, which was performed under a local anesthetic, unless even that type of anesthetic was too much for the fragility of her lungs.

I stayed with Dad a total of 10 days until we knew Mom was stable and in the rehab unit, and that he was all right himself. This hospitalization took a lot of steam out of Dad, and perhaps, in retrospect, this episode allowed the Alzheimer's disease to begin taking control. At the beginning of the ten days, he relied on me totally – to drive, to make decisions, to explain, to discuss what had happened. He wanted to visit the hospital at least three times a day and worried incessantly in the meantime. Once Mom went to the Rehab unit, Dad began to relax, and by the time I left, he was much more like himself. It took Mom six months to recover from this hospitalization, bringing us now to the new issue of Dad's health.

Once I arrived permanently, Mom and Dad's lives ran more smoothly. Their ages at this time were 79 and 81. Occasionally, when doing Mom's hair in the morning, she would have trouble talking or blank out for a few seconds. These little black outs were tiny strokes, called Transient Ischemic Attacks (TIA's). We took Mom to the doctor for confirmation, and she was given Plavix, a blood thinner, as a new medication. Dad's health deteriorated a lot over the first six months to the point that both of them were worried. Mom told me one morning while I was doing her hair that she was very frightened that Dad would die first and leave her a widow. She could not bear to lose him and be left behind without him. Besides breaking out in tears, all I could do was to tell her we just didn't know what was going to happen, but that we would do our best to help him. As she was being affected by dementia (from the TIAs) herself, I explained to her over and over that Dad had Alzheimer's Disease and that she needed to help him by talking gently to him or explaining step-by-step what to do. She would understand but wouldn't always remember.

Health Management and Dad's Diagnosis

Neither Dad nor Mom had a primary care physician when I arrived. Mom had a pulmonologist and Dad had an oncologist (cancer doctor) from a prior incident with colon cancer (from whom he had been released). I am not even sure how they had renewed their medications. This became the first agenda item, after stabilizing their medication routines. We established both of them with a primary care doctor, whose job was to oversee their health and to bring in specialists, as needed. One of the first actions the primary care doctor performed was to have both of them sign a Do Not Resuscitate (DNR) order and placed it on their primary care charts.

Dad's primary care visit immediately created a flurry of blood tests to rule out certain diagnoses, and a referral to the neurologist. It was September by the time we were able to obtain the neurology appointment. The neurologist performed a physical, some verbal testing on Dad, and was able to diagnose Alzheimer's disease from his history and the testing. The verbal testing is called a Mini-Mental State Examination (MMSE). The MMSE consists of thirty simple questions to determine one's mental state and capacity. Types of information that could be asked are: simple questions about their daily life, asking the patient to remember three words for a few minutes (orange, apple, airplane) and then asking the patient to repeat these three words later, giving the patient a pencil and a piece of paper and (under direction) asking him to draw three shapes with specific intersecting points. (Dad actually did pretty well at this part, since he was good at art.) But he looked up at me several times during this questioning and said, "Boy, am I really dumb!" This, from an Architectural Engineer who had run his own business for over twenty years, was excruciating to hear.

The first time Dad took the MMSE in September of 2003, he scored an 11 out of a possible score of 30. My heart broke when I heard the confirmation of the diagnosis of Alzheimer's disease. Dad had always been able to do Math in his head, had owned a successful company, and was so smart. He was always known as an honest man who kept his word. Then, to my surprise, the neurologist turned to me and said, "I bet you thought he had had a stroke." Which, of course, was true. The neurologist went on to explain that highly educated, highly functioning people can hide their Alzheimer's and their failing abilities for some time. Then, suddenly, something will happen and bring the Alzheimer's into focus, and the patient can no longer keep everything together. I have included an example of four actual MMSE questions in Appendix II, courtesy of PAR, Inc.

This type of scenario is what happened to Dad. His condition became unstable during Mom's hospitalization the prior September, and then taking care of her for the six months afterwards was more than he could handle. It was probably an accident, but for us a stroke of fortune, that we had caught the garbled words during telephone conversations, as this caused us to spring into action. Who knows what would have happened otherwise -- a car accident, Dad getting lost while driving, or an emergency even worse than what we encountered or could imagine?

The neurologist also explained that patient's spouses help them hide their disease, either by performing actions for them or by speaking for them. Remember that my Dad was taking care of all the shopping and errands. Mom had broken her other hip about nine years prior to these events, had two surgeries, and no longer drove or went out as often. She had been put on oxygen following that surgery and had quit smoking immediately. So, Dad was the chief "cook and bottle-washer" of the household, so to speak. Mom's cover-up was in the form of conversation and correcting statements that Dad would make.

Dad was initially put on a drug named Aricept. We saw an improvement in Dad's condition almost immediately. These improvements occurred over time, gradually became plateaus, and eventually took downturns into a worsening condition. When Dad's condition would deteriorate, we would try increasing, changing, or adding to his medications to create change. About six months after his diagnosis, he began deteriorating again. This deterioration occurred almost simultaneously with the introduction of a new Alzheimer's drug – Namenda. We began a course of treatment combining the Namenda with the Aricept. Again, an improvement and stabilization occurred in Dad's behavior and abilities.

With both Mom and Dad, this pattern of improvement, stabilization, and deterioration occurred many times. The pattern also showed that once a deterioration occurred, the rise back would not be to as high a level of functioning that once been. The pattern is shown below in Figure 1.

Figure 1: Decline Continuum

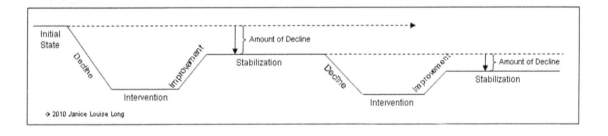

Stabilization periods would be shorter and shorter as the course of their diseases progressed. One can expect many levels of decline over a period of caregiving. Note that improvements may vary from patient to patient.

Dad began to have trouble remembering how to make the coffee, so I would fill up the canister with water and coffee each night, so that all he had to do in the morning was push the "on" button. He was so excited that this process had suddenly become so easy for him and he could still be responsible for making the coffee. We still had a couple of calamities if the filter folded over and the grounds spilled out into the pot or he would forget that there was already water in the canister. He would add more water, turn on the pot, and we would have coffee all over the countertop. I would walk in and the first thing I would hear about is how awful the coffee was or the coffee pot wasn't working. It was easy to "magically" fix it and make a new pot, becoming the "hero" of the morning. Dad would always say, "How did you do that?" in a wondering voice. These small calamities became more frequent over time.

Other times, he could not remember how to shut the car door or buckle his seat belt. He did not know how to take a shower. Shortly after moving to Albuquerque, I realized Dad wasn't taking showers. I began talking to him about needing to be clean. Finally, one day I took him to the shower and turned on the water to get warm. I asked him to take off his clothes, and get into the shower and soap down. He was done in about 30 seconds. I asked him what happened, and he told me he got cold, so he got out. That was when I realized that he had forgotten what to do – how to adjust the water, what to do with the soap, how to rinse off – the entire process.

I felt so bad for him and felt bad that I hadn't recognized the problem earlier. A personal "line in the sand" for me was bathing and toileting my Dad. I felt this was a dignity issue and I didn't want to offend him or take away his dignity. If I didn't have any alternatives, of course, I would have performed these duties. Probably after the first few instances, I would have been more comfortable and it wouldn't have mattered. In the meantime, my brothers would attempt to get him showered on the weekends.

Medical Advocacy

My background was in health care. I had either worked in hospitals as a nuclear medicine technologist or with hospital personnel and systems in health care management my entire career. I was familiar with the health system, its problems, managed care, insurance problems, the role of the primary care provider or gatekeeper, and generally knew enough about medicine to understand any medical language or explanations. Thus, I was the perfect family member to take on the role of medical advocate. I was really happy when Mom and Dad asked me if I could come home to help them. When they did that, I asked them if they wanted to discuss this decision with my brothers – they said – "NO – it is our decision and we will let them know."

I really do not know how families without an internal medical advocate cope with the health care system. I know hospital systems and Hospice organizations have social workers to help out. But, I sincerely recommend that someone in the family (that has a vested interest in the health of the patient) take on this role. <u>I cannot stress this enough</u>. My parents would not only not understand what the doctor said, but wouldn't be able to remember what he said either. I went to all doctor's appointments, monitored their medications, and translated for my brothers. I had explained to Dad and the family what was happening to Mom during her hospitalization and respiratory crash, but it was hard for him to conceptualize the difference between this episode and earlier ones. Mom could understand most of the explanations, but with her low level of dementia, could not remember any instructions. Eventually, the point came that anytime a care provider (nurse or doctor) would ask them a question, their heads would immediately and simultaneously bob over to my direction to answer for them, as they just didn't know the answers.

As we were very ambivalent about placing Mom and Dad in a facility, I began looking for full-time care personnel. At the same time, one of my brothers and I visited three care facilities to be prepared in case we needed to resort to that alternative. About eight months before this period, we had begun hiring evening staff from 4:00 to 8:00 p.m. These staff aides were hired from a local agency (see cost section) and were available seven days a week. The most difficult part of this process was to keep the same staff over time, so that Mom and Dad would be familiar with them. I did receive a few phone calls that Dad had kicked the caregiver out and had locked the door, refusing to let the caregiver back in. Coaxing by telephone calls or visits would then be required to get the caregiver back into the house. Reassurance was the key here. A gentle reminder that the caregivers were there to help them and make sure that Mom and Dad were in bed safely for the night would generally suffice. Also, both of them were insistent about not having me there more than I needed to be, although they were generally glad when I was. I didn't mind being there longer, but their underlying thoughts were that I had my own life too.

As mentioned before, their biggest concern was to remain independent. If they were alone at night and could get up by themselves, that time gave them a sense of independence. They knew that having help was essential, and Mom told my best friend that she worried that I wouldn't stay through the end. I didn't know this until after Mom died. Mom and I always had our differences, and she knew how to get my goat. I have to admit, I did get mad at her a couple of times over the 2-1/2 years that she was still alive, but I thought we did well to only have two brief blow-ups. After all, she knew that I loved them and was trying to do what was best for them. I also think that the arguments between the two of them or between Mom and I were a way for all of us to express worry and the wish for Mom and Dad to stay as healthy as possible. Subconsciously, they were both worried about the other one, but didn't express that worry to each other.

The emotions ran very high for me during this time. It was extremely difficult to watch them decline. Each decline brought a lower level of functioning than before. Adjustments needed to be made with new accommodations each time a decline occurred. Awareness of the level of functioning of each person separately is required at all times. Watch to see what is difficult at the time you are watching. Try to discern what is different. Figure out how to help them acclimate to new situations and keep them as independent as possible. Or, make it seem like they are doing as much as possible on their own, even though independence is not really an issue anymore.

Figure 2 is a picture of the care continuum (the period of care and milestones during that period) that occurred over the four years of caregiving. The care cycle will be different for each person, but this picture should give an idea of the ups and downs and time frame.

Figure 2: Care Continuum

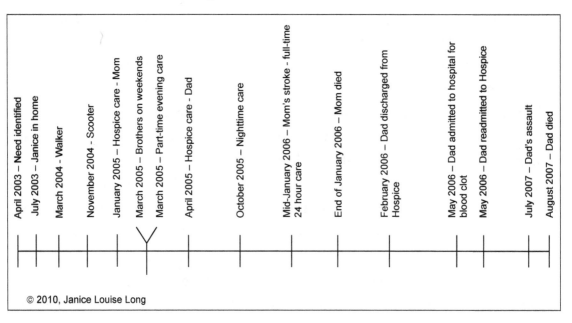

© 2010, Janice Louise Long

By March 2004, safety was again a primary concern. I was receiving more frequent telephone calls from Dad requiring assistance on the weekends. I would normally drop by to check on them at least once during the weekend. But, now, it was becoming obvious that even heating meals in the microwave or making coffee was beginning to be difficult. Mom was having more trouble walking the distance to the bathroom.

One adjustment we made for Mom was to get her a walker with a seat and brakes. That way she could just stop and sit down if she was too tired. Having the walker enabled her to lean on the walker for stability, and to sit on the walker seat to rest as she needed to. The walker also had lockable brakes to push into place to hold the walker steady, however, Mom usually did not remember to use them.

Adjustments to Dad mainly related to making processes easier for him to perform. An example of this was to put the water and coffee in the coffee pot at night. Notes also worked well. Reminder or explanation notes helped Dad to understand what was going on. A note could be as simple as a reminder for a doctor's appointment. Dad would then be ready at the time we were to leave the house and be anticipating the outing. Occasionally, I would travel on business and would leave him a letter (see Caregiving Forms Chapter). The letter would tell him where I went and why, how he could reach me, and when I would return. Not only would he read that letter about 10-20 times per day, he would know when I was returning and would be watching the front door for my entrance. The letter also served to relieve any anxieties he had that I had left him.

About six months later when Mom could no longer breathe well enough to use the walker, we bought a battery operated scooter and put ramps in the house for the step-downs into the living room and bed room. The ramps helped maneuver the scooter up and down the one-step levels into the living room and bed room. The scooter had all puncture proof rubber wheels, which were big enough to traverse the step, but that would have made Mom feel like she was falling off the scooter. The scooter was non-tippable – we tried to show her that it was impossible to tip it over, but she still was not comfortable. The ramps were scary enough! Going into the bedroom required the ramp plus an immediate sharp right-hand turn. Mom often missed this turn, even with our repeated prompting to "turn now". The speed control on the scooter was adjustable (from turtle to rabbit), after the famous fairy tale. A knob with a pin was pushed in or pulled out to start and stop the battery operation. The scooter was both a blessing and a curse!

The scooter gave Mom some independence, but her TIA's were causing increased dementia and she would get confused, nervous, and sometimes scared. Mom had been very familiar with driving golf carts during her golfing days, so it should have been a snap to operate the scooter. For a while, the scooter was a great alternative. The convenience of getting her around the house and being able to stay on the scooter to eat was great. The scooter chair could be turned 45 degrees at a time and would fit at the table or could be turned at a doorway for easier access into the bathroom. This feature decreased the number of times Mom had to get up and down or transfer to another chair.

The battery capacity of the scooter was 10 miles or 2-3 hours of intermittent use. The scooter could be used outside. A buckle on the bottom could be opened and the seat removed, the scooter broken down to load into the trunk of a car. A manual switch could be turned on to operate the scooter by pushing it if the battery died. We quickly found that it was easier to have two batteries and keep the spare battery on the charger at all times. This way, the second battery could easily be put into operation within a minute. It was too hard for Mom and Dad to keep up with the mechanics of what to do when the battery went dead and how to install the new one.

My brothers and I met together in March 2005 and they agreed to take weekend care, bringing lunch to Mom and Dad and to check on them. They would prepare the coffee for the next morning, and overall, provided a safety check.

Between November 2004 (when we purchased the scooter) and October 2005, I had a few emergency calls from Dad related to the scooter. Some were related to the dead battery and some were related to Mom's oxygen. Mom's oxygen tubing was 50 feet long, attached to the 100 pound oxygen tanks in the middle of the house. She would coil the tubing as she went along and drape it over the handlebars of the scooter. Occasionally, the tubing would get caught up in the wheels of the scooter and we would have to stop and unravel it. The key to knowing this was happening was that Mom would start shrieking, as the cannula in her nose would get too tight and would start pulling on her face. When this happened during the evening, Dad would not always be able to untangle the tubing. If the tubing became tight enough, the cannula could come off entirely, and then Mom wouldn't be able to breathe. The other thing that could happen was that the tubing became so stretched that it would get pulled off the oxygen tank.

One time Mom ended up lying on the floor and couldn't breathe. Dad called me, I called 911, as I knew the ambulance could get there sooner than I could. I called back, told Dad to unlock the front door, go back to Mom and tell me what was happening. These calls happened several times and were either related to the tubing falling off or getting wrapped around the wheels of the scooter. I would ask Dad specific questions about how Mom was acting, if the tubing was still on her face or not, and could reassure him until the ambulance arrived. In the meantime, I was racing up to their house myself.

After a couple of these incidents, I was able to talk to them about what had happened and how concerned we were about their safety. The safety issue was much easier for them to understand than the general requirements for caregiving. Mom and Dad finally agreed that we could hire a part-time caregiver for the evening hours to ensure they would get to bed safely. The caregiver would come before I left for the day, give them a snack, and ensure they were in bed and asleep before leaving for the night. (See Caregiving Chapters 4, 5, 6)

I must admit there were a couple of times that I was ready to quit. But, these moments were fleeting. My oldest brother (two years younger than me) became a cushion and sounding board for me. I could call him when I became frustrated or too worried. He would talk to me and calm me down and we would go on. In my heart, I knew I would be there until the end. It was just nice to have an outlet. Caregiving is very stressful, even though the work being performed is not hard.

Caregiving support groups are available, even through Hospice or care-specific organizations, such as cancer or Alzheimer's local chapters. The caregiver must have an outlet to outside activities. Something absorbing that will take the mind completely away from the care issues is excellent. These organizations are always talking to caregivers about protecting themselves. Evidently, caregivers can become ill and die before their loved one does.

Sudden Happenings – When We Least Expect Them

One of the constant questions I always had was ----- what now??? How does this or that incident contribute to Mom or Dad's overall health and well being? Even though one does not like to think about death, I really understood deep down that death would be coming sooner or later. When you are dating and searching for "The Right One," people will tell you to relax – that you will meet the right person when you least expect to. The same thing happens with dying. All of a sudden, an incident may occur that causes a dramatic downturn which may not be recovered from.

Mom was on Plavix once we found out she was having Transient Ischemic Attacks (TIAs), which are tiny, little, short, strokes in the brain. We eventually had to discontinue this drug because she would have nosebleeds – one lasting on and off for almost three days. About five months after discontinuing the Plavix, she had a bigger stroke and died a week later.

When I saw that she couldn't talk, I knew that this was a serious stroke. She did stay in bed that day – we called the Hospice nurse, and one of my doctor (M.D.) friends also came and checked her over. Dad came back to the bedroom, climbed up on the bed next to Mom and laid next to her the entire day, rubbing her chest or her back. That is when we arranged for a hospital bed to be put into the living room, to allow us to care for her more easily, and to help Dad's well-being by keeping him in the living room and decreasing the chance for his Sundowner's Syndrome to occur.

Dad's sudden incident was horrible and very sad. Even with everything we had put in place and done to help Mom and Dad, we still had a huge mishap. Our caregiving supervisor, Arizona, had used up all of her caregiver resources, and we needed a fourth person as a part-time caregiver to relieve the permanent caregivers when they were ill or on vacation. Arizona had recently met a new caregiver (Amy), had talked at length with this caregiver, and thought she would be OK, even though she had not ever worked with her. But, it wasn't!!

I had asked about this person's references (see Hiring Caregivers section) and was assured they were fine. I was not given the references or telephone numbers to call. I should have insisted on seeing these references and points of contact. We hired Amy on a trial basis. The first four to five weeks, she worked 1-2 days each week with no problems. Both Arizona and I watched her closely. Dad seemed to like her and would eat well for her. She would even bring home grown green chili and other vegetables from her garden and would make him green chili hamburgers.

Note that a couple of months before we hired Amy, I had lost my telecommuting position, and was now working in a local office. Having a job outside Dad's house meant I usually could only go by to see him after work. If I needed to take groceries or medications to his house, I would drop them by on the way to work. Since this was a new job, I was in the position at work where I needed to establish that I was dependable, a good worker, and needed to build up sick and vacation time.

About six weeks after hiring Amy, Arizona went out-of-town on vacation during the Fourth of July week. The 4th of July was on a Wednesday and Amy was working that day shift as well as that of Thursday, the 5th of July. I received a frantic telephone call at work from Arizona (on vacation in Ohio) about 10:30 a.m. on July 5. The new caregiver, Amy, had called one of the permanent caregivers (Michelle) to come and fill in, so she could go home. Her excuse was that her husband had beat her up and she was too upset to work. However, Arizona told me that Dad had been hit and was bleeding.

When Michelle arrived, she saw no visible signs of a beating or assault on Amy, but Dad was sitting on the edge of his bed, completely naked, with blood from cuts on his forehead and face, and a completely bruised, purple arm and hand. The sheets were gathered up around him, even the bottom sheet, and blood was spotted on the sheets. I left work immediately upon receiving Arizona's telephone call, arriving at Dad's to find the police already there. Dad was still in the same condition as when Michelle had arrived. (See Dad's Story) Dad lived another five weeks, but this assault was his undoing – he declined dramatically within one day and continued to decline until his death. We found out that Amy had been drinking, both throughout the night of the 4th of July and throughout the morning of the 5th, after reporting to duty. There were empty wine bottles and liquor miniatures on the kitchen counter and on the shelves. She had, in fact, been 45 minutes late to work that morning, but I was not notified.

To summarize, both of my parent's deaths were precipitated by sudden events, one the stroke and the other – the bodily assault. This may not happen in your case, but I tell you these stories to make you aware that this could happen. Even with all our planning and monitoring, we still had this incident occur. One day, you might be wondering how long your parent can continue to suffer, and the next week, they could be gone. Both my parents had long-term illnesses, but I know deaths also occur suddenly from a heart attack or a serious too-late finding of cancer. I would not wish any of these scenarios on anyone, and I wish every reader the best outcome possible for your individual scenario.

Office of the Medical Investigator (OMI)

If a death occurs under suspicious circumstances, or if a death occurs at home suddenly (whether of natural causes or not), the Office of the Medical Investigator (OMI) becomes involved. Specific circumstances might be a murder or a suicide or an unexpected death from any cause.

One example might be when a relatively young person dies of a heart attack. Another example is what happened to my Dad. Because he was assaulted by his caregiver, his case was referred to the Adult Protective Services for investigation. His case was watched carefully over the ensuing weeks. The premise was that if he were to die within six weeks, his death would be ruled suspicious and the OMI would become involved. Since he died about five weeks after the assault, his death was within the OMI window of death of six weeks.

What did this mean? This meant that when Dad died, we called the funeral home. The funeral home called the OMI office. The OMI team came to the house and picked up Dad's body for autopsy. The pathologist performing the autopsy called us to find out the particulars of Dad's health and the assault and factored Dad's hospital information (e.g., the decline) and the police photographs into his findings. The overall finding was that Dad died of pneumonia and Alzheimer's, but that the assault factored into his death at this time.

Early on in the caregiving process, I had been told that if Mom and Dad did not have a Do Not Resuscitate (DNR) order, the possibility existed that an emergency response team would be required to attempt to resuscitate either of them should they die at home. A private telephone conversation with the Administrator of our local OMI office revealed the following information.

The OMI investigation team will be called to the home or site of the death. The team will perform a scene investigation and interview the family and witnesses. They will also contact the primary care physician, review the deceased's medical history, see if there is a possibility of a natural death occurring, and ask the physician if he is comfortable in signing the deceased person's death certificate. All of these findings are factored into the OMI decision of whether or not to do an autopsy. The Administrator also stated that the Emergency Medical Response (EMR) teams are trained to view heart attacks as a natural death. Also, if obvious signs of death have already occurred, they will not resuscitate. However, the EMR team will resuscitate if they feel the circumstances indicate a possibility of survival. Note that it takes several hours for rigor mortis or pooling of the blood in the body to occur.

Source: Personal telephone conversation between author and OMI, February 2009.

Chapter 2:

Mom and the Guardian Angel

Mom was diagnosed with emphysema in about 1994, around age 70. Emphysema is a lung disease in which the lung tissue loses its elasticity and eventually its structure. The smallest alveoli and capillaries supplying the lung tissue collapse and become destroyed over time. The air flow is decreased, air gets trapped in the lungs, and carbon monoxide is not released as readily. Emphysema is also called COPD – chronic obstructive pulmonary disease.

The main outward manifestation of this disease is shortness of breath. Emphysema is a chronic, long-term disease, primarily caused by exposure to toxic substances, which include long-term exposure to cigarette smoking. The chemicals from the smoke invade the lung tissue and deposit heavy black carbon throughout the tissue. This disease is irreversible.

Mom had begun smoking her first year of college away from home. Her smoking continued until about age 69 when she fell in the kitchen, breaking her hip. She had to have surgery to replace the ball joint part of the broken hip. Following the surgery, the doctors had trouble awakening her. Thus, her emphysema was diagnosed. She was sent home on full-time oxygen for six weeks. She quit smoking in a hurry. Fortunately, Mom was in good physical shape, and exercised through golfing several times a week. She played golf both with Dad and with various women's groups. She recovered easily from this surgery, but remained in pain. Two years later, she was back in surgery, receiving the second half (socket) of her hip replacement. Why they didn't replace the entire hip at once was never explained. This second surgery was performed under a local anesthetic, due to her breathing problems.

For a long time, we didn't see too many changes in Mom. She and Dad traveled, taking trips to Hawaii and France, and spent the winters in Phoenix. She did say that the lower elevation of Phoenix did help her to breathe better. They continued to play golf for several years until her breathing worsened, and Dad's hips started to bother him. Eventually, they sold their second home in Phoenix and resumed staying in Albuquerque full-time.

At about the ages of 75 and 77, both Mom and Dad seemed to slow down and stay home more. Dad had had a bout with colon cancer and also an eye stroke, causing him to lose the sight in his right eye. Their lives became much simpler. Mom didn't drive after her second hip surgery, unless she had to. She may have had to drive Dad to the doctor's a few times, but generally he drove. As she was on oxygen, Dad ran the majority of the errands and did the shopping. He loved these outings as he knew all the checkout people and had his favorite one. Shopping became a social outlet for him.

Their meals became simpler, as Mom just didn't seem to cook much anymore. Breakfast was cereal, raisin toast, juice, and the ever important coffee. Lunch could be a sandwich and chips, or some baked chicken, or meatloaf. Lunch became the main meal of the day. About 4:30-5:00, they would have cocktails and a dinner snack, sometimes consisting of chile con queso and chips, cheese and salami, or some other easy-to-fix snack. They would occasionally go out to lunch, most often in conjunction with a doctor visit. Most of the time, lunch was at one of their two favorite Mexican restaurants. Their favorite lunch was green chile chicken sour cream enchiladas with curly fries. After I came to care for them, we would get take-out enchiladas for lunch about once a week. Amazingly, they never lost their love for good green chili or their beloved enchiladas.

In September 2002, about eight years after Mom's first broken hip, she fell again. I received a phone call from Dad telling me she was in the hospital and had had surgery again. This time she had only cracked her hip. I called the hospital to talk to her and she seemed to be doing fine. The next day I was to drive to upstate New York to pick up one of my daughters to bring her home from a vacation. After work, I drove part-way and spent the night with a girlfriend. Upon my arrival at my friend's house, I called Mom's hospital room to check on her and the phone just rang and rang. Strange, as I knew she wouldn't be getting out of bed. A nurse finally answered, sounding very panicked and vague. She didn't exactly say what was wrong, but intimated that Mom was having problems.

I called Dad's house early the next morning and he wasn't there. I called the hospital again only to find out that Mom had been transferred to the intensive care unit (ICU). Her lungs had essentially collapsed and were failing, and she had been put on a respirator (considered a life support mechanism). I met my daughter in Syracuse, gave her the car, and flew to Albuquerque. I arrived about 11:00 p.m. and immediately went to the hospital. Mom was on morphine sedation medication, but the nurses stopped it long enough for her to wake up and hear my voice. I reassured her that I was there and would take care of Dad, which I knew would be her most important concern. I told her I would return in the morning and that the best thing she could do to get better was to sleep and let her body heal.

She was actually put on the respirator so that they could get her to breathe more easily and were sedating her to rest. She had been struggling so hard to breathe that she was panicking. After I left the hospital, I went to Dad's house, and found him waiting up for me. He asked me how Mom was doing. Knowing that Dad doesn't like sugar-coating or to have information hidden from him, I told him that this episode was very serious and even life-threatening. Of course, he was very upset and beside himself. To tell him the severity of Mom's condition was a decision I did not make lightly, but I also did not want him to be surprised if she did, in fact, not live.

Mom was on the respirator (see Chapter on Dying and Life Support) for five days. The pulmonologist (lung specialist) came in late Monday afternoon and explained to us that he was going to test her by turning off the respirator to see how well she could breathe. He woke her up from the sedation and explained to her what had happened, that he wanted to try to remove the respirator and intubating tubing, but that he also wanted her permission to reinsert the tube, if she was not stable. She gave her permission, and the family adjourned to the waiting room.

The hardest part for my Dad to understand was why this had happened. His point was that she had broken her hip before and had come out of that fine. He really was convinced that this event should be the same, even though it was eight years later. Eight years had allowed time for more lung deterioration to occur from the worsening emphysema. This entire episode was a wake-up call to the family. Dad's reaction to Mom's condition and the family trying to keep both him and ourselves calm was the extent of our discussion during the removal of the life support.

After forty-five minutes, Dad and I were allowed back into Mom's room. To our surprise and delight, she was sitting up in the bed, smiling, and talking. The doctor came in and explained that she was very stable, able to breathe on her own, that he would not need to reintubate her, that the five days under intubation had done its job of healing, and that he would be moving her to a step-down unit.

She was moved later that day after the rest of the family had been in to see her. She was extremely weak, of course, and still needed to recover not only from her hip surgery, but to rebuild her lungs and ability to breathe. After five days in the step-down unit, she was moved to the rehabilitation unit for a couple of weeks. Our tremendous joy was being able to bring in a cake and balloons to celebrate Mom and Dad's 55th wedding anniversary while she was in rehabilitation.

I left Albuquerque after 10 days. Dad was doing pretty well, as he knew Mom would be coming home. In retrospect, that episode probably caused his Alzheimer's to begin to surface. I took his lower energy level, his inability to make decisions, and his general malaise to be a reaction to this entire episode. Different though was his insistence to have me drive and to handle any affairs that needed attending to. Mom came home about 10-12 days after I left.

From then on, I called home 2-3 times per week. Mom slowly recovered over the next six months. Her body was certainly more frail and her oxygen needs had increased slightly. While Mom was in the hospital, I had really pushed one of the pulmonologists to give me an estimate of the extent of her disease. He was very hesitant to do so, but I wanted some kind of guideline as to what we were dealing with. He told me that she only had about 25% of her lung function left, which would equate to about two years of expectant life remaining. I probably should not have shared that information with the family, as this upset them, and they felt the doctor should not have said anything. But, I did push him so that I could have some idea of what to expect.

When I flew back to Virginia, I told my boss that I expected I would have to move home in the near future. Fortunately, she completely understood. For the next six months, I held my breath, waiting so-to-speak for the next shoe to fall. I never dreamed that my move home would be precipitated by my Dad's health.

Referring back to the Introduction, it was almost exactly six months later when I was talking on the phone to Mom and Dad and I thought he had a stroke. I happened to be returning home to attend a funeral, and thus began my awakening to Dad's dementia. Upon my return to Virginia three days later, I began the preparation to sell my home for the move to Albuquerque. One of my brothers moved home from Texas to stay with them until I could get there. Mom and Dad wanted me there and were very excited that I was moving home after 29 years.

I was the oldest of four and the only daughter. With my health care background, it seemed natural that I should be the child elected to do so. Fortunately, it was perfect timing for me, and all the pieces fit together so nicely. My children were just out of high school, I was single, and didn't have to uproot a spouse's career. I was glad not to have to travel constantly between Virginia and New Mexico, keeping two households together. I was very fortunate that my job allowed me to move to a different contract and to telecommute from New Mexico. I know this was an ideal situation and will not be so easy to manage for many other families.

Mom and Dad were a very close couple. Mom generally had the power in the household, but Dad was the enforcer, especially if one of the kids really screwed up. Now that Dad had what we expected to be Alzheimer's Disease, this dynamic was even more so in effect. It was very easy to see and to understand that although they knew they needed help, they wanted as much independence as possible. In some respects, their fierce independence made my job easier, and in other respects, harder. Mom and Dad brought us up to be independent, and we were!!

However, because I was a girl, I was still expected to go to college (to have a career to fall back on in case I needed it), to marry, and become a housewife. I became a career woman, married for nine years, and adopted two beautiful girls along the way, divorced when they were toddlers, and remained a career woman. Although Mom had what was essentially a Master's degree in Dietetics, she had quit work as soon as I was born. But, we were from different eras – Dad wanted to be the breadwinner and didn't want Mom to work. Mom still had a very strong and forceful personality. I think there were times in her life that she wished she could work, but in the end, I believe she was satisfied with her life.

So, here I come into this dynamic, ready to be the guardian angel and savior of their health and lives for as long as necessary, knowing that Mom's and my independent streaks were going to butt heads. And we did, especially the first year. It would have been easier if we both had dropped our guards, sat down, and really truthfully told each other what we wanted and felt. But that was not the dynamic in our family. We did the best we could, and did well at that.

Over the 2-1/2 years that Mom was still alive, we only had two shouting episodes, both probably from emotional pain. Mom was an expert at baiting me, and I was an expert in rising to catch the bait. Mom even asked my best friend once if she thought I would stay until the end. I didn't know about that conversation until much later, but I could have told Mom that I would never leave them. It wouldn't have been right and I would not have been able to leave them to fend for themselves. I don't think they fully realized at any one point in time the amount of energy and time it took to keep their lives in good shape. But, then, it was all they could do to get through the day. Of course, I didn't mind helping them, but I did get very frustrated at times.

I would arrive each morning with groceries or medications on hand or goods from whatever errands I had run the night before. I would check on their breakfast, ensure that they were taking their meds, and fix bacon or something extra for them. Microwave bacon is great (expensive, but great) – it takes only three minutes, they loved bacon, and it gave them some extra nutrition. I would start lunch, and then retreat to the office to begin my work day. I would take a few minutes once in a while to check on them, on their lunch, or to stick a batch of laundry in during the morning. At lunch time, I would go to the kitchen, finish fixing lunch and serve it. Then, I would go back to the office. If they needed something, Dad would come back to the office to ask me to come out and talk to them. I could usually tell that this would occur, as I would be able to hear most of their conversations back in the office. At this point, both of them were dressing and toileting themselves, although it was already hard for Mom to do so.

The independence really came to light when Mom would begin calling to me about 4:00 p.m. every day and let me know it was time to leave. I would explain to her that I needed to work eight hours each day, around my caregiving duties to them. Dad would back me up on this, having been a businessman and having owned his own business. But they wanted the house to themselves at night and wanted some privacy. As I was in the office the majority of the day, this was curious to me – I tried very hard not to interfere in their day unless there was a reason to do so.

In reality, I was able to get more work done in this environment than I did in the office as I didn't get interrupted very often, and only had occasional telephone meetings to attend. If I had an eventful day with them and didn't fit in eight hours, I could take work home or come in early the next day. I was very grateful to my boss for allowing me to telecommute, and I wanted to fulfill my duties to my company. I was able to take sick leave for Mom and Dad's doctor's appointments. This system worked very well.

Occasionally, Mom would get up to help fix lunch. This was easily done by letting her sit at the kitchen table, bringing her a cutting board, a sharp knife, and a bowl to put veggies or fruit in. I would then bring her soapy, wet paper towels to wash her hands with. She enjoyed helping, and this was an easy accommodation.

It was very difficult for Mom to stand for long periods of time (more than a few minutes). Their house was a stretched out in a flat V-shape, so to walk from one end of the house to the other (where the bedroom and bathroom were) began to be very difficult for her. She was using her rescue inhalers (Albuterol) too often and because she would panic when she had trouble breathing, she would be using them incorrectly, repeatedly discharging them 3-4 times in a few seconds. The problem with this was that not only would the medication not be delivered to her lungs, but the extra medication would also make her shaky and jittery. She would be stopping in the middle of the hallway to catch her breath.

I had seen walkers with seats on them, but couldn't find one in a store. I found a local representative in the telephone book, and she was kind enough to bring several models to the house and demonstrate them. We bought a snazzy maroon walker with a seat, a basket, lockable hand brakes, and large wheels. If one were walking at a decent pace, the walker could keep up. Although I liked the idea of the hand brakes being able to lock to sit down, or to slow down, in practice, this was a difficult concept for my Mom to remember. Sometimes she didn't have the strength to lock the brakes. She would just turn around and sit down when she got tired. Fortunately, one of us was usually walking beside her and we could stand behind the walker and hold it in place while she sat down.

Mom would also get very claustrophobic easily, due to her emphysema. For this reason, she would not take a shower, she wasn't physically strong enough to get in/out of the bathtub (which was set down lower than the floor), so she was taking "spit baths." She would set herself up at the sink with warm water and soap herself with a wash cloth. About a month before I arrived, she had stopped going to the beauty parlor each week to get her hair done. This may have been for two reasons: one – it took too much energy for her to go out, and two – Dad's driving was probably getting pretty erratic. So, I learned to cut hair.

Cutting Mom's hair was easier than I thought it would be. She had short hair, and liked it to blend smoothly. I had watched hair stylists do my hair for years, so I applied what I had seen. Lift and trim, match the ends of each section to the cut sections, so that they were even. My haircuts turned out nicely and eventually I was cutting Dad's hair as well.

Washing her hair was difficult at first. Initially, Mom would sit in her walker at the kitchen sink for me to wash her hair and stand up to put her head under the faucet when we needed to rinse out the shampoo. This was not easy for her and she was still claustrophobic. So, we tried a new idea, which worked well for the remainder of her life. She would sit in her chair at the bathroom sink. I would protect her with towels, and would wet her hair with warm water using a wash cloth. I would apply the shampoo, let it sit for a minute, and then massaged her scalp for a couple of minutes. She loved this!! I would rinse the shampoo out 3-4 times, again using the wash cloth. I would refill the sink with clean, warm water and continue rinsing until all the shampoo was out. This would only take another couple of rinses, was quick, and comfortable for Mom. I didn't have to fuss with shampoo bowls or systems, and her energy was intact afterwards.

When I washed Mom's hair or spent time helping her to get dressed, we had our quality time together. Occasionally, we would bring up problems or issues; many times we would talk about Dad and his condition. This was actually a learning process for her to understand what Alzheimer's Disease was and how it was affecting Dad. Patiently explaining this disease to her, I tried to get her to understand that when he made mistakes, he didn't know he was making them and he had forgotten how to do things – he was losing the information of how to perform processes in his brain. Many times I was able to intervene and give her a look or say something gently to remind her to be patient. She was able to be more understanding, but in addition, became more worried about Dad as well.

One morning during one of our talks, the middle of one of Mom's sentences came out all garbled. This went on for several seconds. I was calling to her, "Mom, what's wrong? Mom, are you OK?" She couldn't answer me. After about 30 seconds, she looked up at me and started talking normally. In the meantime, galloping thoughts had been racing through my head, trying to figure out what was happening and what my best course of action would be. And then, she was talking normally. I began questioning her about how she felt – she had no symptoms or remembrance of the episode. I suspected that this episode could be a Transient Ischemic Attack (TIA), or mini-stroke.

Mom had not seemed like she had dementia, but sometimes she wouldn't remember details, or some situation. I had initially taken this as simple aging, probably compounded by her inability to breathe. Now, I was on the alert. We made an appointment with her pulmonologist, and he confirmed that the episode was probably a TIA, and that she had probably had many other episodes of them. The TIA is a very small stroke or blood-clot, causing little burn-outs in the blood vessels of the brain, eventually causing enough damage to become Vascular

Dementia (VasD). With Mom's decreased oxygen levels, the emphysema had contributed to the increase in the TIA's. Over time, I only caught one more TIA episode, but once I knew what to watch for, I could usually tell that she probably had them often, and consequently, was also having problems with dementia.

> **Vascular dementia:** "Vascular dementia (VasD) is a degenerative cerebrovascular disease that leads to a progressive decline in memory and cognitive functioning. It occurs when the blood supply carrying oxygen and nutrients to the brain is interrupted by a blocked or diseased vascular system. Vascular dementia generally affects people between the ages of 60 and 75, and affects more men than women. The most common type of vascular dementia is multi-infarct dementia (MID), which is caused by a series of small strokes, or "mini-strokes," that often go unnoticed and cause damage to the cortex of the brain—the area associated with learning, memory, and language. These mini-strokes are sometimes referred to as transient ischemic attacks (TIAs), which result in only temporary, partial blockages of blood supply and brief impairments in consciousness or sight. Over time, however, the damage caused to brain tissue interferes with basic cognitive functions and disrupts everyday functioning. Multi-infarct dementia causes loss of functioning to specific areas of the brain, impairing some neurological and mental functions and not others. When vascular dementia occurs with other types of dementia, such as Alzheimer's disease, it is known as "mixed dementia.""

Retrieved August 2009 from,
http://www.helpguide.org/elder/vascular_dementia.htm

Now, please understand, the vascular dementia (VasD) does not have the same effects on the person as the Alzheimer's disease (AD) does. Mom was very much still herself, but might not remember details of her life, or the current times. Her condition manifested as more forgetfulness and loss of short-term memory, than anything else. The VasD still diminished her capacity to care for herself, but this loss of capacity was also in conjunction with her lung deterioration, due to the emphysema. She eventually did not have the strength to care for herself, but she did not lose her mental capacities.

The pulmonologist prescribed Plavix for Mom to try and decrease the number of TIA's that she had. This medication caused nosebleeds after a couple of months. Mom finally had a nosebleed that lasted on and off for three days. The first day I had her lying in bed, with compresses. Dad came in and laid beside her to keep her company. She got tired of that pretty quickly. I had only seen Mom in bed 1-2 days during the entire time I took care of her. She would get up and get dressed every day. So, then we prepared a bed for her on the living room couch, so she could be with Dad. Telephone calls made to the doctor discontinued the Plavix, and no further nosebleeds occurred. The discontinuation of the Plavix caused the TIA's to resume. Eventually, Mom did have a major stroke.

In December 2004, a friend of mine mentioned Hospice to me. My understanding of Hospice was the typical understanding: the patient is terminal and would die in less than six months. In reality, this belief is based upon the fact that a doctor would have to certify that "the patient would likely die within six months, if the disease followed its natural course." I called a local Hospice in January 2005 anyway.

The Hospice admission criteria is also based upon Activities of Daily Living (ADLs). ADLs include the ability of the person to perform dressing, eating, toileting, bathing, walking, or transferring activities. A registered nurse was sent out to perform an assessment on Mom and to determine whether or not she was qualified for Hospice care. (Note that this assessment may vary among Hospice agencies.). We had just purchased a battery-operated scooter two months before for Mom to ride through the house on, so she wasn't walking more than a few steps at a time. Due to Mom's oxygen requirements and the fact that she couldn't walk without being able to breathe plus her need for assistance with bathing, dressing, and transporting, she was able to qualify for Hospice. The Hospice doctor overseeing her care would have to approve her admission, but because of her ADLs, this was not a problem. And, not only was she able to have the minimum level of support – two aide visits per week, her condition qualified her for five aide visits per week.

These visits were performed in two hour shifts each morning, Monday through Friday. The aide would arrive by 7:30 a.m., about the time when Mom and Dad would be finishing their breakfast. The aide would take Mom to bathe and dress her. The Hospice organization provided a bath bench that sat over the bathtub and extended out onto the floor somewhat. The bench was level with Mom's chair on the scooter. She could turn the scooter chair to move easily from the scooter to the bath bench. A nozzle and hose was placed over the tub spout and Mom once again enjoyed baths for a while. This procedure made her baths easier to manage, was not messy, and helped her to feel cleaner. Eventually, we went back to the spit baths, but the bath bench certainly helped out for about 8-9 months.

About two months later, we implemented part-time caregivers from 4:00-8:00 in the evening to assist in getting Mom and Dad to bed safely. My brothers also began bringing lunches to them on the weekend and checking up on them. Safety at night continued to be an issue and finally we were able to hire full-time night caregivers in October 2005, about six months after beginning the part-time care. These steps are more fully explained in the caregiving chapter. Arizona then came into our lives as our chief caregiver. She was our Guardian Angel, helping our family to survive this difficult chapter.

For the next three months, Mom's breathing became more and more labored. We were helping her do everything except eat. She truly did not have any energy. It was even difficult for her to get up/down from the toilet. She began thinking she was younger and would tell me that she had to pick up my brother's from school. At this time, the two younger brothers were about 46 and 47. This occurrence happened several times. She also talked more about her mother – I asked her if she had seen or talked to her mother and the reply was "Yes." She would be wakeful at night, calling "Yoo-Hoo" to Arizona, talking to her until she was able to go back to sleep.

This is part of the life review and life regression that one goes through prior to death. They may be living their life from an earlier age. This step is important for the dying person to go through. (See chapter on Dying Process) When Dad reached this stage, he often thought he still worked and talked about finishing projects or driving to work. One time before Mom died, they must have been talking about living or growing up in Iowa, as they tried to call someone there on the telephone, even though we had not had family there for over forty years.

Three months after beginning full-time night care, I walked into the house the morning of January 24, 2006 (Tuesday) about 7:10 a.m., saw Dad in the kitchen, but no Mom. I asked Dad "Where's Mom?" He was visibly upset and indicated that Mom had gone to the bedroom. I initially thought perhaps Arizona had taken her to the bathroom and went to check on them. To my great dismay, Mom was lying on the bed with her head propped up. She saw me and tried to talk, but no words came out. (Mom was not one to go to bed or stay in bed, unless she had the flu.) I thought immediately that she had had a stroke.

We called Hospice, even though I knew the aide was due to arrive soon. The nurse came out right away. Fortunately, by that time Mom could speak a few words, there was no paralysis, and she seemed to be coming out of the stroke. Mom began to rally after a few hours, but it was clear that the stroke had taken a toll on her. By the next day, she could again talk, but was still very, very weak. That day we arranged for a hospital bed to be put in the living room – 1) so she could be with Dad, and 2) so that Dad wouldn't be in the bedroom, where his Sundowner's Syndrome was so prevalent. We had a draw sheet under her and could turn her often.

As that long, long week dragged on, Mom became marginally better, but we could only get small amounts of food into her. She could only stand with assistance and couldn't walk. We moved a potty chair into the living room and Arizona would transfer Mom over to it and back into bed. The way that Arizona did this was really neat. She would tell Mom to put her arms around Arizona's shoulders. Arizona would put her arms under Mom's armpits, hug her, pivot and swing her over to the potty chair. Mom didn't have to put any effort into this movement except perhaps move her feet to the side, and Arizona was able to bear Mom's weight without hurting her back or lifting her completely.

By Saturday, Mom was pretty much bedbound 24 hours a day. We moved Dad's recliner next to the bed, so that he could sit next to her and hold her hand. If he was in bed asleep, one of the family or one of the caregivers was sitting there. Mom was only eating soft foods. On Monday, I made homemade vegetable soup and pureed it. We sat Mom up on the side of the bed, as she seemed more alert. She ate two cups of soup! She loved it, and exclaimed how good it was. She later again ate a small amount. Having her do this gave us a small amount of hope that she could get better.

But the daytime caregiver (Michelle) told me – "don't be surprised if that wasn't her last meal. Often people eat well the last day they are alive. This helps them transition to their spiritual life." Sure enough that is what happened. By evening Mom was asleep. My girlfriend took me out to dinner and I went home to sleep for a few hours. Arizona called me at 2:30 a.m. to come right away. By the time I arrived, Mom was gone. To this day, I wish I had gone back to Mom's house after dinner to be with her. But Arizona tells me that people pick how they want to die. If they want it quiet with no one around, then they will die when it is quiet with no one around. She said that Mom had picked her time to die.

A friend of mine lost her husband recently. He had lung cancer and lived for about a year following his diagnosis. She kept him at home and took care of him, until she finally needed a break. The family agreed to put the husband in Hospice for respite care for a week and then return him to home. Even though his death was not imminent at the time, he died in the ambulance on the way to respite care. He had not wanted to die at home, and picked his time to die.

I woke Dad up, had him come out to the living room to see her, called my out-of-town brother and the Hospice nurse. I wish I had given instructions ahead of time to the caregiver to have Dad by her bedside. I just assumed that would happen and it didn't. The caregiver had chosen to wait until I arrived and wanted me to take the responsibility to bring Dad out to the living room. Even in his semi-advanced stage of Alzheimer's, Dad could understand that Mom had died. He spent a few minutes with her, rubbing her chest as he always did. But shortly, he retreated to his bedroom and was inconsolable.

I had called my two in-town brothers on the way to Mom and Dad's house. They arrived shortly after the Hospice nurse, who pronounced Mom's death at 3:30 a.m. The Hospice nurse stayed with us for a while, destroyed Mom's narcotic medications, and removed the comfort kit (see Hospice Care). Arizona bathed Mom and put on the outfit that we picked – a beautiful, lavender pantsuit. We then called the mortuary to come and pick Mom up. They arrived at 6:00 a.m. This was a very long wait. We all said our good-byes before they put her in the body bag and sealed it. Sealing the bag and tagging it protects the loved one and ensuring that proper identification accompanies the body. Do not be surprised if irrational thoughts hit you during this process. Mine was to make sure Mom had warm socks on, as her feet were always cold.

We never really knew the extent of her lung pain or discomfort, due to the emphysema, except when she tried to walk and couldn't breathe. Everything was a tremendous effort for her. But she put on the bravest front that she could.

Chapter 3:

Dad and the Heartbreak of Alzheimer's Disease

After Mom died, we were still in the house caring for Dad. Mom died in the middle of the night, so we had Dad come out to say goodbye to her. He understood what was happening and was wracked with grief. He went back to the bedroom and didn't want anyone near him. It was almost like his Alzheimer's disappeared for a few hours to allow him to understand that Mom had died. One of my brothers was able to go back and sit with him after a while. When the funeral home caretakers came to take Mom to the mortuary, we had him come out to say goodbye to her. He did so very reluctantly.

To minimize the effects on Dad, we immediately took the hospital bed apart and removed it and any other hospital/medical equipment to the garage. We put the couch back in place and made the living room appear familiar and normal. When Dad came out to the living room for the day, he sat at the end of the couch instead of in his recliner (he never sat on the couch, unless we had company). The spot where the end of the couch was sitting was exactly where Mom's bed had been. He sat there most of the day and asked us, "What happened to the woman in the bed?" What a change in him over a few hours! But, somehow, he was still subconsciously connected to her.

I think if Dad did not have Alzheimer's, he would have chosen to stop eating right then and there, just to join Mom as soon as possible. Dad did well during the funeral service, but I am not sure he really knew that it was for Mom. He recognized some of his friends, but he didn't know their names except when I introduced each one to him. After the funeral, Dad became a lot less agitated than he had been for several months, almost leading us to believe that internally he knew Mom's illness was becoming worse all the time. We were able to discontinue the Ativan and never had to restart it. He lived another 1-1/2 years, declining slowly all the time.

He had a great time during those months. We took him to a local Mexican restaurant for both of his birthdays, fed him enchiladas, margaritas, and cake. He always got to wear a large sombrero during the Mexican serenade. In May, a few months after Mom died, my brother remarried. Arizona took Dad shopping and he picked out a beautiful brick red shirt and new shoes. We added a suit and one of his favorite bolo ties. Dad danced with the bride and all the caregivers. It was wonderful to see him have such a good time! We could tell he was really tired by the time we left the party, though. This was his last great hurrah!

Shortly thereafter, Dad was walking down the hall one afternoon when he stopped and clutched his left leg, stating that he was in pain. We sat him down and felt his leg – it felt hard. The next morning, the same thing happened. I took him to the primary care doctor – he was suspicious of a blood clot and referred us for a Doppler scan. A Doppler scan is a type of ultrasound that looks at the blood flow in one's body. Upon arrival, the technician took Dad's blood pressure and pulse. Because the pain was in Dad's leg, he also tried to take toe pulses with tiny little cuffs that fit on the toes. He could not detect any pulse activity in Dad's left leg and only faint pulses on the right leg.

Think of the pulse beat on your wrist or on your neck. These pulses are reflections of one's heart beat and are present in many different areas of your body, including your toes. The Doppler scan was begun, looking for blood clots in Dad's left leg. Sure enough, there was a big clot. So, off we went to the Emergency Room (ER) about 4:30 p.m. We spent about seven hours in a hallway inside the ER area, as no other beds were available. Due to Dad's Alzheimer's Disease and the emergent nature of his condition, he was taken in right away. He loved watching people, so being on a stretcher was probably better than being in a room by himself. Funny, Dad's bed was on the other side of the partition where the doctors sat. Over the seven hours, Dad would become impatient about not being seen or wondering when he was going to get out of the ER. I'm sure the doctors heard him, and helped to get us a room as quickly as possible – seven hours was a short time compared to the current average ER stays.

Radiology (x-ray) performed a low contrast angiogram on his left side. Dad had a pacemaker, so he could not have a Magnetic Resonance Image (MRI). (The MRI machine employs a large magnet to visualize the body fluids and organ systems.) Because of the blood clot, the radiologist did not want to overtax Dad's system with the contrast media, so only performed the angiogram on one leg. Dad tolerated this procedure extremely well.

I was able to talk to the radiologist both before and after the procedure and explained to Dad what was happening. As my initial education was in Nuclear Medicine and Radiology, the radiologist showed me Dad's films and explained his condition. Dad's femoral artery (the main blood vessel from the groin area down to the leg) was completely blocked, along with all the peripheral, smaller blood vessels. Dad should not even have been able to walk. Dad was started on medications to dissolve the clot and was admitted to the hospital for two days. A heart specialist was called in to consult on his case.

I stayed with Dad the entire first 24 hours, and the caregivers came in for their regular shifts. After the angiogram, Dad had to stay on his back for 24 hours – that was truly a trial in getting him to stay still. Dad was hard to understand and the hospital personnel did not have the knowledge, capability, or capacity to handle an Alzheimer's patient. When Dad needed to use the bathroom, the male nurses would come in and explain how to use the urinal and would assist him in doing so. The next day Dad could get up with assistance to get to the bathroom.

Arizona's caregiving skills included knowledge of the use of massage and herbs or oils. When Dad had his blood clot, Arizona mixed up a concoction of oils and would massage Dad's leg daily to improve his circulation. One day (much later on) I was talking to Dad's Hospice doctor about this blood clot and the total blockage of his femoral artery (main blood supply to leg from abdominal area) in his left leg. This doctor told me that most people die within a couple of months after this type of blockage and that they would not be able to walk.

Dad was able to walk with assistance until the day he died and his leg never changed color from lack of circulation. The blockage occurred 15 months before his death and was not a contributing factor to his death. I attribute this entirely to the massage and oil treatments. Arizona shared her favorite oil treatments with me to include in this book (see Appendix IV for Oil Treatment Recipes and Uses). The only concession Dad eventually made was to use a wheelchair in public when he had to walk long distances.

When Dad came home from the hospital, we had him reevaluated by Hospice again, as this blockage was life-threatening. We picked a different Hospice unit that had both in-patient and out-patient care. Even though our prior Hospice group gave us wonderful care, I was concerned that Dad would continue to be admitted, discharged, and then readmitted again. I had called them (the first Hospice) when Dad was diagnosed with the blockage. Their assessment did not show that Dad met their criteria to be readmitted. Thus, the change in Hospice teams.

Our city had several Hospice choices, both private and those directly associated with a hospital system. Note that the Veteran's Administration Hospitals also have Hospice units for veterans. The second Hospice team did admit Dad under the vascular blockage diagnosis – not the Alzheimer's disease. The Hospice nurse we had for Dad the last fifteen months was excellent. Not only was she a good nurse, but she really attached herself to our family, and educated us about each piece of Dad's health as it occurred.

By this time, Dad could no longer read, except basic headlines, he could no longer sign his name, and most of the time watched golf on television. Discovery Channel and Animal Planet were also favorites. He could still tell when a good golf shot was hit, but could not keep up with the scores and who was winning, unless he actually saw the leader board on the screen. Arizona would bring in activities for him, but he pretty much pooh-poohed them.

The winning activity was either a ride in the car, or going out to eat where he could watch and interact with other people. He loved visits from the grand-kids and great-grandkids, as long as they didn't stay too long. Noise and lots of people became very tiring to him, and after a while, he would become very irritable. One thing about Alzheimer's Disease, one would always know where they stood with Dad. He would surely let you know!! His defenses, social amenities, and prejudices disappeared with this disease. On the other hand, Dad could be very funny. He never lost his sense of humor. A new fad about this time was the wearing of goatees on men. Now, Dad had a beard in the 50's, but he didn't remember that! He would just ask people right out, "Why do you have all that stuff on your face?" Or, one could catch him watching a pretty, well-dressed woman walk down the sidewalk.

About two months after his readmission to Hospice, Dad began to become incontinent. At first, the accidents were infrequent. Arizona put him on a two hour bathroom schedule. He would be taken back to the bathroom to try to urinate every two hours. We bought him "a new kind of underwear" (elastic pull-ups). Instead of wearing dress slacks, we bought him stretch pants and switched his loafers for non-skid tennis shoes with Velcro straps. As he became more and more incontinent (both urine and bowel), the pull-up briefs were changed to a diaper like brief with tapes on the sides.

The type of clothes worn should be changed over time so that they become easier and easier to manage as the disease progresses. All of these steps were sure signs that the AD was progressing. The stage I really dreaded was when he wouldn't be able to swallow. Occasionally, Dad would remember to get up and head for the bathroom, but he wouldn't always know where it was. We would guide him there quickly, but sometimes he would surprise us and pee on the floor.

Dad's Sundowner's Syndrome also began occurring more often that spring. When we brought him home from the hospital and was readmitted to Hospice, we automatically asked for a hospital bed. We set it up in the living room where Mom's bed had been, and placed a portable commode next to the bed. This system was manageable for Dad – when he became tired, he just got up from the recliner, walked over to the bed, and laid down. He only went back to the bedroom and bathroom to get dressed or to shower. Dad seemed pretty stable, with the exception of the incontinence. If he became constipated, out came the Milk of Magnesia (MOM) and prune juice (1/2 Tablespoon MOM per ½ cup prune juice). We would give Dad three days and if he didn't use the bathroom, this concoction would be given. This concoction was nicknamed "DynOmite" for obvious reasons. It didn't take long for the constipation to be relieved. It is very important for the bowels to continue moving in very ill patients.

During this time, Dad's appetite also began to decrease and his tastes changed. Some of his favorite foods tasted "blah." When appetite decreases, it is time to move to simpler, finger food, small plates, and small portions. Only one or two foods should be put on the plate at one time, with other foods offered after these are finished. Large amounts of food confuse AD patients and they just don't know what to do with it. They also don't know how to use silverware.

Finger foods make eating much easier. In the last few months of his life, Dad would occasionally spit his food or pills out. His pills would then get crushed and mixed with pudding or applesauce. Other than the incontinence and decrease in appetite, Dad didn't really have any new problems. His memory was assuredly becoming worse over time, but he seemed very content. When the hospital bed was placed in the living room, we estimated that Dad still had 18-24 months to live.

Due to Dad's change in appetite, we were constantly trying to prevent dehydration and malnutrition. We always kept a glass of juice or water near Dad's chair, so that he could take a drink often. Snacks were provided several times a day, in addition to the normal three meal-times. Bribing works too!! "Dad, if you drink this water, I will bring you a Snicker's ice cream bar." Dehydration and malnutrition set the body up for infection or pneumonia, which are not easily detected in the elderly. However, these conditions must be continually watched for and guarded against.

Dad's Caregiving Incident

We didn't bargain for the caregiving abuse incident. When this incident occurred (July 2007), Dad was not able to defend himself. If he were to grab my hand and squeeze it as tightly as he could, his strength would be equivalent to my eight year old grandson. He could wave his arms and bat someone away if he didn't like what they were doing, but he couldn't hurt anyone.

When the incident occurred, Arizona called me at work after receiving a call from Michelle, another caregiver. Although Arizona was on vacation in Ohio that week, Michelle had opted to call her first. Michelle had received a call from Amy to come in and relieve her. Amy said she was unwell and unable to stay at work. When Michelle arrived at the house, she found Dad bleeding and bruised and called Arizona immediately. As soon as I received Arizona's telephone call, I rushed to the house. When I arrived at Dad's house about fifteen minutes later, the police were already there. I went in to see my Dad sitting up completely naked on the side of the bed, with his bare feet dangling over the side. The sheets were no longer on the bed, and were pooled in a circle around him. There were spots of blood on the sheets, Dad's forehead had several bleeding cuts, and his left arm was totally purple from the fingers up past the elbow. Seeing the blood and the bruised arm sent me into a frantic state of mind. We were able to dress him after the police had finished their investigation. Michelle told me that this was the same way she found Dad when she arrived to relieve Amy. Amy had evidently been drinking (see Introduction – Sudden Happenings) throughout the night of July 4th and had also imbibed alcohol from our house. Some old miniatures that had been under the counter were empty and there was an empty wine bottle sitting on the counter.

To digress, Mom and Dad had always had cocktails every evening. Before Mom died, the drink of choice was Black Velvet bourbon and water, primarily because it was easy for Dad to fix it. As the effects of the alcohol became more difficult for their bodies to assimilate, we started diluting the alcohol – eventually to 40% alcohol and 60% water. I often wondered if he continued the practice to help Mom. I now think that the alcohol was a self-medicating process for her to dull whatever pain she was feeling, although she never mentioned being in pain. They started drinking earlier and earlier each day. The past year before Mom died, the first drink occurred when she came out to the living room, dressed for the day. This was about 8:30-8:45 a.m. They didn't drink wine at all anymore and nothing other than this specific kind of bourbon. After Mom's death, Dad would love to drink margaritas when we took him out to eat Mexican food, but we didn't have margarita fixings in the house. He didn't really request alcohol after Mom died – I think he just forgot about it.

It turned out the wine bottle on the counter that day was one I had brought back from the New York wineries four years before. It had been stored in the back of a high cabinet, and would have had to be searched for.

Once I began working outside the house a few months before, the Hospice nurse (Bethany) routinely began making extra visits, especially when Arizona was out of town. When I received the phone call from Arizona, I immediately called her, as she should have been at the house around 9:30 a.m. It was now 11:00 a.m. Bethany (the nurse) told me she had indeed called the house to let Amy know she was on her way. Amy told Bethany that everything was fine and that there was no reason for a visit. Bethany was alarmed, noted Amy's words in her notes, and decided to call later that day. Upon receiving my call, Bethany rushed right over.

Bethany documented the changes in Dad between Tuesday and Thursday, when the attack happened. She did a physical on Dad, and although it did not appear that Dad had any broken bones or extensive damage, she was worried about him. She also wanted to ensure that the incident was medically documented. So, when the police left, we headed for the Emergency Room (ER).

As we were leaving for the ER, I had gone back into the house to get some emergency cash – I kept $40 in a purple greeting card envelope in the bottom of my desk. The money was gone! When I went back outside to the car, Michelle had Amy's backpack in the yard next to the driveway. On top of the backpack was Amy's bloody smock. We carefully picked up the backpack and stored it in the garage. I will never know why Amy called Michelle to relieve her, but I am grateful that she did. She could have just left Dad there and he would have eventually gone outside, naked, hopefully to find someone to help him.

We were placed in a room at the ER immediately. The ER physician called in a police photographer, and later that afternoon, Dad was admitted to the Hospice Unit for five days of respite care (see Hospice section) for observation and for safety purposes. I was so distraught at the Emergency Room that I was in a panic that I didn't have any ready cash to buy Dad snacks or drinks. The ER doctor took pity on me and actually went out to his car and brought in his wallet. I let him give me $20, but he would have let me take every penny he had. The ER staff was very upset about our incident. Of course, I paid him back the next day – but I was really irrational, even though I was trying to be brave and calm.

Mary (the night caregiver) came to the hospital from school, having been called by Michelle. She walked into Dad's room and there was no mistaking the horror on her face. She reported that Amy had been 45 minutes late to work, making Mary late to school. She had hurried off to school, without reporting that Amy had been late. Dad had been comfortably ensconced in bed when she left the house.

By the next day, both Dad's medical and mental conditions declined drastically and his admission was changed from respite status to a medical status. The respite clock stopped ticking at that point. That afternoon, the Adult Protective Services (APS) counselor came to interview me. She asked me to step out of Dad's room to talk to her. As I was leaving the room, Dad yelled out my name. I jerked to a stop in total amazement. I do not remember the last time Dad could call me by name. Whether this was an unusual moment of lucidity due to his condition, or whether he was scared for me to leave him, I do not know. Other family members were still with him. I went back into the room and explained to him that I was going to be in the next room talking to someone, but that I wasn't leaving the hospital. He seemed OK with that, but was obviously glad when I returned and he could see that I was there. Dad had always known who I was – he knew I belonged to him. He could also recognize my brothers, but he hadn't known our names in at least a couple of years, unless we prompted him. I was very shocked! He exhibited this lucidity once again after we took him home.

He remained as a medical admission for about ten days, and then returned to respite status. The next five days of his admission showed good improvement in his condition, even though he was barely eating. We had brought some of his art, pictures of family, and compact diskette (CD) music to the Hospice unit, so that we could have familiar objects around him. We took him home after fifteen days.

He was so glad to be home and seemed to just visibly relax. He continued to not be hungry or eat well even then. About a week after returning home, Dad told me "There just isn't any reason to live any longer." I was amazed that he was able to speak with such clarity, and that his Alzheimer's let him make this statement. This was the second statement that he uttered with such clarity and lucidity. He died about 15 days later.

Dad's breathing was pretty ragged the last 24 hours. We put him on oxygen to help him breathe. He eventually calmed down. A couple of hours before he died, he became very agitated.

This continued without resolve until Michelle stated – "He has some issue that is not resolved. Is there someone he might need to talk to?"

Dad had one sister and they had not really seen each other in years, and had only talked to on birthdays and holidays. I had just put her telephone number into my cell phone when Dad had been injured. I immediately called her and asked if she would talk to him. She said, "Yes." When he heard her voice, he immediately calmed down and breathed more peacefully. After a few minutes, I took the phone back and asked her what she had said. She had told him she loved him, had started praying for him and saying the 23rd Psalm and The Lord's Prayer. Dad died while I was still talking to her. Talking to her was just what he needed.

Dad died a few hours before Mom's birthday and about three weeks prior to their 60th wedding anniversary. I was glad to know they were joined together again in time for them to celebrate these events together.

Dad had had a pacemaker for over ten years. From his biweekly tests, we knew that the pacemaker was active approximately 40% of the time. One question I always had was: would the pacemaker keep him alive beyond what his illness could bear? I was advised by the nurse that Dad would die when it was time for him to and that the pacemaker would not interfere. The pacemaker company advised me that the pacemaker would have to be turned off after death. This is done by placing a magnet over the skin where the device is implanted. It took about two minutes for the pacemaker to turn off. The nurse could tell it was off by listening with her stethoscope. Newer pacemaker devices may require the intervention of a technician or cardiologist.

Amazingly, Dad's autopsy showed pneumonia as one of the causes of death. We did not even know he had it! He had become malnourished over the last couple of weeks, though we were still able to get some fluids into him. He just wouldn't eat. He only had breathing problems the last two days, in the form of shortness of breath. We had attributed that to the dying process and the pneumonia had not been detected by the Hospice nurse. It is unlikely that we could have prevented the pneumonia. This is an example of the easily acquired incidence of pneumonia in the elderly. Heart disease and Alzheimer's disease were the other diagnoses listed. Dad's brain weighed 11 ounces (0.69 pounds) at death – the normal brain weighs between 1300-1400 grams (about 3 - 5 pounds).

Retrieved August 2009, from http://faculty.washington.edu/chudler/facts.html#brain

Chapter 4:

Our Caregiving Continuum

I took care of Mom and Dad for the first 1-1/2 years by being there the entire day Monday through Friday, and visiting them when needed on the weekend. I prepared food during the week for the weekend and left menu notes for them with reheating instructions, if necessary. By the time 18 months had passed, Mom and Dad were occasionally not getting to bed safely or were having trouble with their food preparation. Mom was on oxygen full-time and several times I received a telephone call within an hour after I left that the oxygen wasn't working well. I would ask pointed questions of Dad to assess what had happened. A couple of times Mom's tubing had come off and once she was on the floor. If I was too far from the house, I would call 911 and send an ambulance up there, as they could arrive before I would. I would give Dad instructions to unlock the front door and would keep him on the phone until someone arrived, as I was racing up there myself.

At this point we put in some partial remedies over a two month period. In January 2005, we brought in the Hospice team to evaluate Mom's health status. A friend of Mom's had suggested I call them to see if they could provide any level of care. Her mother had been on Hospice care for a couple of years, and she told me I would be very surprised with the care they could provide. As with many people, my perception of Hospice was that they only provided service when six months of life were left.

This is a huge point to understand. Hospice actually provides care based on how well the patient can perform the Activities of Daily Living (ADLs). ADLs include feeding, dressing, bathing, toileting, transferring (from chair to bed, etc.), and ambulation (walking). The Hospice team visits the home and assesses the patient with regards to the ADLs and what that specific Hospice agency can provide. In Mom's case, she could no longer walk more than a few feet.

In fact, two months previously, we had bought a battery operated scooter for her to transport herself around the house. Most of the time, she needed help with the scooter too. Because Mom could not walk well and especially without running out of breath, this became a main qualifier for Mom to be on Hospice. Another qualifier was that she was on oxygen. She also needed assistance with bathing, dressing, and toileting. She could no longer stand to prepare food. On the telephone, Hospice had explained to me that usually an aide would begin coming to the house two days per week. Much to my surprise, the initial assessment allowed for an aide to come five days per week, Monday through Friday.

In came Nadine, a young mother who was obtaining her RN license from the local university. Nadine came every morning about 7:30 and stayed for two hours, taking over the duties of bathing, dressing, and transporting Mom to the living room. We were very fortunate to have her. She was able to bond with both parents right away, and would joke and visit with both of them before she left for the day. I missed helping Mom get dressed, so several days a week, I would pop in to talk to them and make sure she was doing OK. Mom was very claustrophobic, even from the beginning. The steam from the shower would panic her, and she could not get in/out of the bathtub, so we had been using the sponge bath method.

We had tried having her sit on her walker to wash her hair in the kitchen and only standing up to rinse her hair, but that didn't work very well. It was just too hard. So, I tried different ways to wash her hair without panicking her. The best method was to keep her on the scooter (the chair rotated), dampen her hair with a washcloth, add the shampoo and massage her head (very soothing to her), and use the washcloth to rinse her hair. I would rinse it three times, change the water, and keep rerinsing her hair until there was no more shampoo. Amazingly, this method only required 4-5 rinses. It was simple, easy for Mom and worked really well. She felt no stress from this method. The Hospice aide also adopted this method.

Another benefit of Hospice, which eventually saved us several hundred dollars per month, was that Hospice pays for any medications related to the primary medical condition (the condition that Hospice admitted the patient under). Mom's primary condition was emphysema, so her oxygen, the inhalers, and medications were all paid for. Because of how the MediGap policies (health insurance after Medicare) worked, there was a cap on the cost of medications that were paid for each year, usually about $1100-$1200. Mom and Dad would exhaust this amount by April of each year and I would be paying around $700 per month for medications.

This cost was split between Mom and Dad, as both her lung medications and his Alzheimer's medications were quite expensive.

The Hospice provided one Registered Nurse visit per week. The nurse would take Mom's vital signs each week, and would bring the medications allowed – to support the primary diagnosis of emphysema. Supporting medications included all her inhalers, any lung medications, her blood pressure medicine, and pain medicine or stool softeners as required. Once Mom was on morphine (the last three months of her life), stool softeners were needed, as morphine can cause constipation. (Note - The Hospice philosophy is discussed under Hospice Care.) The nurse would visit with Mom, Dad, and myself to find out how the week had gone, if any issues had arisen, and discuss any personal issues that we had. The best benefit of Hospice is that having this care in the home completely eliminates the process of going to doctor's visits, with the exception of emergency care, such as a fall, eye care, blood clot, etc.

The Hospice organization supports the entire family, offers support in the form of reality checks, to answer questions, or just to provide a listening post or shoulder to lean on. This support was very beneficial to me, and helped me to monitor and come to grips with Mom's true condition. Mom was amazing – she never complained verbally about her condition, and never said she was in pain. Her complaints came in the form of not having enough inhalers, or that the inhalers weren't working quickly enough, or driving the scooter too fast (the maximum speed was 4 miles per hour), or that Dad or I hadn't done something correctly. In retrospect, I think she was masking the effects her disease had on her and was trying to keep it from us.

In March 2005, the four kids had a family meeting and the brothers took over the weekends, making sure Mom and Dad had lunch, preparing the coffee pot to be turned on the next morning, and checking on their safety. Often I had cooked enough during the week that there would be leftovers, but often the brothers brought in outside meals to give them a change. These weekends became treats for them, having special food and the extra bonus of seeing their sons more often. Slowly, but surely, I was able to convince them that if they didn't want me to stay until they went to bed, then I needed to have a caregiver there until they were asleep.

Part of their insistence that I go home every day was a show of independence, but I think their underlying reason was that they didn't want to be a burden to me or my family. What they may not have realized though, was that I worried about them even more as time went by. I could see that they were becoming more and more impaired. The constant worry was difficult for me. After the family meeting, I sat down with them and explained my concerns. I reminded them about the ambulance visits and asked them to consider part-time care, just to be sure they got to bed safely. Neither one could remember the incidents that had occurred. The key point to be made was the importance of their safety. We couldn't have Mom unhooked from her oxygen – she was on 6-7 liters airflow and used about 150 pounds of oxygen a week. We had two big canisters of oxygen (about 4 feet tall x 20 inches in circumference) in the hallway, with 50 feet of tubing extending from the canister. We also made a decision to hire part-time caregivers four hours in the evening through an agency.

The agency lined up caregivers for me. I asked them to be consistent, to try to bring in only 1-2 caregivers, with the same people each week. At first this system worked smoothly. One caregiver would come in five evenings a week from 4:00 p.m. to 8:00 p.m. and another for the weekend nights. I would train them on the procedures and posted instructions in the kitchen. These caregivers were hired as aides, able to assist with ambulation, dressing, toileting, and also fixed snacks for Mom and Dad. Aides are not certified nurse assistants (CNA) and are not allowed to give medications, unless the medications are dispensed into a small container and only contain enough for one administration. We paid the agency $19 per hour for this level of aide. To hire a CNA, I would have been required to pay $35 per hour. A registered nurse would be $50 per hour. These costs add up (see Table 1 below). Be sure and hire the appropriate level of care for the needs that you have. Resources should be factored in as the second consideration. If your loved one needs assistance with bathing and dressing, an aide could come from 7:30-9:30 in the morning and/or 8:00-10:00 at night (or at times that suit the patient's schedule). Arrange for a family member to dispense the medications, if possible.

Table 1: Caregiver Costs

Type of Caregiver	Daily Cost (4 hours)	Weekly Cost (4 hours/day)	Annual Cost (4 hours/day)	Daily Cost (24 hours/day)	Weekly Cost (24 hours/day)	Annual Cost (24 hours/day)
Aide	$ 76	$ 532	$27,664	$ 456	$3,192	$165,984
CNA	$140	$ 980	$50,960	$ 840	$5,880	$305,760
RN	$200	$1400	$72,800	$1200	$8,400	$436,800

Note: These costs were reflective of our area of 2005; costs are area dependent and will vary considerably.
© Copyright 2010, Janice Louise Long

Mom and Dad were of the cocktail generation. She and Dad had two cocktails every night for as long as I can remember. When Dad came home from work, we could greet him and give him any exciting news of the day. We were then expected to disappear, go outside, or go to our rooms to do homework for the next hour. This hour was their time together to watch the news, to review the day, and to have their cocktails. Cocktails could range from martinis to manhattans to scotch whiskey, and on special occasions – margaritas or daquiris. I was therefore surprised to see that now the cocktails were strictly whiskey and water.

I finally realized that Dad no longer knew how to prepare any of the other cocktails. Cocktail hour started earlier now – around 3:30 to 4:00 p.m., especially once the evening caregiving began. Over time, cocktail hour became earlier and earlier – to 2:00 p.m., then 11:00 a.m., then 8:30 a.m. when Mom would get to the living room after dressing. If she didn't get her cocktail, she would really be angry. I believe this was a form of self-medication, but it took me a long time to think this. I was more of a mind to view the tremendous consumption of alcohol as a further signal of danger to them. It was very clear that their bodies could no longer assimilate the alcohol. In fact, I came into the house a few times the next morning to find a chair or table upturned. Neither one of them would be able to recollect what had happened.

When the brothers began helping out with weekend care, we also adjusted the alcohol consumption by diluting the alcohol before it was brought into the house. I would put the empty bottles in the garage closet, my brother would pick them up and refill them and put them in the kitchen. Dad never noticed that he didn't have to break any seals!! We initially diluted the alcohol 60:40 (60% alcohol, 40% water), but gradually arrived at 40% alcohol and 60% water. One time, some friends of Mom and Dad's came by after I had left for the day, bringing martinis. The martinis were way too strong for Mom and Dad. The next morning, I came in and found both the cocktail table and the recliner turned over. I didn't find out for a week what really happened, and then only by accident when I talked to Mom's friend.

Mom and Dad typically went to bed about 6:30 – 7:00 p.m. Once we had the part-time caregivers in place, they began going to bed at 5:30 p.m. and would then tell the caregiver to leave. I think sometimes they even got up out of bed and went back to the living room after the caregiver left. I had to be really firm with both Mom and Dad and the caregivers and set the rule that the caregiver could not leave until they were asleep. This step saved some accidents for a while. But hiring part-time care was the first stepping stone to full-time care. This step took a level of worry away.

I worried a lot anyway, but seeing my parents go downhill added huge levels of anxiety and worry to my shoulders, and over time dragged me down. Eventually, caregivers would be moved around by the agency, or someone would get sick, and a new caregiver would appear. I tried to convince the agency that this was not good for patients with dementia, that we needed consistent caregivers and time to train them. Thank goodness, we did not have too much trouble with caregivers being tardy. Our house was difficult to find the first time, so I had sent a map to the agency that they would give to the caregivers. With the brothers there during the weekend days and the p.m. caregivers, we created a new layer of protection and care for our parents.

We had had a part-time evening caregiver that was Hispanic that Mom did not like at all. She just had an instinctive mistrust of this lady. I never did figure that out – the lady had some missing teeth due to an abusive relationship, and talked funny due to that, but she knew what to do and how to do it. Mom and Dad would get angry with her, cuss her out, and essentially demand that she leave their house. Part of this mistrust may have been due to Mom's paranoia that people in the house would steal. Mom had had previous experiences with stealing by housekeepers who were of Hispanic origin. Please know I mean no slight to the Hispanic people – I have had some great Hispanic friends. It just happened that Mom had primarily had Hispanic housekeepers and I feel this mistrust carried over to our caregiver. This situation added to my feelings later about Arizona (eventually our full-time caregiver) being accepted by Mom and Dad.

Due to Mom's concerns about stealing, I took her jewelry home to my house. She had already given her china sets to her granddaughters, so nothing valuable remained in the house. I kept some spending money in Dad's dresser, as he liked to pay my brothers for bringing lunch to them or to give to them to get something from the store. We kept it in an envelope in a special drawer for knickknacks. Only Dad and I knew where the money was kept (never more that $200), and eventually Arizona knew as well. I was very lucky – none of this money was ever missing.

Dad was in a new decline by this time. Seeing the benefits that we gained from having Mom on Hospice, I began to lobby for them to admit Dad to Hospice. By this time, he had been on Aricept for 1-1/2 years and Namenda for a little over one year. At this time, there were no other Alzheimer drugs available. Another hurdle to cross throughout this entire time was to get Dad to take showers. He insisted he was clean, but Mom would let me know he wasn't taking showers. The brothers had helped out some, but one day I was able to get him into the shower while I was there. I turned on the water and instructed him to take off his clothes, get in, and soap his body. He was out in thirty seconds. He said the water was too cold. That is when I really realized he didn't know what to do in the shower. I was tremendously worried about skin breakdown and uncleanliness.

The Alzheimer's was also causing some balance problems. Dad always looked like he was going to topple over when he walked. Mom had been on Hospice care for about four months when I asked Hospice to assess Dad for admission, as well. They were able to admit him as his condition was declining again, although he barely met the admitting criteria. In fact, he seemed to be declining faster than Mother. Hospice then provided his Alzheimer's medications and a different health care aide, who came in two times per week to assist Dad in bathing. The nurse would do assessments on both of them during her regular weekly visit. Hospice explained to me that the first admission would last six months, with periodic two month reevaluations thereafter. If his condition improved, he could be discharged from Hospice and readmitted later as his condition changed. Fortunately, he was not discharged until after Mom died. He had been exhibiting anxiety and restlessness, which disappeared when she died. It seems that he had still been stressed and worried about her condition, but couldn't express his worry. After Mom died, it seemed like we had a new piece of Dad back.

Adding in these interventions allowed the course of the day to become almost normal again, although it really wasn't. I was able to monitor the care that was given, how Mom and Dad were reacting to the care, to monitor their health, and to continue my work and support my own family. I still managed the shopping, menus, and medications, as well as the finances. The Hospice aide would start the laundry after Mom's bath and I would put it in the dryer and fold it later on. Mom and Dad were so funny. They still didn't like having someone else in their home, but they basically understood that this was necessary. They adjusted their bed time down to 5:00 p.m. Once they were in bed, they tried to shoo the night caregiver out the door. Several times that they were successful in doing this, they would get back up and return to the living room. I had to finally direct the caregivers that they absolutely could not leave until 8:00 p.m. It was very rare that Mom and Dad would still be awake at 8:00 p.m.

Our evening caregiving system did well for about 10 months. Our smooth, but lumpy path continued to move downward. In October 2005, we began talking to Mom and Dad about full-time caregiving. I think they were well aware at this time that they really needed more assistance, and although they really didn't like strangers in their home, they also wanted me to be able to have time to take care of my own family and home. One of my brothers and I actually looked at two assisted living facilities and one Alzheimer's Disease specialty facility. Mother was amenable to moving to a facility and thought she might be able to convince Dad. But, we knew in our hearts that they really didn't want to move, so I tried finding a full-time hiring avenue. Mom and Dad did have long-term care insurance, but only for the nursing home, not assisted living. Assisted living insurance was not available when they purchased their nursing home insurance. The insurance company had sent them an option to add assisted living insurance when it began to be offered, but they did not add it. I assume they either didn't understand what it was, didn't expect to need it, or were totally opposed to even consider assisted living as an option.

I should note that I stayed at their house a couple of nights before hiring a full-time night caregiver, just to see how things really worked for them. It seemed like one or the other of them was up almost every hour of the night. That would wake the other one up and then they would begin to talk. I don't think any of us got any sleep. Knowing how much they were awake at night changed my perception of quiet nights, and increased my anxiety of leaving them alone after 8:00 p.m.

Mom and Dad became used to having people coming in/out of the house: me, my brothers, the Hospice aides, the nurse, the p.m. aides, and the oxygen delivery man. They began looking forward to having people to visit with all the time. Mom was using almost 200 pounds of oxygen a week (two large canisters about 4 feet high and 18 inches across) at a liter flow of 6-7. Each canister could have air flow up to 8 liters, but we were advised that doing so was not efficient for the tank. We were given a "Y"-shaped connector, and ran each tank at 3+3 or 3+4 to maximize the use of the oxygen. Even though we had good control over Mom and Dad's health, I kept thinking another shoe would drop.

I really did not have any idea of how to hire a caregiver outside of an agency. I was lucky though. I called the Alzheimer's Association and asked them how to find a caregiver and how to check their references (meaning – is there a way to check through a professional source). The lady that answered the phone actually knew a full-time caregiver that was looking for a new client. I called this lady and set up a meeting.

We met at Applebee's for dinner – two of my brothers, one of my nieces, and one of my daughters were also there. When Arizona walked in, we were a little surprised to find out that she was black. This raised an immediate concern for me, which I will explain shortly. We let Arizona explain how she viewed caregiving, what she did for her clients, what pay she would require, when she could begin work, and other general questions (see Hiring Caregiver Questionnaire). Her specialty was in working with Alzheimer's patients. Arizona was available immediately, so I set up a time for her to come over and meet Mom and Dad.

Mom and Dad were born and raised in Iowa – in the heartland of the United States. At the time when they were raised, Iowa was predominantly Caucasian and Protestant, and probably still is. We came to New Mexico in 1952 to relieve my asthma by moving to a more temperate climate. During the time that I was being raised, this area was a mix of both Hispanic and Caucasian, with very few black people. In high school, I was not allowed to date either a Catholic or Hispanic person. So, I felt a prejudice would exist with a black caregiver. I was very apprehensive. I explained my concern to Arizona, and she just laughed it away. She told me she had come across this before and had had no trouble handling the situation. The older generations looked upon her as a servant or employee, which didn't bother her at all.

After I checked Arizona's references by calling and talking to all five of them, the meeting with Mom and Dad took place. All of Arizona's references recommended her and one family reported that she went above and beyond normal care. Over time, we certainly found out what that meant. My brothers and I had prebriefed Mom and Dad and were there when Arizona arrived. She took over the conversation right away and had Mom and Dad laughing soon after. She began her caregiving with us that week. Arizona was willing to work full-time at night and had other caregivers she could bring in with her to help. These aides followed Arizona from client to client. She worked 8:00 p.m. to 8:00 a.m. Monday through Friday. Another caregiver came in for this shift on the weekends. This stepped up level of care greatly added to the family's peace of mind.

The premise for Arizona to begin evening care was not only to ensure their nighttime safety, but also that the nighttime would be when Mom most needed help. Even though it was only a few feet from the side of the bed to the bathroom, she was needing more and more assistance and instructional help in the bathroom. By instructional help, I mean step-by-step commands. We would help her get on the scooter, we would turn her chair (telling her we were doing so), holding on to her or guiding her to the towel bar to hold onto, and guiding her onto the toilet. When she had finished, we would have her grab onto the towel bar for stability and we would adjust her clothing. We used a team concept and let her know that together we were a team. She would hold on and we would assist with whatever we needed to. I should have hired a handyman to come in and install handicapped bars on the wall, by the bathtub, and in the shower where Dad took a shower (even though there was a tiled seat available). Installing a handicap handle over tile requires someone who really knows what they are doing, as the tile will probably have to be drilled.

The first night Arizona was there, Dad became sick in the night. Two other nights that week, Mom had problems too. I could not even begin to imagine how they would have dealt with these illnesses on their own or walking into such messes later on in the morning. A caveat here – Mom and Dad were even having trouble using the telephone by this time. By each telephone was taped a sheet of paper listing the 911 telephone number, my telephone number, each brother's, as well as the Hospice 24 hour phone number. (See Forms Section) Part of the written instructions was to call 911, if the emergency dealt with Mom's oxygen. These instruction type pages may be used for any process in the household, and are very helpful for the elderly, and particularly so for dementia or Alzheimer's patients.

Mom liked having Arizona there. When Mom was awake, she would call "Yoo-Hoo" to Arizona. Arizona would reply "Yoo-Hoo" back, bring Mom out to the living room, and let Dad remain asleep. They would sit up talking until Mom was ready to go back to bed. Sometimes, Dad would become confused when they were going to bed and wouldn't know who Mom was. He would say, "Who's that strange woman in my bed?" We would explain, but once the Sundowner's Syndrome kicked in, it was difficult to persuade Dad that Mom belonged there. Mom would stay in the living room then as well until Dad went to sleep.

Once we had full-time care, it became immediately evident that we needed a caregiving system to keep track of each shift and what occurred daily in Mom and Dad's lives. The forms and ideas that evolved in this caregiving system are shown in the Forms section of this chapter. Initially, I had a timetable for the caregivers, showing their schedules. This timetable was taped to the kitchen counter each month. The timetable listed all emergency phone numbers as well as the phone numbers for each caregiver. A sign-in sheet was also taped to the kitchen counter to keep track of caregiving hours for pay purposes.

Log sheets were set up in a notebook to show the caregiver name, the time, what meds were given, and comments of behavior or occurrences during each shift. Even if nothing out of the ordinary occurred, the caregivers were required to add an entry each shift. This also became important for the Hospice nurse and aide. They kept a Hospice notebook in the home, which contained the admission papers and weekly notes. But, they would read all the caregiving notes for the prior week and included any important happenings in their own notes. Our notes, along with the weekly assessment, would lend credence to decisions that needed to be made with regards to changes in Mom and Dad's care.

The overnight caregiving worked well with only a few glitches. Arizona would take a well-deserved week off here and there and we would add the extra hours to the other caregivers and adjust their schedules. I would be nervous while she was gone that something would happen, but we usually managed. One time the hot water heater broke and flooded the garage. That was an emergent phone call at night, which was taken care of the next day. I rarely had a private caregiver not show up for work, although there were times when they might be late. Not being late was a rule (see Caregiver Guidelines) that we established, as taking the time to do a turnover (discuss the shift with the new caregiver) was paramount to good care. Some of our caregivers were attending college and would need to leave immediately to arrive at school on time. We had a backup phone system – the caregiver was always to call both Arizona and myself if there was a problem, even if Arizona was on vacation. Occasionally, we had to reinforce this rule, as the tendency was to call Arizona and let her call me (this worked well too). Fortunately, Arizona and I got along very well and what my goals were for Mom and Dad's health care matched her goals for being a good caregiver. When a caregiver became ill or had a family emergency, we just readjusted the schedule. Personal illness was also a rule – the caregiver was not allowed in the house until 24 hours after the symptoms had disappeared.

A point to mention is that as time went on, many processes became harder and harder for Mom and Dad to perform or understand. Dad had Alzheimer's disease, and Mom had Vascular Dementia. Even though the dementias are very different, the manifestations of the dementias become very similar. I became very conversant in talking one or the other of them through processes step-by-step: using the microwave, dressing, toileting, buckling the seat belt, whatever it was.

I was totally surprised the first time I took Dad somewhere in the car and not only did he not know how to buckle his seat belt or even where to find it, he didn't know how to shut the car door! Another example – one day I was fixing them some cold drinks, and adding ice to the glasses from the icemaker – Dad came in and asked me what I was doing. I replied simply, "Fixing your drinks, Dad." He said, "No, what's this?" pointing to the icemaker. I explained to him that it was an icemaker and all I had to do was push the lever with the glass to get the ice. He was very surprised, exclaiming, "That's never been there before." Another example – I made cinnamon rolls one day, and left some for the next morning. I left Mom a note to heat up two of them in the microwave for breakfast. She did so just before I walked in. The kitchen was full of smoke and the rolls were like black hockey pucks. Mom had set the timer to 20 minutes instead of 20 seconds.

As we now had 24 hour care, no keys were necessary. The caregivers always relieved one another, so the door was answered by one of them at all times. We had obtained two wheelchair placards from the Department of Motor Vehicles (DMV). We used one placard for my car and kept one in the kitchen, along with a spare garage door opener, for Arizona and my brothers' use. Even Arizona did not have a set of keys to the house, although I would have trusted her with them. Arizona was allowed to take Dad out in her car (especially after Mom died to keep him active), but no other caregiver was allowed to do so. Wheelchair placards are obtained from DMV by having the primary care provider fill out the required DMV form. Placards may be temporary or permanent.

The period of time that we had full-time caregiving was from October 2005 to August 2007, nearly two years. Arizona and her team arrived in October 2005 to do night time care. We discontinued the part-time agency care, we still had the Hospice teams during the day, as well as myself. Arizona performed night care, as she had the most experience, and could best assist Mom with her breathing and Dad with his Alzheimer's when I was not there. Arizona had actually concentrated her practice on Alzheimer's patients and currently runs an Alzheimer's unit at a local nursing home. She also continues to take care of other private patients on the weekends. Three months later, Mom's stroke occurred. Following Mom's death, Arizona switched her caregiving to the day to support Dad, and her staff came in for night duty. Thus, we put the most experienced person on the shift that provided the appropriate type of care needed and shifted her around as the needs changed.

During the twenty-two months of full-time care, I was constantly learning more about how to look at Dad's illness, how to talk to him, and how to work with him. As my parents aged and became more ill, they became like children, looking up to me or the caregivers for the right thing to do or say. Just like children, they know when you are upset or anxious and their behavior can reflect your anxiousness. Dad would always know if I was upset or if something was bothering me. Caregivers need to take time outs and find outside avenues for relaxation, so that being an ally and advocate for the patient is possible.

Chapter 5:

Caregiving Overview

The three types of caregivers generally found, whether through an agency or private care, will be a Registered Nurse, a Certified Nurse Assistant, or a healthcare aide.

Registered Nurse (RN): a licensed, college degreed, healthcare professional with the ability to supervise all care. The RN leads the Hospice team under the direction of the physician, reviews the care of all Hospice patients with her team and the physician. The RN is responsible for visiting and assessing the patient. These assessments could be given once a week, or more often as circumstances dictate, or in alignment with the specific Hospice agency guidelines.

Certified Nurse Assistant/Aide (CNA): The aides are usually licensed healthcare aides with the CNA certification, allowing them to give any care needed, including medications with the exception of intravenous care (IV). Many times these aides are also taking college courses to become Licensed Practical Nurses or Registered Nurses. They supplement their income by performing care.

The CNA/aide helps with the Activities of Daily Living (ADLs) – bathing, dressing, toileting, ambulating, feeding – and can also help by starting the laundry or doing small household chores. If the aide is not certified as a CNA, they may not dispense medications. However, if medications have been dispensed into a container (by the family or another licensed professional), like a medication paper cup, they may then give <u>only</u> those dispensed medications to the patient. The CNA/Aide should be able to transfer a patient safely, turn them in the bed, should know first aid, should know how to use a gait belt (a thick, cloth belt with a buckle that may be put around the waist of a patient to aid in walking), and be able to shower or bathe, dress, and shave a patient.

Hiring Caregivers

No system really exists to check on caregiving abilities. I wish there were Statewide Care Registries to check on caregiver reputations, but I do not know of any. Receiving names of caregivers by word of mouth from friends works well and also gives an immediate reference if the friend has used that caregiver. It is similar to finding a good housekeeper!! Tell everyone you know that you are looking for a good caregiver. One should turn up. Telephone calls to local healthcare organizations (Alzheimer's Organization, American Heart Association, American Lung Assocation, American Diabetes Association, American Red Cross, or other disease specific organizations) may also turn up personal caregivers or even the newspaper, e.g., we found Arizona through the local Alzheimer's Organization. The website http://www.craigslist. com is also a good way to advertise for or to find a caregiver.

Each caregiver interviewed should be able to give a list of references, and be able to show copies of their licenses. All references should be called. Call the institutions from which they received training to verify the certificates/licenses that are presented. Each state has a court website, in which a name may be typed to see if any charges have been filed against the person. Call the local police department to find out how to perform a background check. Websites are available to do so online. (See Appendix VI: Website Resources) We found several of our part-time caregivers through our Hospice or agency aides.

During the interview process, all caregivers interviewed should fill out an application. If a caregiver declines to fill out the application, that would be a good clue not to hire that person. Caregivers may not wish to give out their social security numbers, as they like to be paid in cash, and not to report their earnings. Deductions for taxes should include FICA, State, and Federal Withholding taxes. The family should provide unemployment and worker's compensation insurance coverage, as well as homeowner's liability covering employees in the home. Ask all candidates the same questions. Establish yourself as the employer and the boss and make the interview as formal as possible. If the candidate passes the interview stage, ask them for a second interview to meet the patient.

Questions to Ask When Interviewing Caregivers

How long have you been caring for patients?

How many patients have you had in the last two years?

How far do you live from give address or area of caregiving location?

Do you have a car, current license, insurance?

What type of diagnoses have you cared for?

Do you have any experience with dementia or Alzheimer's patients?

What type of medications have you administered?

What is the average length of time you keep a case?

Do you interact with the physician when needed?

Do you have a home telephone? Mobile phone? Pager?

Do you prefer to wear a uniform?

Will you grocery shop and drive patient to appointments?

Will you cook regularly/occasional meals?

Do you keep any type of daily records?

Do you plan to care for anyone else while you are employed by our family?

Do you have a CNA license? CPR Certificate?

Do you have a resume? References?

Why should I hire you?

Retrieved August 2009, from http://www.caregiversdirectory.com. Click on "Health Articles" and then "Helpful Hints for Hiring a Caregiver"

Note: Two questions were added to this list by the author.

As you read on, you will see that some of these questions did not apply to our caregiving situation. I was the patient advocate and took care of the medications, shopping and errands, and interaction with the medical personnel. We only allowed our caregiver supervisor to drive my Dad, but for the purpose of keeping him active and happy, not specifically for caregiving support. We also created our own caregiving record keeping system, which is the basis for this book.

My parents knew they were declining, and fortunately for us, they knew they needed help. Needing help was hard for them to accept, and especially so when it became time for evening or 24 hour care. A few instances of night time illnesses and a couple of ambulance visits helped convince them that having full-time care was important for their safety.

We would again hire independent (private) caregivers, especially if costs were a concern, and if the caregiver was highly recommended. Caregiver references should be checked following the interview (or beforehand if the references are available). Some references (usually family members of the patient) may not wish to give detailed answers, but they should be able to answer the following questions.

1. Did __ Name of caregiver __ give your loved one good care?

2. Did _____ keep your loved one clean and healthy?

3. Did you feel like your loved one was safe under _____ care?

4. Did you ask _____ to perform household chores?

5. Did _____ perform additional services? If so, what were they?

6. Would you recommend this caregiver?

7. Do you have any concerns about this caregiver?

8. Did this caregiver arrive on time?

9. Did this caregiver have outside or family responsibilities that prevented them from performing their caregiving duties?

In addition to personal references, check any professional references given. Most of the time, a professional reference will only be able to tell you that the person worked for them and for how long. Also, check your state's court system for any felony charges. If you have hired a chief caregiver that oversees the caregiving staff, she may perform this step, but be sure and follow-up. Find out how long the caregiver has lived in your state. If the caregiver has only been there a short time, check any other state court systems that apply. One may also choose to check the state licensing agency to ensure this person has a legal driver's license.

Have the caregiver fill out an employment form (see example below), especially listing their address and telephone number. Some caregivers may not wish to give you this information. Ask why. Explain to them that the household will be reporting the caregiving amounts paid to the Internal Revenue Service (IRS). Caregivers not working under an agency can be classified as "Independent Contractors". Independent contractors are required to report income to the IRS.

Independent contractor - People such as doctors, dentists, veterinarians, lawyers, accountants, contractors, subcontractors, public stenographers, or auctioneers who are in an independent trade, business, or profession in which they offer their services to the general public are generally independent contractors. However, whether they are independent contractors or employees depends on the facts in each case. The general rule is that an individual is an independent contractor if the payer has the right to control or to direct only the result of the work and not how it will be done. The earnings of a person who is working as an independent contractor are subject to self-employment tax. For more information on determining whether you are an independent contractor or an employee, see Publication 15-A, Employer's Supplemental Tax Guide.

Retrieved July 2009, from http://www.irs.gov/pub/irs-pdf/p15a.pdf

Independent contractors are required to report earnings between $400 and $106,800 per year from all sources. They must file Self-Employment tax forms each year, paying 12.4% social security tax and 2.9% Medicare tax. The household that the care is being given in can also request an Employer Identification Number from the Internal Revenue Service at 1-800-829-4933 or http://www.irs.gov/businesses/small. Let the caregiver know that the household will be reporting the caregiving income for the year to the IRS under the name of the person being cared for.

The caregiver may ask for an increase in their hourly wage to meet this requirement. Others may choose not to work for you as other families may pay them cash and not report paid-out income to the IRS. Table 2 below shows the change in hourly wages after deductions.

Table 2: Net Hourly Wage for Caregivers

Hourly Wage	SocSec 12.4%	Medicaid 2.9%	Total Deductions	NetHourly Wage
$ 10.00	$ 1.24	$ 0.29	$ 1.53	$ 8.47
$ 11.00	$ 1.36	$ 0.32	$ 1.68	$ 9.32
$ 12.00	$ 1.49	$ 0.35	$ 1.84	$ 10.16
$ 13.00	$ 1.61	$ 0.38	$ 1.99	$ 11.01
$ 14.00	$ 1.74	$ 0.41	$ 2.14	$ 11.86
$ 15.00	$ 1.86	$ 0.44	$ 2.30	$ 12.71

Caregiving Specifics

Caregiving in any form is a hard job and a challenge. <u>Change is constant.</u> However, I strongly believe that caregiving done at home by a loving family member will keep the loved one healthier for a longer period of time. There will be times when the caregiver is very stressed due to worry about the loved one, due to taking care of the loved one's household, as well as their own. If the caregiver (family member) is working, this just adds to the burden. The caregiver <u>must</u> put into place avenues for relaxation and hobbies during each week to give the stress of caregiving an outlet. But, this wonderful, caring job <u>can</u> be done successfully. Remember why you are caregiving – you are caring for a person (parent, sibling, child) that you love and want the very best care for, and you want them to live a <u>quality</u> life while they can, for as long as possible.

<u>Quality of life is the key!</u> Quality is the perception of the loved one, not the caregiver. Even though my Dad had Alzheimer's and he knew he was losing a piece of his mind every day, he never wanted to give up until the last two weeks. He loved music, dancing, and loved to see his grandchildren and especially the great-grandchildren. He loved the little ones to sit on his lap, or be able to yell "Boo" at them when they thought they were hiding from him. He called all of them "George." He still loved his enchiladas and margaritas. If your loved one has dementia, remember they are still that person. They are just a new, different person and one needs to make the best of the world they live in each day. Sometimes their days are lived in a different era, earlier in their life. Acceptance is the key – go with the flow of the day and keep them comfortable and as happy as possible. Chocolate works too!

<u>The patient is always 100% forgiven.</u> The patient may not always act ill or complain, but they do have a disease that is breaking down their body on the inside. Complaints about their daily life, e.g., food, the caregiver (yourself) etc. may be their way of expressing discomfort from their illness. If they become ill or have an incontinence issue, they will most likely be ashamed or embarrassed, and it is your job to reassure them that everything is OK. Yes, it can be messy and the laundry might have to be done every day, but the real issue is that your loved one is well taken care of. Skin breakdowns can cause ugly pressure sores, which quickly become open wounds that take months to heal and requires special care from wound treatment specialists.

The Caregiving System that I developed while taking care of my parents developed over time. I have forms for timekeeping, medications, instructions, health plan letters, explanations, health status, and miscellaneous forms created for specific needs. My goal is to provide these forms to other caregivers to assist them in the care that they are providing and to make their jobs easier. Instructions and forms may be kept in a notebook in the living room. As the notebook fills up, weekly notes pages and timekeeping schedules may be moved to a separate location or back-up notebook.

Caregiver Contract

A simple caregiver contract may be drawn up to specify the terms of the caregiving. We did not do this, as we kept printed schedules in the kitchen of agreed upon hours. However, we did set specific rules for the caregivers, e.g., only the chief caregiver could take Dad out of the house in her car. The contract should specify duties, work schedule, how changes may be made to the schedule, caregiver illness, timeliness, and how payment to the caregiver will be made. The sample contract shown below includes this specification, including notation of the caregiver's automobile insurance.

Sample Caregiver Contract

This is based on a document developed by a law firm in Seattle and copied with permission from the Utah Coalition for Caregiver Support website. A contract such as this below should be carefully reviewed and specific household needs or personal services added or changed, as appropriate. See http://www.caregivers.utah.gov/sample_contract.htm.

Website warning for use of this form: as with any form contract, or, for that matter, any legal information obtained on the internet, it is highly unwise to make uncritical use of this sample. Users are strongly urged to seek legal advice before making any legal arrangement using this sample.

Caregiver Contract

SERVICE AGREEMENT

1.   The parties to this agreement are:

_____, who will be referred to in this document as "Client", who is to receive care and assistance.

Employer, <u>Name of Employer</u>), acting in the name of Client in the following capacity: ☐ guardian ☐ attorney-in-fact ☐ _____.

Employee, _____, who will be referred to as "Caregiver". Caregiver's address and telephone number are:

2.   The purpose of this agreement is to set out the terms of employment and to establish what assistance Caregiver will provide to Client.

3.   Client is a person with impaired abilities, and is a vulnerable person. Client is dependant on Caregiver and is not able to deal with Caregiver on equal terms. Caregiver will take special care not to take advantage of Client and not to unnecessarily influence Client's choices. Caregiver will not negotiate terms of employment with Client. Caregiver will immediately disclose to the employer all gifts from Client, and will return any gifts that the employer decides are excessive. Caregiver will under no circumstances assist Client to write checks unless authorized to do so in writing by employer. Caregiver will not influence Client in any way whatsoever regarding the writing of a will or other estate planning.

4.   Caregiver will assist Client to live at home and to have as much control over the home environment and life as possible, under the circumstances.

5.   Caregiver will be responsible directly to the employer to direct and approve the actions of Caregiver. Services provided may include any of the following:

Personal Services: Assistance with the activities of daily living such as bathing, dressing, feeding, and other activities detailed in the Caregiver'sNotebook.

Personal Care: Assistance carrying out physicians directions regarding care of Client, carrying out the Care Plan, assistance with mobility and transfers, record keeping, preventing Client from wandering or otherwise harming self.

Household Services: Meal preparation according to a plan approved by the employer, shopping, errands, house cleaning, laundry.

Record Keeping: Caregiver will keep records as set out in Caregiver's Notebook and as directed by the caregiving system/employer.

Caregiver will accompany Client on errands and appointments as directed by the employer.

Caregiver will know the whereabouts and the physical condition of Client at all times while on duty, and will keep the employer and the caregiving supervisor informed of any changes.

Caregiver will make a written record of any accidents or other sudden events that bring harm or risk of harm to Client. Caregiver will make use of emergency contact procedures to speak with the employer representative personally about any such incidents.

Other services as agreed between caregiver and the employer.

6.   Driving.

☐ *[check if applicable]* Caregiver states that s/he has a valid <u>insert state</u> State Driver's License, and agrees to provide a copy of such license.

[Choose one]

☐ Caregiver will provide transportation for Client in Client's vehicle to appointments, errands, shopping, and for social purposes. The employer is responsible for maintaining appropriate insurance coverage, unless the caregiver is using his/her own car (see below).

☐ Caregiver will provide transportation for Client in Caregiver's vehicle to appointments, errands, shopping, and for social purposes. Caregiver agrees to provide proof of liability and uninsured motorist insurance with policy limits of at least: $ 100,000.00 for bodily injury, $300,000.00 per incident maximum, and $50,000.00 property damage. Caregiver promises to notify the employer immediately if insurance is terminated. If use of the caregivers auto for work purposes is routine, caregiver will notify caregivers auto insurance carrier,

7.   Work Schedule. Caregiver agrees to work according to a schedule established by the employer in consultation with Client, and will not alter the schedule without at least 48 hours advance notice to the employer (to allow the employer to approve the alteration or make other arrangements.) Caregiver will not revise this schedule without the consent of the employer.

8.   Household Expenses. If Caregiver is provided with funds for household expenses, Caregiver will keep detailed records on forms provided by the employer. Caregiver will only make purchases that are approved by the employer.

9.   Probation Period. During the first three months of employment the employer may terminate this agreement at any time with or without notice and without severance pay.

10.   Termination. This agreement may be terminated at will by either the employer or caregiver with two (2) weeks advance written notice.

        The employer may terminate employment without cause with no advance notice. If this occurs, Caregiver will be entitled to two weeks severance pay at the rate of the average compensation over the past three months.

        The employer may terminate employment with no advance notice and no severance pay if Caregiver has violated the terms of this agreement, or has been negligent, or acted in a way that could have allowed harm to Client.

11.   This agreement will be interpreted according to the laws of the State of _____. In any proceeding in which this agreement is construed or interpreted against its drafter, that construction or interpretation will not apply, and this agreement will be construed or interpreted to give effect to the parties' intent in accordance with the terms of this agreement.

12.   Legal Representation. Caregiver acknowledges that s/he was told that s/he was free to consult with a lawyer to review this agreement prior to signing it and had ample opportunity to do so. Caregiver acknowledges that this is an arms-length transaction in which she was free to negotiate and did negotiate the terms of this agreement.

13.   Attorney's Fees. In the event of any breach of this agreement, the party responsible for the breach agrees to pay reasonable attorneys' fees and costs incurred by the other party in the enforcement of this agreement or suit for recovery of damages. The prevailing party in any suit instituted arising out of this agreement will be entitled to receive reasonable attorneys' fees and costs incurred in such suit.

14.   Hours, Compensation. The hours and hourly compensation of caregiver are subject to change at any time as agreed between Caregiver and the employer. The initial arrangement is as follows:

    Hours/days   _____

    Compensation _____

_____   _____
Employer   Date

Retrieved July 2009, from http://www.caregivers.utah.gov/sample_contract.htm
Note: This form was altered by the author to become a generic form.

Give the caregiver a trial period of two to three weeks. The first two or three shifts should be performed under supervision, either by the family caregiver in charge, or the supervisory caregiver. These initial shifts will serve as training venues, and ensure that procedures are being followed. It is also important for a familiar person to be there to reassure the loved one that this person should be in the house and to get them acquainted. During the trial period, observe how your loved one reacts to the caregiver. Underlying prejudices may come to light that are not expected.

Example 1: We had a Mexican lady come in part-time in the evenings for a while. Her duties were to give Mom and Dad their evening snack and to ensure they got to bed safely. This lady was very nice and had a quiet demeanor. However, she was missing four teeth in the front of her mouth. Mom and Dad had a built-in prejudice (established earlier in their adult life) against Mexican people, thinking them to be poor, shiftless, and lazy. Mom was sure this lady didn't know what she was doing and that she was stealing from them. I assured her this was not the case, but I had to let this caregiver go because my parents could not tolerate her. They would even curse at her and tell her she wasn't qualified to be there.

Example 2: We hired a new caregiver to take care of Dad that was a lesbian. She had a feminine name, was very competent, but she was the male half of her gay relationship. Her hair was cut short and she wore masculine appearing clothes. Well now ------- Dad was convinced she was a man!! And, there was no way he was going to have a man take care of him – changing his clothes and taking him to the bathroom. We even asked this caregiver to wear a smock or lipstick to try and change Dad's perception, but nothing worked. We had to let her go as well, but assured her it wasn't because of her incompetence.

Caregivers will have different levels of expertise and competence. This competence may especially be evident with agency personnel. Oftentimes the agency is just trying to fill a slot and may not match the needs of the patient with the competence of the caregiver. The abilities of new caregivers will be very evident within two to three shifts. Over time, long term caregivers will naturally fall into a ranking system of their own, with the most capable and most willing to accept responsibility rising to the top of the ranking. One may wish to have the best caregiver be a second level of authority (second to the family member in charge). This hierarchy must be carefully and explicitly spelled out. During the period that we had part-time caregivers, I was the only person in charge. If I was out of town, my brothers took over. All of our telephone numbers were posted on the refrigerator and on the timekeeping schedule.

When we transitioned to full-time care, Arizona was named second in charge (after her probation period). Almost all of the other caregivers had worked with Arizona before, so it was natural for them to call her to answer questions or to solve problems. However, all of them knew I was the ultimate person in charge. Arizona and I developed our communication system to the point where all issues or problems were discussed between the two of us, prior to any decision being made. Once a decision was made, she and I enforced it equally and completely. I had override capability. If she and I disagreed, the issue was discussed and a final decision made. Once I made a final decision (even if it wasn't the one she wanted), Arizona backed me up. The goal was still to provide the best care possible for Mom and Dad, no matter what the wishes of the caregivers. Arizona considers it a calling to do the best she can to aide the elderly, especially those with dementia.

Our caregivers were usually not well off or they were going to school. Their personal situations could force them to ask for as many hours as possible. Therefore, we did have two twelve hour shifts during the week and three split shifts on the weekends. As one formulates the caregiving schedule, keep in mind that caregivers will want vacation time, will become ill, or have a sick family member, or just have some personal emergency. We found that the optimum number of caregivers was four. There were three main caregivers and the fourth person was a fill-in person. This fill-in person perhaps worked one weekend shift each week, so that Mom and Dad would know them. This fill-in person was therefore trained to fill in during vacations, illnesses, or emergencies.

If the family member in charge is not on site, I recommend daily check-ins until a comfort level exists with the caregiver. Call at different times of the day and find out how your loved one is doing that day. Talk with your loved one and query him as well, especially about any concerns that the caregiver might have mentioned. Listen to their voices and see if you can detect any underlying anxiety. Reassure them that you will be stopping by later that day or whenever your next planned visit is.

Set rules for what caregiving duties consist of and post these rules. If the person in charge does not live in town, find a family member or close friend that can assist you in monitoring the system. Set up a primary caregiver that is able to run errands and do weekly shopping.

Payment to this caregiver can be made in her weekly paycheck, or by separate paycheck upon presentation of the receipts. One rule that should be very specific is whether or not this caregiver is allowed to take your loved one out in the car.

Our system allowed for this only with Arizona. Taking Dad for rides decreased Dad's problems with Sundowners and may have prevented his need to wander, become anxious, or angry. I do not know this for a fact, but Dad never wandered and was not often angry or anxious. He was usually tired after an outing and would go to bed early. Doing activities, taking them out to eat or for rides in the car can divert their attention from their disease and tires them out to the point where they are ready to go home and sleep. Whether or not Dad would ever have gotten so angry as to be considered violent, I cannot say. I have heard this type of story many times. I know Dad would bat away a caregiver if he didn't want to get dressed at that specific minute or didn't like what they were doing. But, he didn't have enough strength to hurt anyone. I can only think that the care we set in place helped him not to be combative, and I know these same types of plans exist in properly run Alzheimer's units.

Bonuses and Raises

Arizona was given a raise in her hourly salary after she had been with us for one year. We also allowed her liberal privileges in time off, just because she did so much for our family. Giving raises can be done automatically, or on a personal basis, depending on work ethics and skill. We gave bonuses to the caregivers that had been with us for a long time when Dad died to help cover their expenses until they found a new position.

Job Responsibilities

Job responsibilities should be assigned based upon the loved one's schedule and the caregiver's capabilities and hours available. Another way of assigning the caregivers is through an assessment of where the greatest need is. For example, we initially had Arizona perform the night shift because the greatest need was to take care of Mom's breathing and oxygen and to assist them during the night and ensure they were safe. The night hours held the greatest risk for problems. Once Mom died, the greatest need was during the day – to keep Dad active and entertained at his current level of disease. It was important to have someone there that was familiar with Alzheimer's patients and how to work with them.

Basic responsibilities can be: bathing/showering, dressing, hair care, mouth care, cooking meals, laundry, and simple housecleaning. Interaction and entertaining the loved one is of primary importance. The loved one's care is the primary duty; laundry and housecleaning are secondary and may be performed by night staff while the patient is asleep. As I was able to handle my parents' needs at the beginning of this journey, we did not have full-time care until Mom's health had deteriorated to the point where she needed assistance in everything she did.

Household Supplies: Handy supplies to have on hand in the household

Bandaids

Basin, small (used for brushing teeth or washing)

Chux pads or layered cloth pads with plastic bottom

Draw sheet (a folded, flat sheet placed across the bed under the patient – enables turning and lifting for bed sheet changes)

Docusate or Senna or both

First Aid Ointment such as Neosporin or Triple Antibiotic Gel

First Aid Tape

Gait belt (a belt that is strapped around a person's waist when walking and held from the back to keep them from falling)

Gauze

Gloves

Hydrogen peroxide or some form of wound cleaning agent

Milk of Magnesia

Prune Juice

Raised Toilet Seat (available in variety type stores, pharmacies)

Soap and Water/Washcloths

Towels/sheets as needed

Vaseline, A&D Ointment, or Desiten (for rashes, especially in perineum area)

Waterproof mattress pads

Training the Caregiver

Personal training for a new caregiver may be done by a family member or a senior level caregiver that has been trained to family needs and preferred procedures. Special needs should be addressed at a CNA or Nursing level, such as dressing changes, catheter care, colostomy care, Hoyer lifts, wound care, post-surgical care, etc. Forms or instruction sheets can be designed to ensure that expected procedures are followed. Especially important are the following categories:

Caregiver Check-In

Caregiver Guidelines

Caregiver Notes

Caregiver Schedules and Timekeeping

Change in Care/Medication Notes

Emergency Contacts

Equipment Instructions

First Aid Instructions

General Guidelines

Health History of loved one

Incident Reports

Medications, Instructions, and Acknowledgements

Menu Plan

Morning, evening, or weekend instructions

All care should be monitored by a family member, even that of the senior caregiver. <u>Do not schedule important parts of the day at shift change, e.g., medications or medical staff visits.</u> A summary of duties can be printed and placed in a caregiving notebook, along with other forms that are used. This way, all forms are in one place and can be easily referred to. See the next chapter for the forms and caregiving tips.

Chapter 6:

Guidelines, Duties, and Tips: The Forms Related to Caregiving

The following sections either describe caregiving duties or show forms created for specific pieces of the caregiving process. Some of these sections relate to the family, but most relate to caregiving specifically.

<u>Bathing</u>

Bathing or showering should be accomplished 3-4 times per week, more often if necessary. Attach a hand held shower head to the bath or shower head to use for the actual bathing. A skin check should be done at each bath or shower to ensure that no skin break down has occurred. Have a moisturizing lotion handy to rub their skin down after each shower. Many times, elderly people will have aches and pains and the massaging of the lotion will feel good to them. Note that the perineum area should always be washed with soap and water, not baby wipes or other commercial type of cleansing pad. Alcohol or some types of lotions can cause skin breakdown.

A person with emphysema or some other form of lung disease may be claustrophobic in the shower. The mist and heat of the shower can overwhelm them. One way to accomplish a bath is to purchase a bathing bench (or get one from Hospice) for them to slide over onto or a plain bath chair that can sit in the tub. Having a bath chair will prevent falls. Be sure and drape towels over their shoulders to prevent chills. Do not prolong the bath. Pneumonia is a real danger in the elderly and can be undetectable. Towels should be placed on the floor to prevent slipping. Wash the hair after the bath and when the person is dressed and warm.

A person that can still take showers should have a shower chair available to sit down on. If the person being cared for has any form of dementia, find out through questioning if they still understand how to take a shower. Turn the water on while he/she is undressing (if they can perform that act), so that the temperature is easily manipulated once they enter the shower. As Dad had no clue how to take a shower, the caregiver walked him through each step with gentle hints and conversation in a calm, soothing tone. As Dad's dementia progressed, he would more loudly protest the showers, especially when the caregiver was soaping him down. But, they both managed to live through it.

As the patient becomes weaker or more helpless, two other forms of bathing are possible. The most common is the spit or sponge bath. A spit bath is accomplished with a wash cloth and a warm basin of water. The bath may be given while the patient is either sitting in a chair or lying in the bed. Again, only have the area being washed exposed to prevent chills. The second form of bath is actually a shower. Have the person sit on the toilet lid (with it down, of course). Pack towels around the toilet and across the floor to prevent water seepage onto the carpet and to prevent slipping. Bring the shower head (on a long hose) out into the bathroom and shower the person on the toilet. Obviously, this is a messy process, but it does work

Use the bathing process to make the patient feel special – treat them carefully. Massage their skin. Mom loved to have her head massaged, and Dad his back. Put a nice smelling lotion on them or a special after shave on a man following his shave. Everyone likes to look nice and appear well to their families and friends.

Breathing

Breathing problems can occur with any terminal illness and oxygen may be required. Oxygen is provided by the health care provider or Hospice and is delivered to the home. Instructions will be given to the family and patient by the oxygen service. If the patient has lung disease, other breathing treatments and medications will also be necessary.

Mom used a saline nasal spray every morning (in each nostril) to help keep her nasal passages clear, as well as Advair – a long-acting control medication for both lung constriction and inflammation (asthma, bronchitis, chronic obstructive pulmonary disease, emphysema). In addition, she was given breathing mist treatments through a breathing machine called a nebulizer. The nebulizer changes the liquid medication to a mist and allows the mist to be breathed into the lungs. Mom had 3 nebulizer treatments a day, for seven minutes each. The nebulizer medication can be combined with saline to create enough liquid volume for the nebulizer to be effective. Both the medication and the saline are provided in small plastic vials, from which the top can be twisted off and the medication poured into the nebulizer cup. Shortness of breath or changes in breathing should be reported to the patient's physician.

Caregiver Check-In

A sign-in sheet may also be posted for caregivers to sign in and post the number of hours worked. This system enables weekly pay to be made easily. Although I kept duplicate checks, I wrote "Paid" next to the hours, as a checking mechanism. (Changes in care or medication notices may be posted next to the sign-in sheet for caregiver initialling as they check-in for duty.)

Caregiver Sign-in

Date	Day of Week	7 am - 3 pm	3-7 pm	7 pm - 7 am
17-Mar	Friday	Name (8-4)	Name (4-7)	Name
18-Mar	Saturday	Name (7-4)	Name	Name
19-Mar	Sunday	Name	Name	Name
20-Mar	Monday	Name	Name	Name

Different color used each week – caregivers are to sign their initials next to name.
Different hours are indicated in brackets. The hours were totaled at the end of each week for pay purposes.

Abbreviated Caregiving Form 1
© Copyright 2010, Janice Louise Long

A monthly calendar was kept in the kitchen to help Mom and Dad know what activities were going on that day, whether the oxygen was due to be delivered, or if the cleaning lady was coming. I usually bought a calendar that featured hummingbirds, as Dad had a hummingbird feeder outside the kitchen window. Both parents enjoyed watching the hummingbirds. One time the calendar must have been thrown away accidentally. A monthly calendar was generated on the computer to use in the interim. Notes were added to the calendar to alleviate questions or worries. Please see below.

Mom & Dad's Schedule

Monday	Tuesday	Wednesday	Thursday	Friday	Saturday	Sunday	Comments/Notes
					WEEKEND		
Oct 19	Oct 20 Janice out of town James doing lunch Phone #:	Oct 21	Oct 22	Oct 23 **9:00 Dr. Chapman Both Mom & Dad**	Oct 24	Oct 25	
Oct 26	Oct 27	Oct 28	Oct 29	Oct 30	Oct 31 Halloween 	Nov 1	We already have the candy ready for Halloween

Abbreviated Caregiving Form 2
© Copyright 2010, Janice Louise Long

Caregiver Guidelines

Establish clear guidelines for the caregivers that let them know what the household will allow or not allow. We let the caregivers eat with us and provided food for them. Sometimes they would bring in their own food. If the caregiver was staying overnight, they would often lay down on the couch to rest or quietly watch television. I never had a problem with them not waking up if Mom or Dad woke up or needed them. Driving Mom or Dad in their own car was not allowed, unless special permission was given. Arizona had special driving privileges with Dad after Mom passed away. Michelle was allowed to drive Dad to my brother's wedding, to allow Dad to leave early if he became tired, but that was a one-time permission due to the circumstances.

CAREGIVER GUIDELINES

Priority: Dad's health and care is the #1 Priority
– nothing else comes ahead of that!!

---

1. **Dad's care is the #1 priority.** Please keep him clean at all times, and get him up to walk 3-4 times per day. Failure to do so will cause instant dismissal.

2. **Additional duties:** As time permits, the house should be kept clean. Vacuuming may be done during the day. Dusting and cleaning should be done daily. Bathrooms should be cleaned once a week. Laundry is done as needed.

3. **Timeliness**: Be on time for your shift, preferably arriving 10 minutes prior to your shift start time for turnover.

   a. Respect the person you are taking over from. If they have been here 12-16 hours, they are ready to go home and have other schedules to keep.

Abbreviated Caregiving Form 3
© Copyright 2010, Janice Louise Long

We were very fortunate that our caregivers were, for the most part, very compassionate and wanted to take care of elderly people. Arizona provided the food after Mom's funeral service and would not let us reimburse her for it. She also set up the reception after Dad's funeral. All of the caregivers attended the funerals, with one exception.

Caregiver Notes

Once we hired a caregiver, we set up a system to allow all the caregivers to know what had occurred during any shift. Notes pages were created with annotations available for medications. Menu pages were created to show what foods had been eaten and also for menu planning (see Menus.) Medications pages showed the evening medications that were to be given, as these changed each night. The caregivers were required to initial each day, and list the medications given to ensure that the appropriate medications were given. These notes were placed in a notebook and were read each week by the Hospice staff (once we were admitted to Hospice), and became a complementary process to the Hospice system. The Hospice staff members were quite pleased with our system. They could immediately assess what had occurred during the week, and their job was made much easier. They often commented on how well we took care of our parents.

If I needed to add to these notes or make a special notation of something that had occurred during the day, I would write my own notes in this journal. (Notes were handwritten)

Caregiver Notes

Date	Day of Week	Meds Given (Type & Time)	Vitals (if taken)	Comments	Initials

Abbreviated Caregiving Form 4
© Copyright 2010, Janice Louise Long

Example of special notes by family: "Dad forgets what a plate is and has trouble pouring milk and coffee in the morning. Sometimes pours milk instead of orange juice. Sometimes puts his coffee cup on the place mat instead of on the saucer." " Dad is dizzy today. I had washed the sheets so that the cleaning lady could put them back on the bed, and he laid down without any sheets. He didn't eat any breakfast or take his pills. Mom doesn't have very much energy, and is worried about Dad. She didn't finish her breakfast."

Changes to caregiving processes should be posted on the kitchen counter or in a place where the changes will be read. I found the best place was next to the timekeeping sign-in sheet. Each caregiver should sign change sheets to verify that they have read and understood them. The change sheets should be dated and state when the change is effective.

Another type of daily note is the daily medication sheet. We used this sheet to keep track of medications that were given separately from the morning medication box. (I don't remember any time that the morning medications were not taken. However, any abnormality would be noted in the caregiver notes pages.) The legend at the top of the nightly medication sheet shows the type of medications available by letter. Dad had previously had colon cancer and didn't always have bowel movements daily. If he didn't have one that day, we gave him two pills each of senna and ducolax (morning and night). If two doses were given, then two "S's" were noted on the medication sheet. A "Y" for yes or "N" for No were annotated to indicate whether or not a bowel movement had occurred that day.

Dad's 4:00 pm Medications   H=Haldol, S=Senna/Ducolax, T=Tylenol, L=Lorazepam

Year:

Date	Time	Medications	BM	Initials
8/3	4:00 p.m.	HST	Y	jle
8/4	4:30 p.m.	HSST	N	jle
8/5				
8/6				
8/7				
8/8				
8/9				
8/10				
8/11				

Year:

Date	Time	Medications	BM	Initials
8/12				
8/13				
8/14				
8/15				
8/16				
8/17				
8/18				
8/19				
8/20				

The time the medication was given should be noted; the initial for the medication listed; a "Y" or "N" indicated for Yes or No that Dad had a bowel movement; and the caregivers initials filled in. If no medications given, the word "None" should be written in under the Medications column.

Abbreviated Caregiving Form 5
© Copyright 2010, Janice Louise Long

If Mom or Dad were ill or in a decline, vital signs were taken every few hours. These vital signs were recorded on a separate chart. The vital signs column in the notes pages was for biweekly notations of normal care.

Vital Signs

Date	Pulse	Respiration	Blood Pressure	Weight	Initials
17-Apr					
1-May					
15-May					

Abbreviated Caregiving Form 6
© Copyright 2010, Janice Louise Long

Once Mom started using morphine as a rescue medication to relax her breathing, an oxygen saturation chart was used to record the date, time, if a nebulizer treatment had been given, what her oxygen saturation level was, whether or not morphine was given and how many drops, whether or not she had a bowel movement, and the caregiver's initials. Morphine can be constipating, so the bowel notation was added. Hospice likes to know this information as well, so incorporation into a daily chart is most helpful.

Mom's O2 Saturation

Give blue morphine tablet and 1/2 tab of Atavan at 8 pm -- DO wake up to give this. Please give 4-8 drops of morphine prior to nebulizer treatment. Give neb treatment at night when she wakes up (now given 4 times/day) -- <u>does not need to be awakened for this</u>. Please record bowel movements (BM).

Date	Time	Nebulizer (if Yes)	02 Sat Reading	Morphine (# of drops)	BM	Initials

Abbreviated Caregiving Form 7
© Copyright 2010, Janice Louise Long

Caregiver Schedules and Timekeeping

Timekeeping may be performed several ways, depending upon whether the care being given is part-time or full-time, and if care is private or agency care. A schedule for private care may be prepared and posted each month. Preparing the schedule ahead of time gives everyone time to arrange for substitutions. Discourage changes to the schedule as keeping the same caregivers in the same time formats is easier on the patient. Agency time scheduling can be done on a day-to-day basis. Keeping track of the person, the date, and number of hours will be helpful when confirming agency billing.

Also, create a record showing the invoice number, check numbers, dates and amounts paid, and whether or not the check was cashed by the agency's home office. This record will give proof that the agency bill was paid and will assist in avoiding discrepancies between the agency's billing office and yourself. I received several duplicate bills, and had to backtrack through my records to ensure that these bills had been previously paid.

Part-time schedules may be maintained in different ways. A general calendar schedule can be posted in the kitchen or taped to a free counter space. This schedule is useful for both the family and the caregiver. If both hospice and agency care is being used, the agency name may be added to the caregiver's name in each time slot. Agency caregivers often work only part-time, and would be glad to work supplemental hours, if allowed to do so by their agency.

Part-Time Caregiving Schedule

Agency/Hospice Schedule					Friday 10/7	Saturday 10/8	Sunday 10/9
7 am - 9 am					Name of caregiver (Agency name)		
9 am - 4 pm					Family	Family	Family
4 pm - 6 pm					Name of caregiver (Agency name)	Name of caregiver (Agency name)	Name of caregiver (Agency name)
6 pm - 7 am							
	Monday 10/10	Tuesday 10/11	Wednesday 10/12	Thursday 10/13	Friday 10/14	Saturday 10/15	Sunday 10/16
7 am - 9 am	Name of caregiver (Agency name)	Name of caregiver (Agency name)	Name of caregiver (Agency name)	Name of caregiver (Agency name)	Name of caregiver (Agency name)	Name of caregiver (Agency name)	Name of caregiver (Agency name)
9 am - 4 pm	Family	Family	Family	Family	Family	Family	Family
4 pm - 6 pm	Name of caregiver (Agency name)	Name of caregiver (Agency name)	Name of caregiver (Agency name)	Name of caregiver (Agency name)	Name of caregiver (Agency name)	Name of caregiver (Agency name)	Name of caregiver (Agency name)
6 pm - 7 am							

This form was used to keep track of hospice and agency part-time personnel, so we knew which person was coming on which day. Agency name denotes the name of the Hospice or the private agency. Telephone numbers were listed below the chart.

Hospice contact telephone #: _____

Agency contact telephone # _____

Emergency contact: Name & # _____

Abbreviated Caregiving Form 8
© Copyright 2010, Janice Louise Long

Note: After we discontinued part-time agency care, we did hire some of the agency caregivers to work occasional nights/weekends. The caregivers are not allowed to work for the family

This form was used to keep track of attendance and problems with part-time and agency caregivers. Because of the continual changeover in caregivers and problems with attendance, we elected to hire private caregivers when the time came for full-time caregiving. Hours were consistently 4-8 p.m. so only attendance was kept track of. This chart was used to double-check agency billing.

Caregiver Attendance

Hospice	Agency	Month	1	2	3	4	5	6	7	8	9	10	11	12	13	14	15	16	17	Comments
Alfreda		January																	X	Quit
	Elvida	January																		New person
	Isabel	January												X	X	X				New person
	Cathy	January															X			Weekend person; can't come on Sundays
	Isabel	February	X	X	X	X														New person
Christine		February		X	X															

Abbreviated Caregiving Form 9
© Copyright 2010, Janice Louise Long

Caregiver Hours Worked

Date	Day of Week	Name 1	Initials	Name 2	Initials	Name3	Initials	Name4	Initials
2/1	Sunday	Off	XX	8a-4 / 8	XX	4p-10 / 6	XX	10p-8 / 10	XX
2/2	Monday	7a-7 / 12	XX	Off	XX	7p – 7 / 12	XX	Off	XX
2/3	Tuesday	7a-7 / 12	XX	Off	XX	Off	XX	7p -7 / 12	XX
2/4	Wednesday	7a-7 / 12	XX	Off	XX	7p – 7 / 12	XX	Off	XX
2/5	Thursday	7a-7 / 12	XX	Off	XX	Off	XX	7p – 7 / 12	XX
2/6	Friday	7a-3 / 8	XX	3p – 11 / 8	XX	11p – 7 / 8	XX	Off	XX
2/7	Saturday	Off	XX	7a-3 / 8	XX	11p – 7 / 8	XX	3p – 11 / 8	XX
	Total for Week	56		24		46		42	
2/8	Sunday	Off	XX	8a-4 / 8	XX	4p-10 / 6	XX	10p-8 / 10	XX
2/9	Monday	7a-7 / 12	XX	Off	XX	7p – 7 / 12	XX	Off	XX
2/10	Tuesday	7a-7 / 12	XX	Off	XX	Off	XX	7p -7 / 12	XX
2/11	Wednesday	7a-7 / 12	XX	Off	XX	7p – 7 / 12	XX	Off	XX
2/12	Thursday	7a-7 / 12	XX	Off	XX	Off	XX	7p – 7 / 12	XX
2/13	Friday	7a-3 / 8	XX	3p – 11 / 8	XX	11p – 7 / 8	XX	Off	XX
2/14	Saturday	Off	XX	7a-3 / 8	XX	11p – 7 / 8	XX	3p – 11 / 8	XX
	Total for Week	56		24		46		42	

Hours to be worked are shown. Following each shift, each caregiver is to write in the number of hours worked and initial in the block provided. The hours are added up at the end of each week. Paychecks were written on Monday mornings for the hours recorded. At the side of this form, the caregiver telephone numbers were listed, as well as those for the family points of contact.

Abbreviated Caregiving Form 10
© Copyright 2010, Janice Louise Long

Weekend Schedule for Mom & Dad (see note below)

1. Bring lunch on Saturday and Sunday, call to remind them that you are coming; they like to eat by 12:00 (sooner is OK, too). If you bring hors d'oeuvres, you can just bring them for that day.
2. Please empty dishwasher (door will be locked if dishes are clean)
3. Fill coffee pot with 7 cups of water and 4 scoops of coffee on Saturday, 8 cups of water and 4.5 scoops of coffee on Sunday. Coffee and filters are in same cabinet as the glasses.
4. Check mother's oxygen before you leave by pushing button on top of canister. You need at least 4-5 lights on the indicator to get through 24 hours. All you need to do to change it is to move the hose from one tank to the next and turn it on to a level of 5. Be sure and turn the old one off.
5. Check milk and juice levels to see if it needs replenishing. I will get groceries through the week, but will leave an envelope for grocery money by the list in case you need to get something. Please add to list as needed.
6. James brought extra whiskey and it is in the garage closet. Ralph is making a set of car keys for each of you.

Schedule So Far

Dates	Person
Feb 14-15	James
Feb 21-22	Ralph
Feb 28-29	Ron
Thurs, Fri Mar 4-5	James
Sat, Sun Mar 6-7	Janice
Mar 13-14	
Mar 20-21	Ralph
Mar 29-30	
Apr 3-4	
Friday, Apr 9	Dad's Birthday
Apr 10-11	
Apr 17-18	Ralph
Apr 24-25	
May 1-2	
May 8-9	Mother's Day
May 15-16	Ralph
May 22-23	
May 29-30	Memorial Day weekend

This schedule was used for the family members, so each one of us would know who had the weekend coverage. A copy was posted in the kitchen and also emailed to each family member. Instructions can be added as needed.

Janice's contact numbers: _____

Caregiving Form 11
© Copyright 2010, Janice Louise Long

Change in Care/Medication Notes

Instruction or change sheets may be made up both for the caregiver and for the person being cared for. Change sheets can be used for any change – a change in medication, a change in diet, a change in doctor – any change should be published and signed by all caregivers. Instruction sheets for the patient should be in a large enough type for them to read.

MEDICATION INSTRUCTION CHART

WHEN	WHO	WHAT	HOW MUCH
7:30-8:00 AM	Mom	Serevent (round green inhaler)	1 puff
7:30-8:00 AM	Mom	Rhinocort Nasal Spray	1 spray each nostril
7:30-8:00 AM	Mom	Breathing machine 7 minutes	2 vials of medicine on kitchen counter
Breakfast	Mom & Dad	Pills in boxes on kitchen table	
11:30 AM	Mom	Breathing machine 7 minutes	2 vials of medicine on kitchen counter
4:00 PM	Mom	Serevent (round green inhaler)	1 puff
4:00 PM	Mom	Breathing machine 7 minutes	2 vials of medicine on kitchen counter

Note: Shapes indicate the type of inhaler to use.

Mom may take at any time the orange "Ocean" nasal spray or her Albuterol (blue) inhalers.

No more than 2 puffs of her blue inhalers at one time.

Albuterol should be taken 1 puff at a time, slowly inhaling following puff.

Puffs should be at least 30 seconds apart.

Caregiving Form 12
© Copyright 2010, Janice Louise Long   Caregiver initials: _____ _____ _____ _____ _____

Mom's Inhaler Schedule

Check blocks off when you take each dose

Time	Inhaler	# of Puffs	Monday	Tuesday	Wednesday	Thursday	Friday	Saturday	Sunday
When you get up	Serevent 7 am	1							
When you go to bed	Serevent 7 pm	1							
Breathing Machine (Nebulizer)	1 vial of medicine (on kitchen counter)	3 times per day	8:00 am 1:00 pm 6:00 pm	8:00 am 1:00 pm 6:00 pm	8:00 am 1:00 pm 6:00 pm	8:00 am 1:00 pm 6:00 pm	8:00 am 1:00 pm 6:00 pm	8:00 am 1:00 pm 6:00 pm	8:00 am 1:00 pm 6:00 pm

Mom: You may take 2 puffs of the white inhaler (Albuterol) if you are short of breath. Take one puff at a time and wait at least 30 seconds (one minute, if possible) between puffs.

This form was to help Mom remember to take her inhalers and nebulizer treatment during the day. The form was printed on an entire page (landscape) to ensure that the text was large enough for her to read.

Caregiving Form 13
© Copyright 2010, Janice Louise Long

As of April 29: MEDICATION CHANGE NOTICE

Inhaler Schedule:

Both Atrovent and Albuterol inhalers are now only used "as needed."

Serevent: (round, green inhaler in bathroom) Morning and Night

Breathing machine: Take lid off of plastic breather – pour in 1 vial of combination medicine (on kitchen counter – Atrovent + Albuterol) and put lid back on.

Attach to breathing machine and turn on "black button." Mom should breathe normally for 7-1/2 minutes.

Do this 3 times per day – breakfast, lunch, and bedtime.

Caregiver Initials: _____ _____ _____ _____

Caregiving Form 14/29
© Copyright 2010, Janice Louise Long

Cutting the Hair

Cutting the hair at home can be done easily with a haircutting comb, barber's shears (scissors), and a pair of clippers. If none of the caregivers have any haircutting experience, perhaps a family member will volunteer. Sometimes it is possible to hire a stylist to come to the home or the designated caregiver can go to a salon and observe the procedures and gain tips from the stylist. I cut both Mom and Dad's hair. Mom had a simple, short hair cut and Dad was mostly bald with a fringe around the bottom. It was actually harder for me to cut his hair than it was Mom's.

Drape a towel around the shoulders. Wet the hair slightly – this can be done by dipping a comb into a glass of water. Pull up a section of hair around the cowlick area – top, middle of head. Estimate the desired amount to be cut (¼– ½"). Trim only this amount. Pull up the section next to the first. Comb through both sections, lifting hair above the head. Trim the second section so that it is even to the first. Continue doing this until all hair is trimmed. Clean the hairline with clippers. For men, also trim the sideburns. Use a small pair of scissors to trim men's eyebrows and nose hair. Shampoo after cutting. Men's hair may be trimmed with scissors or with the clippers. Select a tooth comb from the clipper set that meets the desired length. Turn on the clippers and move them up from the bottom to the desired area.

Dehydration

Dehydration can easily occur in the elderly, particularly as their appetite decreases. Symptoms may include nausea, dizziness, confusion, hallucinations (which can also be due to constipation). Fluids are necessary at all times as the ability to feel thirsty decreases with age. Dehydration can cause nausea and constipation in the elderly. Dehydration can also occur from vomiting, diarrhea, or fever.

Denture Care

Mouth care can include denture care. Dentures should be brushed each morning and soaked at night. Sometimes the elderly may not want their dentures taken in/out. Sometimes the denture no longer fits as well. A visit to the dentist may be required for adjustment. Dad used to grind his teeth the last couple of months, but I believe that this was a repetitive behavior due to his Alzheimer's, not because he needed dental care. Common sense is still key in these situations.

Dressing

Lay clean clothing out before the bath or shower, so that the clothing is ready immediately after the lotion massage. Place a towel on the bed for the patient to sit on during the dressing process. Have the patient help in picking out the clothes for the day. Assist the person in dressing, as needed. Their ability to dress themselves will change over time. Increase the level of help in response to the person's ability.

Emergency Contacts

We had leased a medical alert system (see http://www.lifelinesys.com). The company sends a monitoring system to be placed in the home and attached to the telephone line. A wristband or necklace with a touch button is provided for each patient that will use the device. If an emergency occurs, the person need only touch the button. The button signal is picked up by the monitoring system, which sends a signal to the home office of the alert system. The operator will come on the line of the monitoring system and call the person by name, and ask if they are all right. If there is no answer, the operator will call the nearest emergency response team. Other companies also have this system – search the internet using "medical alert" as the search term.

When the medical alert device is installed, the patient's name, telephone number, name of physician, locations and telephone numbers of the nearest emergency response team and fire station will be provided by the family. Also, an emergency spare key will need to be placed outside the home, with the location specified to the company. We kept this system intact, although Dad would not wear the wristband and Mom's necklace broke. She did, however, keep it at her bedside. If either of them had been living in the house alone, I would have been more insistent about their wearing the alert devices. As events turned out, we went to full-time care anyway and my parents were never alone again.

Other medical alert devices are available, such as bracelets for diabetes, allergies, etc. An Alzheimer's Safe Return program exists. A bracelet is provided with a note about memory impairment and an 800 telephone number. The patient is registered with the MedicAlert + Safe Return program (fee based). If a patient wanders, the family can call the 800 number to report the incident. When the patient is found, the bracelet will alert the person to call the 800 number. This system works similar to the Amber Alert for children. The local

Alzheimer's chapter will help to locate the missing person as well. A picture of the bracelet is shown below.

Image courtesy of the MedicAlert Foundation

Also, next to all telephones, we posted an emergency instruction for Mom and Dad's use, both to help her with her breathing and for emergency contact purposes. This form was printed with large type (not shown here) – using a type font that the patient can read is important.

<u>EMERGENCY</u>

1. Push Life Line button
   a. Keep on at all times – button is waterproof
   b. Lifelines will call an ambulance if needed and then will call us

<u>SHORT OF BREATH??</u>

2. Slowly inhale <u>up to</u> 3 puffs of white inhaler (Albuterol)
3. Turn oxygen tank up to 6
         (turn knob toward bedroom)
4. If no relief, call one of the following:
   a. Emergency (911)
         or
   b. Daughter at home (list phone #)

   c. Son at home (list phone #) or at work (list phone #)

Abbreviated Caregiving Form 15
© Copyright 2010, Janice Louise Long

<u>Emergency Room Visits</u>

Emergency room visits are on the rise in the elderly population, with the patients exhibiting true emergency needs.

Retrieved October 2009, from

http://www.emergencycareforyou.org/YourHealth/ElderlySafety/Default.aspx?id=1572

Common reasons for emergency room visits could be due to falls, medication errors, pneumonia, or dehydration. Ten recommendations when taking your elderly parent to the Emergency Room from the American College of Emergency Physicians (ACEP) are shown below. These recommendations will not only make your elderly relative more comfortable, but will also assist the physician and medical personnel in making the right diagnosis and in giving the right care.

1. Medical History Form: Either use the Health History form in this chapter or go to http://www.emergencycareforyou.org/EmergencyManual/Medical Forms/Default.aspx?ekmensel=c57dfa7b_150_166_btnlink and obtain a form (click on Medical History form) that you and your parent's physicians can help you complete. On the form you will list what medications your parent is taking, allergies as well as past and current medical conditions. Bring this form to the emergency department with your parent and give to the emergency physician. Also keep track and make sure your parent is taking medications correctly.

2. Bring Reading Materials: Make sure you have a book, magazine, or a newspaper to read while you are waiting for results or to see a physician. It will make the time pass more quickly and help keep your stress level lower.

3. Anticipate Admission: Bring a change of clothes and some personal items in case your parent is admitted to the hospital. You can always leave them in the car.

4. Know Physician Contacts: Do you know all the names of the doctors your parents see? You should. Take some time now and find out their names, contact information, why your mother or father sees them and how long they have been seeing them. Write it down and hand it to the doctor or nurse in

the emergency department. If you are traveling, have copies of the most recent doctor summary and a copy of an EKG if it is abnormal.

5. Convey Parent's State of Mind: You know your parent better than the doctor. If he or she seems confused, explain to the physician what "normal" behavior is like. If the doctor is talking to you, make sure you are talking to your parent. Do your best to make sure they understand what is going on. The doctors may have to run tests, conduct an examination or admit your parent to the hospital. Keep the conversation open with your parent.

6. Consider Living Wills: A difficult thought, but important nonetheless. It's one to prepare for. If a condition is life-threatening, you need know what the plan will be and what your parents' wishes are. Do your parents have living wills or known care desires if conditions become critical?

7. Report on Recent Surgeries: Keep track of surgeries, especially ones involving implanted devices such as hip replacements, or pace makers.

8. Simplify Insurance Information: Have a single sheet of paper with insurance and identification information.

9. Resist Downplaying: Realize that elderly patients often will talk down their symptoms to doctors or nurses and only tell it like it is to family members. Be ready to fill in the additional information if necessary.

10. Be Patient: Realize the more the complaints (almost always the older the patient), the longer it takes to work up the problems. Be patient with your physicians and your parent.

Retrieved October 2009, from http://www.acep.org/pressroom.aspx?id=46727. Note that this link refers to increased emergency room visits for elders. The link for the above list will be retired by ACEP in 2010. Permission was granted by ACEP to use this information.

When I took my Dad to the Emergency Room for his blood clot, I stayed with him the entire time due to his Alzheimer's Disease. He was much more comfortable, did not complain about being in the hospital, but did complain about the wait. It was quickly evident that hospital personnel are not trained in dealing with Alzheimer's Disease, nor do they have the personnel to do so. We waited in the hallway of the Emergency Room for seven hours before being admitted to a room in the hospital. After the first 24 hours, I went home to rest for a while and one of our caregivers relieved me. Our being there for the three days that Dad was in the hospital made his stay easier, he had no complaints about following the instructions we were given, and tremendously helped the hospital personnel.

Emergency Packs

When taking a patient in the car, have an emergency kit or pack ready at all times. Included in the emergency pack should be panty liners, change of underwear, change of clothes, socks, and perhaps an extra pair of shoes. Copies of medical identification cards and identification should be carried by the driver. An envelope with these forms can be kept in the kitchen, along with the handicap parking placard and the garage door opener.

Family Meetings and Updates

Updates to the family may be performed by email, telephone conversations, or informal family meetings. If important issues need to be discussed, such as overall health status, a change in caregiving venues, or even the possibility of assisted living or nursing home placement, an agenda may be used to ensure all issues are discussed and the meeting kept on track. See the example below. I think sometimes my brothers thought I was too dramatic or too verbal – I let them know of any changes in Mom or Dad's conditions, but also tried to explain the medical ramifications of the changes. It is kind of like a double edged sword – you want to know yet you don't want to know. But, I tried to keep them informed.

Family Meeting Agenda, <u>Date</u>

Things to Discuss:

Goals:

a.   Overall: Keep them together and at home as long as possible

b.

c.

Current Status:

a.   Mom's health

b.   Dad's health

c.   How well are they managing

      a.   Alcohol

      b.   Meals

Safety

Cleanliness

Next Steps: What is realistic?

a.   Acquire information – nursing homes, Alzheimer's, Support Groups, reading

b.   24 hour care

c.   Home Care Evaluation – MD requested

d.   Assisted Living – also have Long Term Insurance

      a.   Must be MD certified

      b.   @ $4500/month for both after Long Term Care Insurance reimbursement

      c.   Could have extra charges for meds, special needs

e.   Home Health Aid 2-3x/wk; Physical Therapy, Occupational Therapy

f.   Hospice

g.   Caregiver assistance

      a.   Help on weekends

      b.   Vacation in May

Caregiving Form 16
© Copyright 2010, Janice Louise Long

Familiar Items

When caring for a person with dementia, think about the era they were born in and what types of things might be familiar to them, as compared to new types of items on the market. A good example of this is the soap dispenser. The person may not remember what liquid soap is and may be looking for a bar of soap. If they don't see a bar of soap, they may not wash up. Watch for signs that indicate confusion about a process, and try to figure out what part of the process is bothering them. Then accommodate to the patient's needs.

Financial Issues

Any company that is telephoned to discuss business or financial transactions will require a copy of the Durable Power of Attorney (DPOA) or a verbal authorization from the loved one that these matters may be discussed with the particular family person placing the call. The DPOA may be faxed or mailed to these companies when it becomes viable. However, the current representative on the telephone may not be able to locate it. If possible, I would send a scanned copy of the DPOA to the representative while I had them on the telephone.

Often, I had an insistent representative ask to speak to my Dad to verify that I was allowed to discuss his financial business. It would break my heart when I had to do this. The representative would usually ask him for his name, his date of birth, his social security number, and his verbal permission for them to talk to me. Even though I would explain that he had Alzheimer's Disease and that he wouldn't be able to answer these questions, they would insist on talking to him. I would write down the desired information on a piece of paper and hand it to him to read to them. It would be very obvious to the representative that I would be guiding Dad of what to say in the background.

Each company will have its procedures that are required to be followed, and the DPOA may not be able to be located by the specific person on the phone. One can try to be organized and stay ahead of the caregiving continuum as much as possible, but there will always be a monkey wrench. This was my monkey wrench. If there was anything I could do to alleviate this situation, I would try to get a national Alzheimer's registry organized, listing the person's name, birthdate, social security number, their authorized point of contact, and DPOA for companies to refer to.

October 3, 2003

Prudential Financial
General Correspondence

Re: Contract Number (List #)
(List name of policy holder)
SSN: (List SSN of policy holder)

Dear Sir:

I am faxing to you a Power of Attorney showing myself (Mr. L's daughter) as his representative. Our files show an insurance policy with the above contract number. I would appreciate having an explanation of this policy if someone could contact me by telephone.

Sincerely,

Janice L. Long

List Address and Telephone #

Caregiving Form 17
© Copyright 2010, Janice Louise Long

First Aid/Special Care Instructions

Bowel Management

Proper bowel management is crucial to an elder's health. Changes in diet (less fiber) or decreased fluids can cause constipation. A bowel movement should occur at least every three days. Medications such as Senna or Docusate given to soften bowels should be given sparingly until a "known" dosage is figured out. Any great change is liable to reverse the process, causing diarrhea, which in turn dehydrates the individual. Try giving pieces of fruit or granola bars as snacks. Be sure and provide some type of liquid with the snacks. Fluids can also be given in the form of "Ensure" or similar beverage. Ensure can be provided by Hospice or may be purchased in a grocery or drug store. Milk of Magnesia (2 tablespoons) combined with ¼ cup prune juice can be given on the 3rd day following the absence of bowel movements. Microwave for fifty seconds or at least until the mixture is warm. Have the patient drink the mixture. Results should occur within an hour. Be prepared – this mixture is known as Dyn-O-Mite!

Bruises, Scrapes, and Cuts

Clean the area as well as possible, ensuring that any debris is removed from any open sore. Smooth any torn skin over the area with a Q-tip or sterilized tweezers. The skin wrinkles up like a pleated shade. Several times, we were able to heal a nasty scrape more rapidly by retaining as much skin as possible. Use triple antibiotic cream or Neosporin, plus gauze and medical tape that doesn't tear the skin. Clean the area and change dressings daily. As the skin heals over, leave the wound exposed to air some each day until the wound is able to be totally exposed.

Nose Bleeds

If nose bleeds occur, follow the instructions below. Continue until bleeding stops. Be careful about having them lay down as a serious nose bleed can cause choking. Assess possible explanations about why the nose bleed occurred, e.g., new medication, dry nasal passages, etc. K-Y Jelly may be used or a physician can prescribe an estrogen based ointment to use in dry nasal passages. Mom would have occasional nose bleeds due to dry nasal cavities. We alleviated that problem with the use of a saline nasal spray (available over the counter in drug and grocery stores). Her most serious nose bleed was due to a new medication, used to prevent strokes.

NOSE BLEED INSTRUCTIONS

1. Have patient blow all matter out of the nose as hard as he/she can
2. Have her/him lean forward and pinch her/his nose
3. Nose should be pinched for periods of 3 minutes, then 5 minutes, then 10 minutes
4. If nosebleed does not go away in a reasonable period of time, call (<u>list number for Hospice or primary care physician</u>)

   Also, list patient name, medical identification number, and birthdate.

Caregiver initials: _____ _____ _____ _____

Abbreviated Caregiving Form 18
© Copyright 2010, Janice Louise Long

Pain

The caregiver should be aware of any pain that occurs and a note should be entered into the daily notes as to the severity and location of the pain. The caregiver should alert the Health Care Power of Attorney (HCPOA-see Legal Forms) immediately and a determination made as to whether or not a call/visit to the doctor is in order (or to the Hospice nurse, if applicable). Pain or discomfort should also be watched for if a fall has occurred or some type of bruising occurs. If a fall occurs, the caregiver should know how to assess the patient for broken bones BEFORE allowing the patient to be moved.

Dad could not put any weight on one leg all of a sudden. He had not fallen. The pain lessened with an oil massage, but returned. We took him to the doctor, who was concerned about a blood clot. We were referred to a laboratory for a Doppler scan of both legs. This was followed by an Emergency Room visit and an admission to the hospital (see Dad's Story).

Pain Management

Once a patient is admitted to Hospice, a comfort kit will be brought to the house. The comfort kit includes nausea, vomiting, pain, anxiety and agitation, and shortness of breath medications to be given at the direction of the Hospice nurse. These medications may include morphine, haldol, ativan, and suppositories. The purpose of the comfort kit is to avert a crisis or symptom change and to eliminate a physician or pharmacy visit. Directions for these medications are given by the Hospice nurse (available 24 hours per day by telephone).

Morphine, a liquid pain medication, may be given orally under the tongue. A small amount makes a huge difference, not only in pain management, but also in ability to breathe. Mom would panic when she couldn't breathe, which just made her breathing worse. The morphine would allow the muscles to relax and more oxygen to become available within 30 seconds to a minute. Initially Mom was afraid the morphine would be addicting, but when she saw how a tiny dosage of a few drops would help, she was not so against taking it. The nurse explained that it would not be addicting in this type of circumstance. The most we ever needed to give her was four drops 3-4 times per day.

Pressure Sores

Pressure sores, also called bed sores, are extremely difficult to manage and heal very slowly. Pressure sores are usually caused from being in one position too long. Sores will result in any area that rests directly on the bed or chair surface without being shifted. These sores are extremely serious open ulcers, which can become easily infected. Call for help immediately. A bed ridden patient should be turned at least every two hours and more often if possible. Pressure sores require care by a licensed nurse or wound care nurse.

Food and Menus

If the caregiver is preparing meals, have a list of suggestions and menus for favorite meals. Menus may be prepared a week at a time, not only to plan the shopping, but also to note what foods and quantity of food that the person has eaten (see menu charts below). As an elderly person deteriorates, the heaviness and amount of food required decreases. If the patient has dementia, their taste of food changes and favorite foods may begin to taste awful. However, their taste for sweet foods stays the same or even increases. Mom and Dad loved chocolate, especially Mrs. See's chocolate. I was initially buying two 2-pound boxes each month, then five 2-pound boxes, and eventually ten 2-pound boxes. They were offering them to the caregivers as well, but often were eating several pieces at once because they didn't remember eating that many. I am not sure how that much candy disappeared in a month, but it was gone!

At least, they were consuming calories and at their age, who cared? Breakfast and lunch were balanced meals with protein, salad, and fruit or vegetables. Desserts were not generally served except on special occasions. Favorite meals were prepared until tastes changed. Fats should probably be decreased and vitamin supplements added (Vitamin C, Vitamin E, and multivitamin), if they are not already being taken. I have seen some discussion that vitamin supplements may help delay Alzheimer's Disease.

As a person becomes more frail, or with the dementia patient, swallowing difficulties or lack of appetite may occur. Foods may be pureed/blended and softer foods served. A good way to get calories in is by serving milk shakes with malt added to them. Use whole, homogenized milk, a good quality ice cream, and a tablespoon of malt (available in grocery stores). Chocolate syrup may be added as well. We could get Dad to drink a large glass of this concoction almost every day.

Homemade vegetable soup or other soups are also easily eaten and well received by the patient. The size of the food servings and the amount of food on the plate can also become daunting.

Split up the meal into sections, giving one section at a time. Begin with no more than two foods, take the plate away, and serve a third food if the person is still hungry. Cut foods into finger sized bites when silverware becomes too hard to handle. Sweetened ice tea, juice, or fruit drinks will help, as well. As tastes change, try new and different foods. Foods not previously enjoyed may be liked now, as the memory may not be there that they didn't like that food before. Dress up a salad with cheese cubes, hard boiled egg, pickled beets, chicken pieces, or shrimp. The general principle is to make eating less confusing and easier to manage. The higher the level of diet and the number of calories consumed will keep your loved one healthier for a longer period of time. Replacement beverages (available in grocery and drug stores) can also keep fluid and calorie intakes at a higher level. My Mom and Dad loved the cheesecake bars that are available in the grocery store.

Some sample recipes are printed in Appendix V. Snacks throughout the day can also add calories, e.g., cheese and crackers, kielbasa sausage (buy in store, slice, heat in frying pan), balsamic chicken, fajitas, sloppy joes, vegetable soup, ham pinwheels, tortilla roll-ups, shrimp cocktail, croissant bites, deviled eggs, Greek lemon soup, linguine with chicken and mushrooms, meat loaf, pulled barbeque pork, pot roast, chile con queso, and quesadillas. A good high calorie dessert is the Black Forest Ice Cream Cake.

Week of: _____

Dad's Meals	Monday	Tuesday	Wednesday	Thursday	Friday	Saturday	Sunday
Breakfast							
Lunch							
Dinner							

Comments:

Foods consumed and quantities

	Monday	Tuesday	Wednesday	Thursday	Friday	Saturday	Sunday
Breakfast							
Lunch							
Dinner							

Comments:

Caregiving Form 19
© Copyright 2010, Janice Louise Long

<u>Health History</u>

From the information that I had, I created a health history for both Mom and Dad. This health history could be printed whenever we went to the doctor, changed health plans, or when we incorporated Hospice into the home. The health history should include name, date of birth, medical insurance identification #, surgeries, current status, medications, diet, who the Durable Power of Attorney is, who the Health Care Power of Attorney is, and who the main point of contact in the family is. Be sure and note any vaccinations (flu or pneumonia), allergies, alcohol and tobacco use, implants or devices, e.g., dentures, cataract lens, hip or knee joint replacements (or screws), or pacemaker.

<u>Health History Form</u>

Name <u>Date</u>

Medical Identification # <u>list number</u>

Medicare Identification #_____

DOB: _____

DNR: Yes/No (circle one)

Allergies: None

Tobacco Use: 50 years, stopped 1995

Alcohol Use: 3-4 drinks each day, whiskey

Vaccinations: Flu vaccine, November 2005

Surgeries:

Appendectomy – as a teenager

Tubal Ligation – <u>List Date</u>

Pregnancies (delivered): <u>List Dates</u>

Back surgery (disc?) - @ 1980-1982

Partial hip replacement (left) @1990; diagnosed with emphysema

Partial hip replacement (left) @1992

Hip repair (right) – Sept 2002

Sept 2002 major hospitalization – following hip surgery to insert screws to hold cracked hip, contracted pneumonia within 24 hrs, oxygenation decreased to 60's (%), was kept in ICU on ventilator for 5 days, in hospital a total of 3 weeks. Began liquid oxygen at 3-1/2 to 4 liters.

Current issues/status: NEED APPROVAL FOR HOSPICE HOME CARE

Has been on oxygen @ 5-1/2 years. Now on oxygen liter flow of 6 to 6-1/2; began use of wheelchair Nov 2004; diagnosed with micro-vascular disease in Sept 2004 with large, dense area of disease noted on CT scan– Aricept course (scored 21 on diagnostic test) began at that time. Pulmonologist estimated lung capacity @ 20% in November. New oxygen/nebulizer/wheelchair service in process.

(continued next page)

(Health History – continued)

Current Medications: Liquid oxygen – 6 tanks (4 filled 1st week, 6 filled 2nd week, etc.). Tubing is Doubled to 2 tanks at a time for more efficient flow and ability to turn to higher levels if needed, just acquired pulse oximeter – oxygenation at 94-98%; pulse rate 80-109. Had 5-6 courses of Prednisone during past 12 months; last course was in November. Have been starting course at 80 mg, as 40 mg course does not work well enough any more. In Oct/Nov timeframe had an 80 mg followed by a 40 mg course back-to-back.

Nebulizer: Albuterol + Ipatropium Bromide – 3x/day

Albuterol Inhaler – 2 vials/month –

Aricept, 10 mg

Cimetidine, 400 mg

Norvasc, 5 mg

Rhinocort Aqua

Serevent, 2x/day

Multivitamin

Calcium, 600 mg + D

Aspirin, 325 mg (increased from 81 mg by Dr. G., January 5th)

Plavix, 75 mg – began in August 2004, discontinued in November 2004 due to several nosebleeds in one week, lasting 4-10 hours, (have 22 pills at home)

Prednisone – have 38 pills at home

Diet: Small breakfast (toast & juice); good balanced lunch (appetite decreasing x 8 weeks); snacks at dinner time with cocktail hour (alcohol consumption estimated at 2+ drinks/day @ 2 ounces each).

All care given at _____ Health system 1/1/05. Daughter Janice is daily caretaker since 7/03 and has Durable and Health Care Power of Attorney. Her phone #'s are <u>list telephone numbers.</u>

Caregiving Form 20
© Copyright 2010, Janice Louise Long

(Note: Highlight any issues that need to be discussed with the Hospice provider.

Health Plan

During the caregiving process, the family may need to change health plans or request medical records for their loved one. The health plan will usually require thirty days notice, especially for the automatic bank deduction to be discontinued, and any medical equipment picked up. This transition time will also be necessary for the new health plan to have new equipment in place, e.g., oxygen delivery and spare tanks, wheelchair or walker, potty chair, etc.

December 20, 2004

Name of Health Plan
Senior Plan

RE: Names and Medical Records #'s

Dear Health Plan (can address to specific name, if known),

We are dissatisfied with our primary care and are switching to _____ Health Plan as of January 1, 2004. We understand that a 30 day transition period will allow the transition of care to be accomplished smoothly. This is very important to us as Mrs. X uses oxygen and other durable medical equipment.

Our primary care managers keep leaving the Health System and we are having to go in to get reestablished every time this happens. We finally found a Primary Care Manager that understood what "managing our health" actually was and helped us a lot. Now even he (Dr. _____) is leaving after we have been with him only 3 months. We have found our specialty care, especially Dr. _____ and Dr. _____ to be superb. However, it is not fair to them to try and manage our daily needs.

We have signed up for (Name of new health plan) Health Care as of January 1, 2005. Please disenroll us from this Senior Plan as of December 31, 2004 and ensure that our automatic payment is stopped, as the December 2004 payment has already been made. Thank you for your assistance in this matter,

Sincerely,

Dad's name   Mom's name

Address and telephone #

Caregiving Form 21
© Copyright 2010, Janice Louise Long

December 20, 2004

Health Plan
Senior Plan

RE: Names and Medical Records #'s

Dear Medical Records,

We are disenrolling from the _____ Health Plan as of December 31, 2004 and transferring to the _____ Health Plan. Please find enclosed authorizations to transfer our medical records to the _____ Health Plan.

We authorize the transfer of all records, including laboratory, x-ray, CT, doctor's notes, hospitalizations, etc. Please also send film or CD copies of our CT scans and other x-rays as well. Please send copies to our home address as well.

If you have any questions, please do not hesitate to contact us.

Sincerely,

Dad's name   Mom's name

Address and telephone #

Caregiving Form 22
© Copyright 2010, Janice Louise Long

Hospice

When Mom or Dad were admitted to Hospice, a needs list and questions were prepared. A copy of the health history (see above) was supplied to the Hospice nurse. Hospice would review the medications and decide which medications were to be supplied by Hospice. <u>Once Hospice is in the home, Hospice is the first source contacted for any problem, even before 911 is called</u>. If Hospice deems that emergency care is required, they will let the family or caregiver know to call an ambulance. It is imperative to keep in mind that Hospice deals mainly with the admitting diagnosis. Hospice is responsible for all care given and the costs associated with that care. If an emergency occurs, such as a fall or blood clot which requires emergency attention, Hospice may discharge your loved one during that time and readmit him/her when he/she returns home. Hospice is paid a daily fee from Medicare to take care of your loved one. All medical costs then come out of this daily fee. Obviously, a hospitalization or surgery could not be covered by this fee, hence the discharge and readmission.

Occasionally, the Hospice nurse will give new instructions for medications. A change notice may be written up for the caregivers, such as the ones below. The chart below is an example of a medication change. This chart also appears in "Oxygen" section.

OXYGEN/NEBULIZER

1. All of the Oxygen/nebulizer equipment and LUNG (only) medications are now supplied through Crossroads Hospice.

2. The oxygen tanks hold @ 33% more than the old tanks. Oxygen deliveries are now twice a week, Tuesdays and Fridays. Thus, fewer tanks. Liter flow is currently 6-1/2. The vaporizer is now attached to one machine. If you switch the tank flows to even out the tank volume, make sure the vaporizer is on the higher flow machine. You will have to switch the green nozzle as well. Fill the water with distilled water (in kitchen) when the water level gets below the minimum mark. Fill only to the minimum mark.

3. The nebulizer top screws on and off of the medicine cup. Unscrew the top and put the two vials of medicine in the medicine cup. Screw back on and turn on the black button. Wash out the components following each treatment and put back on machine.

4. There are two portable oxygen machines in the dining room. To fill, place unit on top of one of the oxygen tanks. Push down slightly to seat it on the tank. There is a tan 1" x 3" lever on the side of the tank. Lift up on that to fill. When you hear a change in the noise of the oxygen flow and see a puff of vapor, the tank is full. Close the lever. Hold the tank by its strap and look at meter to ensure tank is full. Fill both tanks as they are joined to give Mom enough oxygen flow.

5. Call (list Equipment supplier name/phone number) if any questions or problems.

   List Patient Name, SSN, Medical ID#, Date of Birth, Medical Points of Contact (e.g., Daughter), Primary Care physician name and telephone number

Caregiving Form 23
© Copyright 2010, Janice Louise Long

New Oxygen and Medication Instructions
<u>Date</u>

1. Check oxygen level every 2-4 hours. Note level on oxygen notes. If oxygen level is lower than 90, check to be sure cannula is in her nose and that it is hooked up properly to the machine.

   1a. If oxygen level is in the 80's, increase oxygen flow to 4 or 5.

   1b. If oxygen level is in the 70's, increase oxygen flow to 4 or 5 if it has not yet been increased already. Give 0.5 mg (1/2 tablet) Lorazepam.

   1c. If oxygen level is in the 60's, give 0.5 (1/2 tablet) Lorazepam (Ativan) AND 0.25 ml Roxanol.

2. As needed: can give Lorazepam 0.5 mg every 4-8 hours AND Roxanol 0.25 cc every 3-4 hours – ONLY AS NEEDED FOR ANXIETY, RESTLESSNESS. Please confirm with Janice, Arizona, or Hospice before you give an extra dose.

3. You may call Hospice at any time for guidance or assistance. Please request a nurse visit at any time, if you are uncomfortable or if you feel Dad needs a nurse visit.

Caregiver Name/Initials/Date: _____ _____ _____ _____

HOSPICE <u>List phone #</u>

JANICE <u>List phone #'s</u>

Arizona <u>List phone #</u>

Form 24
© Copyright 2010, Janice Louise Long

Household Duties

Household duties should be secondary to direct hands-on caregiving. Once full-time care begins, light cleaning and laundry can be performed while the cared one is sleeping. Laundry, of course, may be started throughout the day, should an immediate need arise. Duties should include meal preparation, as needed. A housecleaning team can be hired 1-2 times per month to perform heavier cleaning at a reasonable fee.

Incident Report

We had one incident between caregivers. One of the caregivers had come on duty and found that Dad had not been cleaned properly. The two caregivers got into an argument about what happened. Each of them reported the incident to Arizona and myself, but with two different stories. I wrote up the incident for documentation, considered each story and the implications of the care for my Dad. I did let the one caregiver go, after much thought. Another incident occurred, probably for an outside jealousy spat, between two caregivers. One of them became very angry and cussed up a storm in front of my parents. She was let go, as well. Perhaps my decisions were hasty with regards to these incidents, but underlying reasons existed as well. My ultimate goal was the safety of my parents and for them to have the best care possible. I needed the caregivers to be professional at all times and not to let their personal issues cause substandard care.

<u>Incident Report</u>

Date Occurred: _____

Caregiver(s) Involved: _____

Reporting person: _____

Summary of incident:

Corroborating/Disputing Evidence: (List names of those providing information)

Conclusion:

Action:

_____

Signed/Date

Note: Can add signature lines for caregivers, if they will sign

Caregiving Form 25
© Copyright 2010, Janice Louise Long

Instructions for Parents

Neither Mom nor Dad could remember or keep instructions straight. However, they could read and understand information or instruction sheets. Examples in this section include several types of instructions that were used at different times in the caregiving continuum. The instructions became more prescriptive, as the need arose. The instructions were taped to the bathroom counter, kitchen table, night stand, or wherever the particular instruction was needed.

Scooter instructions were written for Mom when we purchased the scooter. We only needed them for a while, as she basically understood what to do. Her hand would accidentally move the speed button while she was riding on it, and occasionally she would panic. Because of her oxygen tubing, one of us walked beside her while she was moving through the house. That way we could keep the tubing clear of the wheels and also give her gentle instructions on the scooter use.

SCOOTER INSTRUCTIONS

CONSOLE:

(Make a copy of the brochure and paste a picture of the console here)

STANDBY MODE:

If your scooter has been sitting for a while, it will be in standby mode. Take the key out for 2 seconds and put back in; scooter will start again.

GETTING INTO/OUT OF THE SCOOTER:

Arm rests lift up.

Pull up the lever on the right side of the scooter, just below the middle of the seat. You may then turn the chair to the direction (e.g., sideways or backward) desired.

SPEED:

SLOW = Turn speed knob to left to TURTLE

FAST = Turn speed knob to right to RABBIT

TO GO FORWARD/BACKWARDS: Push on throttle control lever (flat lever below console)

LIVING ROOM RAMP:

May need to turn speed up (turn knob to 1:00 position towards the rabbit).

Can "touch and let go" forward lever to go slower

CHARGING THE SCOOTER:

Charger is plugged into the wall behind the TV.

Take the key out of the console. Put front end plug into the charging slot on the middle, front of the battery. The battery is on the floor of the scooter, below the seat. The charging slot is on the front side, in the middle. Plug in for 3-4 hours. Put key back into the console.

Caregiving Form 26
© Copyright 2010, Janice Louise Long

Occasionally, Dad would ask me to give him an update on what was happening in their lives. His requests were generally related to health or financial concerns. I would give him a verbal report and also write what I said in a one page summary, so both he and Mom could read and internalize what I had told them. They really liked this idea. When I occasionally had to travel for business, I would write a note to them about where I was, what I was doing, how to contact me, and when I would return. Dad would read these travel notes 10-20 times a day and be able to understand that I was out-of-town and hadn't left him. He would be watching the front door for my return.

Once Dad understood that he really couldn't remember daily events, we had an arrangement that I could write a note and we would both sign that we had agreed on something. He could then verify that I had discussed the situation with him. He had begun accusing me of lying to him. I would say, "Dad, why would I have a reason to lie to you?" I was always upfront and honest with him and never hid information from him. When I explained to him about his health, he just looked at me and said, "That doesn't sound very good, does it?"

LIFE STATUS

Date
The following is an explanation (which you asked for) about the status of your life.

Health
Mom has Emphysema (disease of the lungs), which causes her difficulty in breathing. She also has tiny strokes in her brain, which cause her to be forgetful and to lose her memory. Her health is OK, but not good.

Dad has Alzheimer's, which is a disease in the brain that causes the thoughts to get disconnected. This process causes memory loss and also causes you not to remember how to do things, like make the coffee. This disease gets worse as time goes by. Dad's physical health is otherwise good.

Dad's Job
Dad retired from <u>Name of Company</u> about 16 years ago. The company paid him stock options for about 7-8 years. We are no longer receiving stock options. Dad sold an office building about 6 years ago, for which we receive $677 a month. We will be receiving those funds for one more year. We are fortunate that you saved enough money for your retirement that you no longer have to work. We also receive <u>list amount</u> each month from Social Security.

Money
Your money is split up between cash, investments, life insurance, and the house. All together, these assets total just at <u>list amount</u>. The house is worth about $250,000 to $275,000. We have enough money for you to live at least 10-12 years longer, without doing anything. Janice moved here 2-1/2 years ago and has been taking care of your bills, investments, groceries, and medications since that time. Your sons have also been helping by bringing lunch on the weekends.

Care
Because of the health and memory problems, we now have Arizona, Bethany, Michelle, and Katrina coming in to help you at night with anything that you need.

Caregiving Form 27
© Copyright 2010, Janice Louise Long

Medications, Instructions and Acknowledgements

Medications should only be dispensed by a family member or chief caregiver. Weekly or daily pill boxes are available at drug and grocery stores. A different color may be used for each person and/or for evening medications. Once the medications are parceled out, a parent can take each day's pills himself. If the morning newspaper is available, the parent can determine the day of the week. Make sure prior newspapers are stored elsewhere or disposed of to avoid confusion. A daily calendar may also be set up with the prior days crossed off to help parents keep track of the day. Included on this calendar can be doctor's appointments, birthdays, holidays, scheduled deliveries, aide visits, or cleaning lady dates. Only caregivers with a Certified Nursing Assistant (CNA) license or higher level are allowed to dispense medications. Aides without a CNA license can give medications <u>already dispensed</u> into a designated container. All medications dispensed or given during a shift should be recorded. We found the easiest system was to dispense two weeks at a time – each week stored in a separate box. This gave us leeway in both the dispensing and ensuring the medications were available and also arranging for refills to be purchased. Night medications were dispensed daily into small medication cups.

Elderly are very susceptible to changes in medications or medication overdoses. Overdoses can occur easily when an elderly person takes their medications twice in one day, just because they could not remember if they had already taken them or not. Conversely, not taking medications can cause problems, as well. Always watch the person being cared for carefully. Watch for any changes from day-to-day and speculate on why the change may have occurred. Quiz the caregivers about what happened the day before and the current day to find out if something could have triggered the change. Try to have the same caregiver give the medications each morning or each evening. Do not schedule medications to be given at the time of a caregiver shift change.

We created an evening medication sheet once evening meds were begun. Evening meds primarily dealt with agitation or bowel problems. As Dad's Alzheimer's progressed (in concert with the progression of Mom's emphysema), he became more and more agitated. We were giving him Haldol and Lorazepam (prescribed by Hospice) to help him calm down and sleep. Because Dad had trouble with constipation, we gave him Docusate and/or Senna to regulate his bowels. We gave different meds in the evening on an every other day basis. The medication sheet kept track of which medications to give and also served as a means for the evening caregiver to sign that the medications had been given.

If medications become hard to swallow, crush them up and mix with a soft food like applesauce, pudding, peanut butter, or milk shakes (small amount). The hard part is finding a food that is tolerated. Some medications, especially capsules should not be opened or crushed. Advice should be sought from the local pharmacist. A mortar and pestle (Figure 3) is the best way to crush pills. Mortars and pestles are available for purchase through the internet.

Figure 3: Mortar and Pestle

Image courtesy of American Educational Products, http://www.amep.org

As Mom's breathing became more labored, she would begin to panic that she could not catch her breath. At this point in time, Hospice recommended that we give her a few drops of liquid morphine under her tongue. The morphine was kept in the refrigerator in the comfort kit that Hospice had provided at the time of admission. This dosage of morphine was very small and not addicting. We quickly found out that the morphine allowed Mom's muscles to relax, for the panic to ease, and for more oxygen to be inhaled. We might have to give the morphine 2-3 times per day, but it was a lifesaver.

Note that change is constant in the world of elder care. A decline or short-term medical need can necessitate medical changes. For example, Mom had cataract surgery about a year after I arrived. An eye drop schedule was developed so that she could easily understand when to take her eye drops, how many drops to take, and which kind of eye drops were to be taken. The eye drop schedule was different for each day for three weeks. Mom would cross off each dose and each day as it occurred to keep track of where she was on the schedule. This eliminated duplicating dosages or not taking a specific dosage. Developing a form like this needs to be simple and easy to understand and follow. Going over the draft instruction form with your loved one will show you whether or not the instructions can be followed. Make adjustments to the form until this is accomplished. Daily verbal reminders may be needed to ensure that the medication is being taken correctly.

Mom's Eye Drop Schedule
Take only in right eye

Sunday	Monday	Tuesday	Wednesday	Thursday	Friday	Saturday
			March 23 - Day of eye surgery	March 24 1 drop of Maxidex (pink) at 8:00, 10:00, 12:00, 2:00, 4:00 and 6:00 AND 1 drop of Vigamox (tan) at 8:00, 12:00, 4:00 and 6:00	March 25 1 drop of Maxidex (pink) at 8:00, 10:00, 12:00, 2:00, 4:00 and 6:00 AND 1 drop of Vigamox (tan) at 8:00, 12:00, 4:00 and 6:00	March 26 1 drop of Maxidex (pink) at 8:00, 10:00, 12:00, 2:00, 4:00 and 6:00 AND 1 drop of Vigamox (tan) at 8:00, 12:00, 4:00 and 6:00
March 27 1 drop of Maxidex (pink) at 8:00, 10:00, 12:00, 2:00, 4:00 and 6:00 AND 1 drop of Vigamox (tan) at 8:00, 12:00, 4:00 and 6:00	March 28 1 drop of Maxidex (pink) at 8:00, 10:00, 12:00, 2:00, 4:00 and 6:00 AND 1 drop of Vigamox (tan) at 8:00, 12:00, 4:00 and 6:00	March 29 1 drop of Maxidex (pink) at 8:00, 10:00, 12:00, 2:00, 4:00 and 6:00 AND 1 drop of Vigamox (tan) at 8:00, 12:00, 4:00 and 6:00	March 30 1 drop of Maxidex (pink) at 8:00, 10:00, 12:00, 2:00, 4:00 and 6:00 AND 1 drop of Vigamox (tan) at 8:00, 12:00, 4:00 and 6:00	March 31 1 drop of Maxidex (pink) at 8:00, 11:00, 2:00, and 5:00	April 1 1 drop of Maxidex (pink) at 8:00, 11:00, 2:00, and 5:00	April 2 1 drop of Maxidex (pink) at 8:00, 11:00, 2:00, and 5:00

This form was used to remind Mom of when to take her eye drops (and which ones) each day following her cataract surgery. This schedule lasted five weeks, with eye drop frequency changing over time. She would check off each individual time and kept the eye drops on the table next to her chair. (The pink and tan notes refer to the color of the top of the eye drop bottle.)

Abbreviated Caregiving Form 28
© Copyright 2010, Janice Louise Long

Medication Changes

When any medications are changed or a new medication added, a notice can be posted in a central location, such as the kitchen, with a place for all the caregivers to initial that they have read the change notice. A primary reason for the change notice is to alert the caregivers that a medication has been changed. This could be due to a dosage change, a subtraction of a medication or an addition of a new medication. Medication changes should also be listed in the caregiver daily notes pages. If the new medication or change in medication venue causes a change in the patient, either positive or negative, the change should also be recorded in the caregiver daily notes.

As of April 29: MEDICATION CHANGE NOTICE

Inhaler Schedule:
Both Atrovent and Albuterol inhalers are now only used "as needed."

Serevent: (round, green inhaler in bathroom) Morning and Night

Breathing machine: Take lid off of plastic breather – pour in 1 vial of combination medicine (on kitchen counter – Atrovent + Albuterol) and put lid back on.

Attach to breathing machine and turn on "black button." Mom should breathe normally for 7-1/2 minutes.

Do this 3 times per day – breakfast, lunch, and bedtime.

Caregiver Initials: _____ _____ _____ _____

Caregiving Form 14/29
© Copyright 2010, Janice Louise Long

Another note:

Caregiving Status Note: Tuesday, December 7

Caregivers,

Mom and Dad got up about 5:00 a.m. and Mom has been acting angry all day. Not sure what is bothering her or if she feels bad or is just tired. She was regressing in time a little bit, which she hasn't done for a couple of weeks. She did not eat any lunch – maybe 2 bites and said she wasn't hungry.

After lunch, I gave her the nebulizer treatment about 1:00 (instead of noon) and she thought she was talking on the phone. She kept saying she was tired of talking. I gave her ½ tablet of Lorazepam about 1:20 p.m. I tried to get her to take a nap in the chair, but she wanted to go to bed (very unusual). She did sleep for a while and Dad went into the bedroom about 3:00 to be with her. The 4:00 nebulizer treatment can wait for a while, if she is still asleep.

If you have ANY CONCERNS AT ALL, call Hospice first at (list telephone #) and then call me. Please initial below that you have read this notice.

Thanks very much,

Caregiver Initials: _____ _____ _____ _____ _____

Janice

Caregiving Form 30
© Copyright 2010, Janice Louise Long

Oxygen

Over the time that Mom was on oxygen, she went from an in-home oxygen generator to five small tanks to two large tanks. The change from the generator to the small tanks occurred because the generator could not produce enough oxygen for her consumption. The change to the two larger tanks occurred for several reasons. Two tanks are easier to manage, do not take up as much space, and the oxygen line didn't have to be changed. On the smaller tanks, we always had to watch the level of oxygen and change the tanks in the evening to ensure that

Mom would have enough oxygen to get through the night. She, understandably, was very paranoid about this. With the two larger tanks, the "Y" shaped connector was added, with the tanks running simultaneously at a lower capacity. Running at a lower capacity makes them more efficient. For example, if Mom's liter flow was at 6, each tank would be run at a flow of 3 for a total of 6 liters. The two tanks would last the entire week without worry or any need to change the line. The tank capacity was 8 liters, so as Mom's oxygen needs increased, we could easily change the level of each tank accordingly. We also changed the nasal cannula tubing twice a month, or more often as needed, and the fifty foot tubing once a month. The oxygen company kept us supplied with tubing.

Oxygen instruction sheets were created at the different care levels. One instruction was written for my brother's use when they came on the weekends. Another was written for Mom and Dad for their understanding and for general use. We tried using a distilled water vaporizer occasionally, but found they did not work well, causing tank operation problems.

We kept portable tanks for use when we took Mom out of the house. One of the green tanks (about two feet high) could last about four hours. An extra tank was kept in the back seat of the car, in case of delay. If we were going to a medical appointment, we would ask for her to be put on in-house oxygen to preserve our oxygen tanks. Often, this was an available option. I would periodically reassure Mom that her oxygen tank level was fine and remind her that we had an extra tank in the car.

OXYGEN TANK INSTRUCTIONS

1. **James and Ralph will switch the tanks when needed (on the weekend).**
2. **Tanks are connected by a "Y" shaped connector; when moving them, go to 2 new tanks**
3. **Tanks only need to be switched every 3 days**
4. **Turn each tank to 3**
5. **Can move up one tank to 4 if Mom is short of breath**
6. **See general instructions for doctor and oxygen supplier, etc.**
   List Oxygen supplier name and telephone #

Caregiving Form 31
© Copyright 2010, Janice Louise Long

OXYGEN/NEBULIZER

1. All of the Oxygen/nebulizer equipment and LUNG (only) medications are now supplied through Hospice.

2. The oxygen tanks hold @ 33% more than the old tanks. Oxygen deliveries are now twice a week, Tuesdays and Fridays. Thus, fewer tanks. Liter flow is currently 6-1/2. The vaporizer is now attached to one machine. If you switch the tank flows to even out the tank volume, make sure the vaporizer is on the higher flow machine. You will have to switch the green nozzle as well. Fill the water with distilled water (in kitchen) when the water level gets below the minimum mark. Fill only to the minimum mark.

3. The nebulizer top screws on and off of the medicine cup. Unscrew the top and put the two vials of medicine in the medicine cup. Screw back on and turn on the black button. Wash out the components following each treatment and put back on machine.

4. There are two portable oxygen machines in the dining room. To fill, place unit on top of one of the oxygen tanks. Push down slightly to seat it on the tank. There is a tan 1" x 3" lever on the side of the tank. Lift up on that to fill. When you hear a change in the noise of the oxygen flow and see a puff of vapor, the tank is full. Close the lever. Hold the tank by its strap and look at meter to ensure tank is full. Fill both tanks as they are joined to give Mom enough oxygen flow.

5. Call (<u>Name of Supplier and telephone number</u>) if any questions or problems.

Name of Patient:

SS# _____, Medicare # _____

Date of birth: _____

Hospice # _____

Health Plan Member # _____

Primary Care Physician: (List Name, Address, and Telephone #)

Caregiving Form 32
© Copyright 2010, Janice Louise Long

Nebulizer Treatments

A nebulizer is an electric machine that allows a patient to breathe medications through a mouthpiece. The medications are supplied in small plastic vials. The liquid medication is poured into a nebulizer cup, the mouthpiece placed in the patient's mouth, the machine turned on, and the medication delivered in a mist as the patient breathes in. See picture of nebulizer use below – Figure 4. Mom received three of these treatments each day for seven minutes each.

Figure 4: Nebulizer Use

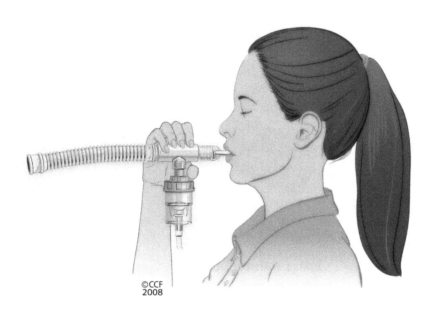

©CCF
2008

Reprinted with permission, Cleveland Clinic Center for Medical Art & Photography © 2008-2009. All Rights reserved.

Potty Chair

A portable potty chair may be placed near the bedside for use at night, or near the hospital bed (wherever it is placed in the home). The potty chair is much easier to use and clean if a solution of toilet bowl cleaner and water is poured into the basin (1:4). Once the potty chair is used, the solution can be directly emptied into the toilet and refilled. It should be cleaned at least once a day. The potty chair may be supplied by Hospice, if applicable.

Pulse Oximeter

We checked Mom's oxygen level with a small device called a "pulse oximeter." The pulse oximeter (Figure 5) could be put on Mom's finger and would show her oxygenation level (O_2 saturation level) and also her pulse. If her oxygen level was too low, we could give her an extra nebulizer treatment, in addition to the three treatments she already received each day. Pulse oximeters may be purchased from a medical supply store.

Figure 5: Pulse Oximeter

Image courtesy of Clinical Guard,
http://www.clinicalguard.com/oximeters-for-home-use-p-36.html

Safety

Falls are very dangerous for seniors. Many falls cause broken bones, requiring surgery, hospitalization, and often, rehabilitation care prior to a return home. Falls can be a precursor to or an indication of an elderly person's failing health. According to the CDC:

- Among older adults, falls are the leading cause of injury deaths. They are also the most common cause of nonfatal injuries and hospital admissions for trauma (CDC 2005).
- In 2005, 15,800 people 65 and older died from injuries related to unintentional falls; about 1.8 million people 65 and older were treated in emergency departments for

nonfatal injuries from falls, and more than 433,000 of these patients were hospitalized (CDC 2005).

- Nearly 85% of deaths from falls in 2004 were among people 75 and older (CDC 2005).

Retrieved August 2009 from,

http://www.cdc.gov/HomeandRecreationalSafety/Falls/adultfalls.html

Adults can help by doing the following:

- Exercising regularly; exercise programs like Tai Chi that increase strength and improve balance are especially good.
- Ask their doctor or pharmacist to review their medicines–both prescription and over-the counter–to reduce side effects and interactions.
- Having their eyes checked by an eye doctor at least once a year.
- Improving the lighting in their home.
- Reducing hazards in their home that can lead to falls.

Retrieved August 2009 from,

http://www.cdc.gov/HomeandRecreationalSafety/Falls/adultfalls.html

CDC also publishes a home safety check list to survey the home and remove potential fall hazards. This safety check list appears in Appendix I.

Retrieved August 2009 from, http://www.cdc.gov/ncipc/pub-res/toolkit/CheckListForSafety.htm

Safety hazards within the home can also include electrical appliances and cleansers. A person with even a low level of dementia can forget how to use an appliance as simple as a coffee pot or microwave. The stove can be left on and forgotten. Misuse of cleansers can cause a chemical hazard. Forgetting to take medications or overdosing accidently on medications can cause problems in mental status, dehydration, depression, dizziness, or other problems.

Getting into a shower in which the water temperature has not been monitored or lowered at the water heater can cause burns. Slipping in bathtubs or showers can be prevented by placing non-slip rubber mats on the floors, both inside and outside of bathtubs and showers. Non-slip placemats can also be placed on eating tables to prevent dishes being pulled onto laps or the floor. Be watchful for problems and make care choices to accommodate for them.

Watch for problems with toilets. Toilets that are backed up may be flushed repeatedly by elders in an attempt to obtain proper flushing. Backed up toilets may run over onto a carpeted floor that will need to be sanitized or cleaned. We actually replaced the carpet in the bathrooms with tile to help alleviate this problem.

Safety Tip

Put your car keys beside your bed at night

This tip retrieved from the internet can be a good safety measure, both indoors and outside. My Dad's neighbor fell on her patio, broke her hip, had to drag herself inside and then passed out. Her telephone shorted out, and she lay there 18 hours. If she had her keys with her, she could have pushed the alarm button and someone would have come to help her. Some cars may not be able to be triggered from inside the house, but it may be possible to come up with an alternative alarm system.

If you hear a noise outside your home or someone trying to get in your house, just press the panic button for your car. The alarm will be set off, and the horn will continue to sound until either you turn it off or the car battery dies. This tip came from a neighborhood watch coordinator. Next time you come home for the night and you start to put your keys away, think of this: It's a security alarm system that you probably already have and requires no installation. Test it.

It will go off from most everywhere inside your house and will keep honking until your battery runs down or until you reset it with the button on the key fob chain. It works if you park in your driveway or garage. If your car alarm goes off when someone is trying to break into your house, odds are the burglar/rapist won't stick around. After a few seconds all the neighbors will be looking out their windows to see who is out there and sure enough the criminal won't want that. And remember to carry your keys while walking to your car in a parking lot. The alarm can work the same way there. This is something that should really be shared with everyone. Maybe it could save a life or prevent a sexual abuse crime.

Retrieved May 2009 from, Personal Email Circulation

Shampooing

Shampooing the hair can be done very easily without forcing the patient to stand and put their head under a faucet. Sit the patient in a chair close to a sink and drape towels around their neck. Fill the sink with warm water. Using a wash cloth, dampen the head with warm water. When damp enough, massage in the shampoo. Use a nice smelling shampoo. Massage the head for at least a minute to give comfort and to allow the shampoo time to work. Gradually remove the shampoo with the washcloth by rubbing the washcloth through the hair. Rinse often. After about three rinses, fill the sink with clean, warm water. Continue rinsing the shampoo from the hair until all the shampoo is removed. This takes about 4-5 rinses total. Style in desired manner.

Shaving

Once Dad had too much trouble using his electric shaver, we reverted to shaving him with a safety razor. A basin of warm water, shaving foam, and a towel is all that is needed. The patient may be shaved sitting up or lying down. Be sure and use a nice smelling aftershave afterward. This helps the patient to feel special.

Shopping and Errands

Shopping and errands were only performed by a family member until the last 1-1/2 years (after Mom died). Before she died, neither one of the parents would leave the other. Excursions were saved for doctor's appointments or lunch out. Dad would attend all of Mom's doctor's appointments, even if he couldn't understand what was said. One of the brothers would come and take Dad for a drive each weekend to get him out of the house. Dad's care was better facilitated by taking him out of the house for short periods of time. At this time, we allowed Arizona to run errands or get groceries. Sometimes she would take Dad to breakfast or lunch as well.

Our neighborhood grocery store knew our family well. This store allowed me to write a letter giving Arizona permission to buy groceries with a check signed by me. I found out it never hurts to ask for help – you might get what you want. This was a great social outing for Dad, as he knew all the grocery store personnel by sight.

As Mom got less and less able to go out, she would let me take Dad to his doctor's appointments and leave her at home. If I knew the appointment was going to take a long time, I would arrange for one of my brothers to come and stay with her. Otherwise, I would make sure she had been to the bathroom before we left, had a glass of water and snack, and she would situate herself in her recliner. I would call her every hour on the cell phone to check in with her, make sure she was OK and give her an update on Dad's appointment. I would then reassure Dad that she was doing well, otherwise, he would have been in a big hurry to get his appointment over with and go home.

Signage

Signs showing where the bathroom is or emergency contact signs are important to the person being cared for. Patients with dementia may forget how to get to the bathroom or where it is. Having signs directing the way will help avoid accidents. A list of important phone numbers may assist them in calling the right person – they may not be able to remember phone numbers, but they may still know how to use a telephone. Likewise, signs on drawers can help the person find their clothing, or items in the bathroom or kitchen.

Stress, Caregiving

Caregiving stress goes with the territory. I would never be able to count the numbers of times I was asked if I was OK or if I was taking care of myself. Caregiving takes its toll, and especially so if the caretaker is dealing with patients with forms of dementia. The Alzheimer's website has a caregiver stress questionnaire, with resource tags. Any questions that are answered "Yes" are linked to resource websites that will help the caregiver deal with their feelings of stress. Caregiver stress is exhibited by "denial, anger, social withdrawal, anxiety, depression, exhaustion, sleeplessness, irritability, lack of concentration, and health problems." Two lists are shown below. The first is ten steps to manage caregiver stress courtesy of the Alzheimer's Organization. The second is twenty-five ways to eliminate stress courtesy of Elder Independence of Maine.

Step 1: *Understand what's going on as early as possible*

Symptoms of Alzheimer's may appear gradually. It can be easy to explain away changing or unusual behavior when a loved one seems physically healthy. Instead, consult a doctor when you see changes in memory, mood or behavior. Don't delay; some symptoms are treatable.

Step 2: *Know what community resources are available*

Contact your local Alzheimer's Association office. The staff can help you find Alzheimer care resources in your community. Adult day programs, in-home assistance, visiting nurses and meal delivery are just some of the services that can help you manage daily tasks.

Step 3: *Become an educated caregiver*

As the disease progresses, new caregiving skills may be necessary. The Alzheimer's Association offers programs to help you better understand and cope with the behaviors and personality changes that often accompany Alzheimer's.

Step 4: *Get help*

Trying to do everything by yourself will leave you exhausted. Seek the support of family, friends and community resources. Tell others exactly what they can do to help. The Alzheimer's Association 24/7 Helpline, online message boards and local support groups are good sources of comfort and reassurance. If stress becomes overwhelming, seek professional help.

Step 5: *Take care of yourself*

Watch your diet, exercise and get plenty of rest. Making sure that you stay healthy will help you be a better caregiver.

Step 6: *Manage your level of stress*

Stress can cause physical problems (blurred vision, stomach irritation, high blood pressure) and changes in behavior (irritability, lack of concentration, change in appetite). Note your symptoms. Use relaxation techniques that work for you, and talk to your doctor.

Step 7: *Accept changes as they occur*

People with Alzheimer's change and so do their needs. They may require care beyond what you can provide on your own. Becoming aware of community resources – from home care services to residential care – should make the transition easier. So will the support and assistance of those around you.

Step 8: Make *legal and financial plans*

Plan ahead. Consult a professional to discuss legal and financial issues including advance directives, wills, estate planning, housing issues and long-term care planning. Involve the person with Alzheimer's and family members whenever possible.

Step 9: *Give yourself credit, not guilt*

Know that the care you provide *does* make a difference and you are doing the best you can. You may feel guilty because you can't do more, but individual care needs change as Alzheimer's progresses. You can't promise how care will be delivered, but you can make sure that the person with Alzheimer's is well cared for and safe. Visit your doctor regularly. Take time to get regular checkups, and be aware of what your body is telling you. Pay attention to any exhaustion, stress, sleeplessness or changes in appetite or behavior. Ignoring symptoms can cause your physical and mental health to decline.

Step 10: Call Alzheimer's Organization 24 hours per day/7 days per week at 1-800-272-3900 for reliable information and support or email info@alz.org.

Courtesy of: © 2009 Alzheimer's Association. All rights reserved.

The elder independence of Maine website lists twenty-five ways to eliminate stress. Retrieved August 2009, from http://www.elderindependence.org/eim_caregiverstress.html

"Twenty-five Ways to Eliminate Stress!

1. Have fun to reduce stress.

Do things for the sheer fun of it. Each day, plan to something "just for you." Even if you only have 30 minutes of fun time, don't let anything stop you from your 30 minutes. Find the "kid" inside you whenever possible and have fun! Sing out loud in the shower! Dig in the dirt! Play catch with a child! Dress up the next time you go out for dinner….so many possibilities! Having fun recharges those batteries!

2. Laugh to reduce stress.

Interact with people who make you laugh to reduce tension and boost the immune system. Learn not to take life so seriously. Smile with your mouth and eyes, and smile while you are talking on the phone. People will notice the change in you.

3. Learn to say "no" to reduce stress.

When requests and invitations become a burden instead of being enjoyable, it is time to say "no." If you believe a request could damage your own mental well-being, say "NO"

4. Simplify your life to reduce stress.

Move closer to your work, hire a maid, order out once a week or shop by internet. Clean out the clutter in your home and your life. Make lists, but throw them away when you completed the tasks. Organize so that everything has its place. You will feel better.

5. Delegate responsibility to reduce stress.

Sharing duties allows time together and gets the job done faster. Don't assume people know what you want done. Come right out and tell them what you need.

6. Learn to disconnect, let go and relax.

Try to visualize calming scenes; bring a calming picture to work and practice work station meditation. Stretch and take deep breaths. Play your favorite music. Take a brisk walk. Soak in the tub. Find a tool that you can use to disconnect from stress going on around you so that you are able to relax.

7. To reduce stress, don't be a workaholic.

Find a healthy balance between work and play.

8. Break tasks into segments to reduce stress.

Break down tasks into easy-to-handle segments and problems. It is easier to eat an elephant one bite at a time.

9. Keep your job skills current to reduce stress.

If your job skills are up date, new work tasks will be easier for you and also help with advancement.

10. Take care of your family and friends to reduce stress.

Having relationships in your life is less stressful.

11. Examine work habits to reduce stress.

If you are constantly stressed at work, examine your work habits. Maybe you are wasting time.

12. Drink water.

Consume 8-10 glasses of pure water daily.

13. Eat sensibly to reduce stress

Eat healthier foods and be aware of bad eating habits.

14. Get quality sleep to reduce stress.

Sleep is an essential recovery mechanism. Sleep on your back or sides, not on your stomach. Go to bed on time. Before you drift off to sleep, think of all the things in your life you are grateful for.

15. Stop smoking.

Stop smoking and don't use drugs. Limit alcohol and caffeine. Remember that food is a drug, also.

16. Schedule time to reduce stress.

Allow enough time to reach the place or goal you wish without rushing. Schedule time just for you to relax every day. Take One day at a time, pace yourself and slow down!

17. Exercise regularly to reduce stress.

Take a vigorous walk, jog, or swim for an average of 20 minutes daily or 45 minutes three times a week.

18. Control your attitude to reduce stress.

About the only part of your life you can control completely is your own attitude. One BIG Tip is to keep quiet when you should not or don't need to be involved in someone else's business. Bite that tongue if you have to! Be kind to unkind people- (they probably need it the most.) Develop a forgiving attitude- (Most people are really trying the best they can) Be genuine and always say exactly what you mean… in a nice way.

Here is a great exercise to try at home: Next time a telemarketer calls, answer in a happy, bubbly voice - interrupt their script right away and say- "Hi! Listen, I am a very busy person and not interested, but I hope you sure have a GREAT day! "And hang up. You need to know that that person is sitting in a cubicle somewhere in the world smiling. You may even find yourself smiling for handling that call so well.

19. Be prepared to reduce stress.

Don't stick your head in the sand. There are always going to be bumps in the road of life. Being prepared stops stress in advance. Have backups-keep extra keys, stamps, money, emergency numbers handy. Keep vital information in a folder or box so you can grab at a moments notice.

20. Think positive to reduce stress.

If something is stressful, make a list of every positive aspect of your situation. This doesn't mean you should go through life as a Pollyanna, however. Then you will rarely, if ever, be prepared--see number 19!

21. Improve yourself to reduce stress.

Broaden your knowledge through reading, seminars, and self- improvement courses. Carry a backpack with a book and read when you wait in line. Talk less and listen more- you'll learn a great deal that way.

22. Live within your means to reduce stress.

Constantly overspending and worrying about money is definitely stressful.

23. Save money to reduce stress.

Knowing you have a "nest egg" makes you less stressed.

24. Consider a career change to reduce stress.

Burnout can be very stressful. If that has happened to you, consider changing careers.

25. Handle stress now to reduce stress.

Putting off stressful events only makes them more stressful. Settle matters that are troubling you "as they occur." Procrastination usually leads to increased stress."

Retrieved October 2009 from,
http://www.elderindependence.org/eim_caregiverstress.html

Many websites have information on caregiver stress. The caregiver just becomes overwhelmed. Trying to work and caregive and take care of a family and run errands plus the worry just takes it toll. The caregiver may become greatly fatigued, short-tempered, forgetful, and generally feel like their mind is in a fog. My neighbor has been taking care of her mother full-time for only two months. Her mother is between Stages 6 and 7 of Alzheimer's. My neighbor is already experiencing depression and is worn down. Caregiver's must have breaks or ways to leave the house to take their mind off of the worry and stress. Their health will probably suffer anyway, but without respite, the consequences can be devastating.

I was tired for sure and worried. I did play competitive bridge (card game) 1-2 times per week, which entirely took my mind away from the problems for a few hours. My brain certainly did feel like it was in a fog the last year. It took many months after Dad's death before I felt more like myself, and even now I still feel like I am recovering. I am not sure my brothers ever understood the toll caregiving takes on a person. How I felt didn't mean that I wanted to give up the caregiving – just that it was taking a toll on me. Hiring caregivers helped immensely, but that doesn't take away the responsibility or worry. I have heard reports of caregivers becoming ill enough not to perform the caregiving or of dying before the person they are taking care of does. The family tries to understand, but the only way for them to truly understand is to take over the caregiving duties for a few weeks. I was not good at delegating – it was easier for me to just take care of things, as I was there every day. Asking my brother's to take over part of the responsibility would have taken them away from their jobs and their families. It might help to just delegate up front before the responsibility is set in place.

Types and Signs of Elder Abuse

Elder abuse is quite common in the United States, although we don't like to think of this type of abuse. According to the Helpguide website 500,000 to 1,000,000 elders are abused each year and for each elder abuse case reported, approximately 12-13 cases are not reported. Primary signs to look for are excessive bedsores, uncleanliness of the elder, bruising or fractures, or inability to get out of bed. Elder abuse can occur anywhere, in the home or in a facility. It is less likely to occur in a facility, as signs for abuse are watched for. Because of the importance of elder abuse, I have taken the following information on types and signs of elder abuse from Help Guide. Elder abuse may be reported by calling the Eldercare Locator at 1-800-677-1116.

"Signs and symptoms of specific types of abuse"

Physical abuse

Physical elder abuse is non-accidental use of force against an elderly person that results in physical pain, injury, or impairment. Such abuse includes not only physical assaults such as hitting or shoving but the inappropriate use of drugs, restraints, or confinement.

Emotional abuse

In emotional or psychological senior abuse, people speak to or treat elderly persons in ways that cause emotional pain or distress.

Verbal forms of emotional elder abuse include

- intimidation through yelling or threats
- humiliation and ridicule
- habitual blaming or scapegoating

Nonverbal psychological elder abuse can take the form of

- ignoring the elderly person
- isolating an elder from friends or activities
- terrorizing or menacing the elderly person

Sexual abuse

Sexual elder abuse is contact with an elderly person without the elder's consent. Such contact can involve physical sex acts, but activities such as showing an elderly person pornographic material, forcing the person to watch sex acts, or forcing the elder to undress are also considered sexual elder abuse.

Neglect or abandonment by caregivers

Elder neglect, failure to fulfill a caretaking obligation, constitutes more than half of all reported cases of elder abuse. It can be active (intentional) or passive (unintentional, based on factors such as ignorance or denial that an elderly charge needs as much care as he or she does).

Financial exploitation

This involves unauthorized use of an elderly person's funds or property, either by a caregiver or an outside scam artist.

An unscrupulous caregiver might

- misuse an elder's personal checks, credit cards, or accounts
- steal cash, income checks, or household goods
- forge the elder's signature
- engage in identity theft

Typical rackets that target elders include

- Announcements of a "prize" that the elderly person has won but must pay money to claim
- Phony charities
- Investment fraud

Healthcare fraud and abuse

Carried out by unethical doctors, nurses, hospital personnel, and other professional care providers, examples of healthcare fraud and abuse regarding elders include

- Not providing healthcare, but charging for it
- Overcharging or double-billing for medical care or services
- Getting kickbacks for referrals to other providers or for prescribing certain drugs
- Overmedicating or undermedicating
- Recommending fraudulent remedies for illnesses or other medical conditions
- Medicaid fraud

Signs and symptoms of elder abuse

At first, you might not recognize or take seriously signs of elder abuse. They may appear to be symptoms of dementia or signs of the elderly person's frailty — or caregivers may explain them to you that way. In fact, many of the signs and symptoms of elder abuse do overlap with symptoms of mental deterioration, but that doesn't mean you should dismiss them on the caregiver's say-so.

General signs of abuse

The following are warning signs of some kind of elder abuse:

- Frequent arguments or tension between the caregiver and the elderly person
- Changes in personality or behavior in the elder

If you suspect elderly abuse based upon the information above, but aren't sure, contact your primary care physician, your Hospice agency (if applicable), or your state Adult Protective Services office.

Retrieved August 2009, from
http://www.helpguide.org/mental/elder_abuse_physical_emotional_sexual_neglect.htm

Task Instructions

Before we had full-time caregiving, my brothers or daughters filled in during the evenings or weekends. Task lists gave instructions of what care was to be given in the mornings, evenings, or weekends. These instructions were written as a checklist to ensure that all Mom's and Dad's needs were taken care of. These instructions were also used as training devices for the part-time caregivers. We also posted a schedule to show who was covering weekend duty. Several formats are shown below.

WEEKEND INSTRUCTIONS

1. Check oxygen: currently at 6-1/2 liter (4 on one tank, 2-1/2 on second tank); can even our oxygen flow by switching dials if enough oxygen left

2. Breathing machine: Times are now @ 8:00 am, 11:30 am (before lunch), and 4:00 pm

3. Give Mom her Serevent to take @ 4:00 pm (round, green inhaler on kitchen table)

4. Mom is no longer taking Plavix at lunch

5. Fix some kind of snack for the afternoon

6. Wheelchair: easier to maneuver if large wheels are taken down ramps first (Mom leaning back in chair, rather than forward); go gently – she gets nervous. Mom can walk around bedroom and bathroom with walker. Take wheelchair into bedroom for her to transfer (not on landing before step). The rest of the time, she is in the wheelchair for transport to living room or kitchen.

Caregiving Form 33
© Copyright 2010, Janice Louise Long

WEEKEND SCHEDULE FOR MOM (Used for part-time caregivers)

Breakfast	7:00-8:15 (approx)	1. Takes Serevent, 1 puff
		2. Takes Rhinocort nasal spray, 1 squeeze
	Check to see if she took her breathing treatment and medications	3. Takes breathing machine, 7-1/2 minutes
		4. Takes medications from pill box with orange juice
		5. Usually eats 2 slices of raisin bread with coffee
		6. Transport to bathroom
	8:15 - 10:00	1. Bathe (as needed) and dress
		2. Curl hair
		3. Assist with bathroom
		4. Assist with electric scooter
		5. Vacuum bedroom/make bed/tidy up

Clothes: Usually changes outfits 2-3x/week; may change more often

Hair: Wash with shampoo in green bottle; put on a small amount of mousse before drying. Wash hair by dampening with washcloth; rinse with washcloth. Take wet towels off shoulders as soon as possible and let her put on her blouse.

Lotion: Pat lotion onto dry skin as needed (lanolin), do foot bath 1x/weekend.

Sheets: Check for soils; wash if needed. (secondary duty; only if time permits)
Do not start laundry if you cannot complete the drying and folding; it will not be finished by them

Dishes: Dad does dishes, but doesn't get them clean; if you can beat him to them, please put in dishwasher (may need emptied); hand wash coffee cups and juice glasses.

Quart bottles: Fill juice and milk quart bottles, if needed

Schedule: Check calendar in kitchen and remind them which brother is coming to do their lunch

Caregiving Form 34
© Copyright 2010, Janice Louise Long

A couple of times when I was out of town (prior to full-time caregiving), my daughters would take turns and go by to check on Mom and Dad. Special instructions were drafted for them. Morning, Afternoon, and Evening tasks may also be separated on different pages for caregivers.

Grandpa and Grandma Tasks

<u>Morning:</u>

1. Check to see if they took their pills from the pill box.
2. Check to see if Mom took her nebulizer treatment (2 vials of liquid medicine – put in container and time her breathing for 7-1/2 minutes); vials are labeled by day of week and time (7:30 am, 11:30 am, 4:00 pm) and are either on the kitchen table or on the counter across from the refrigerator.
3. She is also to take 1 puff of Serevent (round, green inhaler) at breakfast (should be on kitchen table but may be on their table in living room).
4. Caregiver will get her dressed and bathed. Monday through Friday attendant comes between 8-8:15. Mom is usually impatient about waiting for them to get here. Just remind her they come and help her so she doesn't run out of energy and that they give her a bath. Sat-Sun attendant usually gets here by 7:30 am.
5. Try to do the kitchen dishes or put them in the dishwasher if the dishwasher will be run that day.

<u>Noon:</u>

1. Have lunch ready by 12:00 noon. I suggest going one day to Albuquerque Grill and picking up 2 orders of green chile chicken enchiladas, 1 order of curly fries (no beans/rice) and 2 iced teas. The other day you can order a pizza (Special) and salad from Dion's. I will give you the $$ for it.
2. If you get there about 11:00 then you don't need to call and remind them that you are bringing lunch. Call and order lunch and pick it up. They probably won't remember you were there in the morning.
3. Give Mom her 11:30 nebulizer treatment (same as morning). Wash the nebulizer container before or after each treatment. This treatment may be given either before or after she eats.
4. Clean up the dishes and start dishwasher, if needed. I run the dishwasher every 2 days or they will run out of dishes.

Afternoon:

1. Give Mom her 4:00 pm nebulizer treatment. Also, take the Serevent (round, green inhaler) to her and have her take a puff.

2. Set the table for breakfast – small plate, knife, small juice glass, coffee cup.

3. Put nebulizer machine, vials of medicine for 7:30 am, and Serevent on the table at Mom's place (closest to garage door) after she is done with her treatment.

4. Make the coffee – put in 6 cups of water and 3 scoops of coffee (filters and coffee are in cupboard above coffee maker. That way all Dad has to do is turn it on in the morning.

5. Give them some kind of snack – pizza, bisquit with ham and cheese and mayonnaise, or fruit (in bottom drawer of refrigerator). Can also make a quesadilla (2 tortillas with cheese in the middle – heat up in toaster oven). Potato chips are in cabinet on top of the oven.

Other:

1. Caregivers may start laundry while they are here. You will have to take it out of the dryer and hang it up or fold it. Mom's towels go on her bath chair in her room; her clothes get hung up in the closet and Dad's in his closet (in the room where my office is). Her underwear goes in the top right hand drawer of her vanity (next to the window). Dad's underwear goes in the 3rd drawer of his dresser (down from the top).

2. The oxygen tanks are filled on Tuesdays and Fridays. The guy that delivers it knows what to do, so you don't have to worry about that.

3. Emergency phone #'s and health care information is on the kitchen counter by Mom's meds.

Caregiving Form 35
© Copyright 2010, Janice Louise Long

Morning Tasks

1. Assist Mom to bathroom and out to kitchen – give meds as needed.

2. Get raisin bread, butter, and juice out of refrigerator. Pour coffee. Microwave 1 pouch of bacon for 3 minutes.

3. After breakfast, check to see if they took their pills from the pill boxes on kitchen table.

4. Give Mom her nebulizer treatment (2 vials of liquid medicine – put in container and time her breathing for 7-1/2 minutes); vials are labeled by day of week and time (7:30 am, 11:30 am, 4:00 pm) and are either on the kitchen table or on the counter across from the refrigerator.

5. She is also to take 1 spray of Flonase in each nostril and 1 puff of Serevent (round, green inhaler) at breakfast (should be on kitchen table but may be on their table in living room).

6. Assist Mom in bathing and dressing. Please curl hair with curling iron and comb out. Use slight teasing on top and smooth with comb/brush.

7. Please clean up kitchen table and put dishes in the dishwasher; hand wash juice glasses if dishwasher not being started.

8. Do not start any laundry that cannot be completed, as laundry would not be completed and will sit in washer/dryer until next day.

9. Assist with scooter as needed – Mom may need help getting oxygen tubing out of the way, going up and down ramps. Check battery level (on top monitor). If battery is getting into the yellow/red area, please put in a new battery (in living room). Hook up old battery to the charger (by living room door, next to TV).

Caregiving Form 36
© Copyright 2010, Janice Louise Long

Evening Tasks

Give Mom her afternoon meds – in plastic cups on kitchen counter, Serevent inhaler, her nebulizer breathing treatment at 4:00 pm. The Serevent should be on the kitchen table (please put back there for breakfast). The nebulizer treatment is on the middle kitchen counter with all the meds. Please put the breakfast dose for the nebulizer on the table by Mother's placemat and return the nebulizer machine to the table as well, and plug it in. Please wash out the mouthpiece and place in nebulizer.

Please make the coffee for the morning (8 cups water + 4-1/2 scoops of coffee). Coffee and filters are in the cabinet above the coffee maker. Extra coffee is in the lower cabinet between the oven and the dishwasher.

Please set the kitchen table for breakfast: juice glasses (there are only two), coffee cups and saucers (the wheat patterned saucer and the plain white cup is Mother's), small plates, and knives. Please put muffins on table, if there are any (usually on middle kitchen counter).

Try and get them to eat a snack. They don't eat as much as they used to. A snack could be a sliced apple, a leftover from lunch, a tortilla (add cheese and salsa and fold in half. Cook in toaster oven and cut into four pieces), fruit (e.g., cantaloupe, strawberries, peaches, pears), shrimp (in freezer) – shrimp sauce in door of refrig, sausage and crackers, kielbasa (in freezer -- will have to be cut up and heated in frying pan). Potato chips and crackers are above oven.

Check battery on scooter – if on yellow or red, change batteries. Hook up the one you take off of scooter to the charger. A battery usually lasts 3 days. One of the cases is cracked, so if you hold the silver pin down in the back, it should align enough to put the charger in.

Check oxygen tanks to ensure they are connected when they go to bed. Occasionally, the tubing gets disconnected or Mom runs over it with the scooter.

Please stay until they are in bed. Assist as needed. Go out through the garage and make sure front door is locked. Don't need to lock kitchen door to garage.

Janice's cell phone:

List all important telephone #'s:

Caregiving Form 37

Travel

The letters to Dad process worked very well. One of the main uses for them was when I needed to travel for my work. I always wrote a letter to Dad, telling him where I was going, where I would be, when I would return, and how to reach me by telephone. I would also let him know who to call for help (with the appropriate telephone number), and any other general information that I thought he needed to know. I especially told him I loved him and would miss him while I was gone. I always left spending money for him (@ $100.00) in a special drawer. The letter would tell him there was spending money in his special drawer. He knew where it was, and knowing that he wouldn't be out of money was always able to give him a sense of security and extra piece of mind. A similar letter may be written to the caregivers. Be sure and use large font for text so that the patient can read it easily. Sign the letter.

Neither my Mom nor Dad could travel any longer by the time I came to care for them. However, many seniors (even those in Assisted Living facilities) do travel, especially in group tours. Be sure medication lists, names and contact information for physicians, as well as legal contacts (e.g., Health Care Power of Attorney, Durable Power of Attorney) are placed in their luggage. The amount of belongings should be contained in one lightweight suitcase. Trips can become very long, especially if tours require lots of steps or walking. Often, the traveler will be lugging their own suitcase around, especially if the trip is overseas. Airports can be daunting, requiring long walks, especially if customs requirements are being met. Check with the tour company to ensure that wheelchairs are available and that there will be someone to assist if the need arises. Give assurance to your parent that using a wheelchair and accepting help is OK. I recently traveled with 9 other people – five of us were about the same age and the other five ranged in age from 78 -92. By the end of our trip, all five of them were in wheelchairs with one of the younger five wheeling them about, as well as caring for the luggage.

Thursday, February 16

Hi Dad,

This note is to remind you that I will be flying to Washington DC tomorrow for business meetings and a couple of days with my friends. I will miss you a lot!! There is plenty of food in the refrigerator and freezer. I have put extra money in your drawer, in case you need it.

I will call while I am gone, but you can call me anytime at _____. I am staying with a friend named Alice and you may need to call me through her if you cannot get me on the cell phone. Her number is _____. If I am not there and am at work, she will take a message for me.

You can also call James at _____ or Ralph at _____ if you need something.

I will be flying back on Monday, February 27. I arrive at the airport about 3:15 and will come here to see you before you go to bed.
I love you and will miss you!

Caregiving Form 38
© Copyright 2010, Janice Louise Long

Travel instructions were also left for the caregivers or brothers.

WHERE I WILL BE:

Staying with Alice: List telephone numbers

My Cell phone:

Daytime telephone #:

OXYGEN:

Oxygen will be delivered on Thursday.

If any problems or delivery is late, call Jim at _____ (will need to give him your name, Mom's name and address). He is a supervisor at the oxygen supply company. James and Ralph will take care of switching oxygen tanks.

MEALS/ANYTHING YOU NEED:

Saturday/Sunday: Call Ralph at _____

Monday through Thursday: Call James at _____

LAUNDRY:

I will do when I return on Friday – you can leave dirty clothes in the bedroom or on the washing machine

APPETIZERS:

1 éclair in refrigerator

2 canteloupes in fruit drawer

3 chile con queso in freezer (James can make more)

MEDICINES:

I will refill the pill boxes on Friday when I return

Breathing medicines: All vials are labeled by day and time on counter: there are extras in case Mom becomes short of breath or if you lose one.

Serevent: (green, round inhaler in bathroom) – should run out on Wednesday – new canister on bathroom counter.

If Mom gets short of breath, have her take 2 slow breaths on her white inhaler (in cart) or an extra breathing treatment

DOCTOR:

If you need a doctor: Dr. _____ (weekdays) or _____ (weekends – ask for pulmonologist on call)

Mom's medical records #: List number

Dad's medical records #: List number

Caregiving Form 39

© Copyright 2010, Janice Louise Long

Vaccinations

Ensure that the patient(s) have their flu vaccinations each year, usually available after October through the primary care provider. If the patient has a history of allergies, heart or lung disease, asthma, immunosuppressed system, kidney failure, HIV, diabetes, alcoholism, or certain Native American or Alaskan natives, the pneumonia vaccination should be given and updated in a timely manner. Guidelines for the pneumonia vaccination change, based on the current vaccine. Generally, the pneumonia vaccination should be given at least every ten years. If the patient is 65, this vaccination should be given no later than five years after turning age 65, and updated regularly. Pneumonia is an insidious disease among senior citizens and is not always detectible.

Summary

The number of forms presented here may seem overwhelming. Take each section as it is needed, figure out what the present need is, and incorporate the appropriate form. Many examples are given, but perhaps only a few forms are needed or an adaptation of a form may be created. Forms and current caregiving news are available on my website: http://www.dyingtherightway.com. Please email me through my website if you have ideas for new forms or if you would like a form individualized to your situation.

Above all, remember, caregiving is an overwhelming task. Do not be afraid to ask for help, protect your health and well being, and take each day one at a time. Also take each caregiving task one at a time. Take deep breaths for calming purposes. Remember, common sense and kindness prevail!!

Chapter 7:

Residential Facilities: What Each Type Offers and What Questions to Ask

Mom and Dad's perception of nursing homes was probably of the old style – dark, smelly, rooms where no one pays attention to you, coma-like patients lining the hallways. Both of their mothers had been in nursing homes, and this probably left a bad taste in their mouths. Neither one really explained why they were so adverse to being in one though. If I hadn't been able to move home to take care of them, we would have had to look at the assisted living/nursing home alternatives.

There were actually two occasions that we did consider placing Mom and/or Dad in a facility. The first was at the point when we needed to transition to full-time care, about 2-1/4 years after my arrival. The second time was later on in Dad's disease progression, shortly before he died.

We visited three homes before we hired a full-time caregiver. The first two were assisted living (AL) types of homes, in which Mom and Dad would have their own apartment. Assistance would be given with bathing and dressing. Meals were provided in the general dining room. Giving medications were an extra charge. The staffing ratios were generally 8 to 10 patients to one caregiver.

The main advantages/disadvantages to these assisted living homes were that:

1. Mom and Dad could both stay together in the same room. Rooms were available with one or two bedrooms, each bedroom having its own bathroom. A small living room would usually separate the two bedrooms in a unit.

2. Social events were available for them to participate in, and new friends could be acquired at mealtime.

3. Both of these homes had separate locked Alzheimer's units.

4. Mom would have had a hard time getting around the home due to the size of the facilities – she would have required assistance in traveling to meals. Dad would just get lost all the time.

5. The Assisted Living facilities do not always have advanced care when needed. For the two AL facilities, we would have had to transfer them to a separate facility for more advanced care.

6. The rooms that were available would be the ones we would have to take, whether or not they were close to a staffing area.

7. The rooms were basic, but nice and could be furnished with our own personal belongings.

It was difficult to tell how personable these homes were. They were decorated nicely, the staff members seemed friendly, and the patients seemed dressed nicely and cared for. I imagine that some staff members would be better caregivers than others. Even though Mom and Dad would not be used to the idea of again having a social life, I thought they would enjoy having the ability to meet new friends.

The third home we visited was dedicated to the care of dementia and Alzheimer's patients. This home was quite amenable to having both Mom and Dad there, as Mom also had some dementia. However, at the time we were looking, a double room was not available. This home was our favorite alternative of the three facilities we looked at. The country-styled home was divided into two square buildings, with a courtyard and grassy area connecting them. The courtyard had picnic tables for family gatherings. Each building had bedrooms encircling three sides of the square, all with windows and a bathroom, and open areas in the middle. The open areas were separated into living rooms for television, music, arts and crafts, and another area set up as a dining room. The bedrooms opened up into the center, so that patients could be checked on easily at night.

The patients had access to the courtyard, but could not leave the courtyard or their unit as a locking system was in place. The staffing ratio was 5:1 and no extra charges were applied – all care was inclusive to the price. Amenities also included home cooking. This home is the only one who called to ask our impressions and to follow up later on placement. The main disadvantage to this home was that some of the Alzheimer patients were very advanced in their diseases. We were worried that Mom and Dad would be upset by this. Also, we could not shake the feeling that Mom and Dad in a facility could cause them to decline faster.

The Decision of What Type of Caregiving should be Instituted

I realize that many do not have the resources to either hire caregivers or to place the parent(s) into assisted living care. This book will hopefully give suggestions for helping your parent(s) through their last, most difficult period of their lives. The biggest obstacle for them is their loss of independence. When I sold Mom's car, she worried about how to get to the doctor or hospital, even though she knew I would take them and that we still had Dad's car. I play bridge and several senior players have expressed to me how hard it is for them to stop driving, even with macular degeneration or extreme arthritis. Most of them hate to have to depend on others to help them out, even though even a small amount of assistance can make their lives so much easier to manage.

Below are explanations and illustrative costs of the different types of homes, to give one a feel of the different alternatives that are available. Please note that costs will be different in many areas of the country. The decision of which alternatives to consider comes down to cost (what alternatives are affordable) and type of care needed.

If your parent does not quite need a facility or there is a waiting list prior to moving into a facility, perhaps local senior services are available to fill in until they can be moved to a facility. Local Senior Affairs centers or agencies may offer outside services provided to elders such as: fitness centers, sports programs, meals, senior trips, companion services, special social events, classes, transportation to doctor's visits, income tax assistance, meal preparation, light housekeeping, etc. Day care centers are also available.

When making the decision of which care avenue to pursue, think about the financial resources that are at hand. Do your parents have Long Term Care (LTC) Insurance? Does it cover Assisted Living facilities? How much per day does the insurance cover, compared to the costs in the area that your parents will be placed? When was the Long Term Care Insurance started? My parents had LTC coverage, but they had signed up for it long before Assisted Living (AL) alternatives became available. A waiver to sign up for AL was offered to them, but they declined the waiver. I imagine this was because they intended to stay at home and probably they didn't understand what AL was. Therefore, if we placed Mom and Dad into an

AL home, we would have to pay the full cost – nothing would be reimbursed until one of them needed long term care. See Table 3: Residential Care Costs below.

Table 3: Residential Care Costs

Type of Care	Incurred Costs*
Assisted Living	$3,000-5,000 per month ($36 -60,000 per year)
Full Care – Assisted through Nursing Home	$50,000 – 60,000 per year
Continuing Care	Initial buy-in of $80,000-$100,000 per person; $2,000 - $3000 per month thereafter (dependent upon size of unit)
Private Home Care (6-8 patients) (in a separate home)	$2,800 per month ($33,600 per year)
Alzheimer's Unit	$5,000 per month ($60,000 per year)
Hospice Care	Paid for by Medicare
Agency Care at Home	Aide: $19.00/hour CNA: $35.00/hour ($305,760 per year) RN: $50.00/hour ($436,800 per year)
Private Home Care (at your home)	CNA: $10-15.00/hour ($87,000 -130,000 per year)

The costs listed in this chart are example costs for our area. The chart shows the range of costs for different alternatives. Other areas, such as Los Angeles, Washington D.C., or New York City will have much higher costs. These costs are increasing each year and should be evaluated at the proper time.

© Copyright 2010, Janice Louise Long

Our long term care insurance also only paid for <u>certified</u> agency care and would not reimburse for private care. There is a catch to this. If agency care is used, up to $50.00 per day will be reimbursed. This reimbursement rate made having agency care prohibitive, as noted in

Table 3 above. I would not settle for any type of care less than a Certified Nurse Assistant that is licensed to give medications. Therefore, hiring an agency CNA for $35.00 per hour would cost us $5,880 per week less $350 reimbursement from the LTC insurance or $5,530 per week, about $24,000 per month, and about $285,000 net cost per year. Hiring an agency aide that was not licensed to give medications would be just a little over half of these figures. Be sure to check the policies of current Long Term Care Insurance plans, as caregiving options and restrictions vary from company to company.

We did initially hire agency care for four hours per day to ensure Mom and Dad would get to bed safely for about six months before we went to full-time care. Most of the time, the caregivers were very nice, cared about Mom and Dad, but occasionally, caregivers would not show up, or were late. About half of the time, the agency would know the caregiver would be late and would let us know. The agency did not always know the caregiver had quit without notice. Even though great care was taken to ensure that the schedule was clear, mistakes were made. Unfortunately, in caregiving, not having a caregiver show up or having to deal with a replacement caregiver not used to our situation really threw a monkey wrench into the situation. Mom and Dad did not like to have caregivers in the first place, but would become used to the same people coming in. If a different person showed up, this would confuse them and they didn't know how to handle it, even if I explained to them what was happening. Consistency is definitely an important factor.

Before visiting any care facility, be well versed in the type of care your loved one will need. Do you expect these needs to increase over time? Once you have narrowed the facilities to two or three favorites, visit each facility a couple of times unannounced to check on staff availability, friendliness of staff, cleanliness of the facility, and odors within the facility. Are the residents sitting around in the hallways unattended or placed in a circle in front of the television? Make arrangements to take your loved one to visit and view the facilities, activities, and have the family eat a meal together at the facility. Factors you may wish to consider are the size of the facility, the proximity to the immediate family (distance), levels of care available, cost, activities offered, and religious preference.

In some cities, homes are available by religious preference. Generally, members of that religion may have first choice of units as they become available. Facilities also exist that are industry related (based on one's career). Examples of these types of facilities may be a Presbyterian, Methodist, or Catholic home that offers independent living and assisted living services. Hospice services may also be faith-based. Military retirees with disabilities have access to Veteran's Administration (VA) Hospital services, which include Hospice care. VA services require documentation and an application to be filed. Some churches within cities have bonded together to create a faith-based continuum of care setting, offering services from independent living through nursing home care.

Note that for Independent Care and Assisted Living levels of care, facilities usually allow the residents to bring their own furniture and belongings.

Independent Living – The Best Life

Independent Living occurs when a <u>parent is still fully capable of caring for themselves</u>, but would like to have their affairs settled before it is too late. Doing so allows them to make friends and be involved in facility activities, to not have to prepare meals, to downsize their living arrangements, and ensure their property is disposed of according to their express wishes. Parents may also wish to remove the "burden of care" from their children.

James Michener wrote the book "Recessional" in 1994, describing life in The Palms, a three-floor resident facility which encompassed independent living, assisted living, and nursing home living. The book describes life and personalities within the facility and shows how relationships are formed not only with other residents, but with the personnel within the facility as well. After all, older people have had extensive life experience and have great stories to tell. Four of the men formed their own group to discuss complicated topics, and actually decided they could build their own airplane – and they did. This book might be worth reading to get a glimpse of everyday life within a facility. The three major types of care – independent living, assisted living, nursing home care – are discussed.

This type of care is like living in an apartment, but in a facility that is available for assistance when it becomes needed. Independent living alternatives may be an apartment in a building with a common hallway, or may be a townhouse on the grounds of the facility separated from the common building. Units may offer choices of one or two bedrooms, each with a bathroom. Independent living allows residents to prepare their own meals in their apartments. Laundry facilities, beauty salon, postal service, and activities are part of the facility.

Facilities are much more welcoming and offer many more senior services than the old paradigm of "sitting in a smelly place" and waiting to die all alone. Facility activities and meals are available as part of the package, with the costs prorated based upon the services chosen. Often, it is easy to handle breakfast and lunch in the apartment and go to the dining hall for dinner and socialization with other residents. Other fees may be assessed, based upon the needs of the occupant(s), e.g., medication assistance, laundry, housekeeping, etc.

Some facilities offer two bedroom units for two adults, but require that once one of the residents dies the other resident moves to a one bedroom unit. This move may occur as early as one month following the death, which could be an additional disruption to an elderly person. Other facilities do not have this requirement.

Looking for and deciding where placement should be made should be done early – before the need becomes an immediate one. Once a particular home has been decided upon, begin the arrangements for placement. Many homes have waiting lists – often up to six months or a year. Waiting to make arrangements until the need is emergent may cause your loved one to be placed in a second or third choice home.

Assisted Living (AL) – Life is Still Good

Assisted Living is just that. The resident needs assistance with part of their day, e.g., dressing, bathing, taking medications, walking, etc., but can still be alone in their room. The resident is not ill enough to require nursing care, but does need help with daily living activities. Assisted living rooms may be an efficiency type room and bathroom, large enough to hold a twin bed and other furniture, or may be a full one bedroom/one bath larger room. Some may have small kitchens, but at this stage, cooking could be a safety hazard. Simple meals, like cereal and toast, sandwiches, and snacks would work well. These rooms are closer to the nursing staff, are usually located in wings dedicated to AL care. The assisted living rooms are often located in a specific wing, with access to a nursing station. Many facilities offer both independent living and assisted living, with the ability to move into assisted living from independent living. The resident may also be able to transition from assisted living back to independent living, if some medical situation has been resolved that caused the transition to assisted living. The doors of apartments in AL units may not be locked to give the nursing staff access and ability to check on residents throughout the day and night.

In both Independent Living and Assisted Living care, the apartments can be self-furnished. Often residents will sell their main home and use that income to live on and pay the facility fees. Favorite furniture and belongings are taken from the main home to the facility to keep a familiar atmosphere. Many facilities have name tags by each door with a personal decoration made by the resident hanging there as well. I have also seen resident paintings hung in the hallways.

Nursing Home Care – Life Sucks

Full nursing care occurs when the resident is either bedridden, or no longer has the faculties to care for him/herself. All care modalities (called skilled nursing care) are offered for this type of resident. If your loved one requires hospitalization or surgery, and returns to their care facility, temporary nursing home care or rehabilitative care might be required. Bear in mind that nursing home care is not offered at all IL/AL facilities and illness or surgery may require several moves for your loved one. Some facilities offer all three types of care and residents may move from one type to another as care is required.

Rehabilitative Care – Why Can't They Just Leave Me Alone

Rehabilitative care is not a home alternative, but a type of care that often follows hospitalization. Rehabilitative care often occurs following a stroke, or surgical repair of a broken bone. If the patient lives alone or cannot manage well enough to return to independent or assisted living, then rehabilitative care will offer support, retraining, and physical therapy until the patient can return to their regular living arrangements.

Continuing Care – Aaahhhh, Now I Can relax

Continuing care facilities are becoming more common. Continuing care facilities offer all levels of care, from Independent Living to Assisted Living to Nursing Home care, and may have Rehabilitation care. These homes offer alternatives to move in/out of the different levels of care as space is available. Transferring to new care levels may require a shift to a different wing, but the facility and services offered will be familiar. The parent will not have to leave this facility unless hospitalization is required. In other words, these residence facilities guarantee the applicant a place in any level of care for the remainder of his/her life.

These facilities may be of a higher quality than other facilities and may require an upfront down payment buy-in. This buy-in price will be the price for one person, with a decreased amount for the second person (perhaps 25% of the original buy-in price). Often, seniors will sell their home to pay the down payment. A monthly fee is required thereafter, but the monthly fee can be a set fee for the rest of the life of the patient. Depending upon life expectancy and physical condition of the senior, this alternative may be cheaper in the long run than another type of home. Due to the in-processing charge, the monthly fees are generally smaller than that of facilities that do not charge this fee.

Licensed Private Home Care – I Can Live with This

Small group homes exist that offer specialty care (e.g., Alzheimer's) or long term senior care. These homes are generally approved for 2-8 residents, and offer a home-like place to live. Residents may have their own bedroom or share a bedroom with one other person. Residents share the rest of the household. Care provided is usually up to and including full care. In this type of home, hospitalization and rehabilitation would be separate, but return home placement could occur sooner, due to more intensive staffing levels. These homes are run by a minimum of 1-2 people, with other caregivers added based upon occupancy. Some private home care facilities are gender specific.

Agency Care – Too Expensive

I would recommend agency care for bathing/dressing needs or for short time intervals, e.g., 3-4 hours per day. If the type of care needed is at the aide level (not able to give medications), this works well. Have a family member give the medications. Doing so will save the family money. Agencies have a pool of caregivers to draw from at all levels (Aide, CNA, RN). If a caregiver is ill, they can fill the time slot with a caregiver from the pool. I found that it was easier for my folks to work with the same caregivers than to try and deal with short-term strangers. The agency we worked with also had high turnover. The caregivers typically receive about 50% of the funding that is being paid to the agency. This type of care would be very useful for a homebound parent to allow the caregiving parent time to shop, run errands, or just take a break. Many agencies offer companionship services, as well

Alzheimer's Units – Sometimes Necessary

Many facilities not only offer IL/AL, NH care, but also have separate Alzheimer's units. I would view these units with care. The Alzheimer's units are locked units to prevent wandering of patients. Assess these units for safety, types of activities offered, kitchen accessibility, home-like atmosphere, personalization of rooms, holiday functions, outings, ability to be outside, and prevention of wandering. An activities director should be available to keep Alzheimer patients active and busy. Find out from the activities director what activities are available.

If the parent has lived in a town for a long time or is active in church activities, many times friends of theirs will have preceded them to a local home. Thus, your parents may already have a very good idea of what facilities are well-liked. Assess the needs of your parent(s) carefully. Facilities that offer IL or IL/AL combinations require that the parent be moved to a different facility for an increased care level. Moving can be quite devastating for an elderly patient, especially one that is ill, and may itself cause a new decline.

Check the accreditation level of the facility. All facilities are required to be inspected and licensed, both under state and national standards. The state licensing agency is probably the State Aging Agency. The national licensing agency is the Joint Commission for the Accreditation of Healthcare Organizations (http://www.jcaho.org). Facilities may be put on probation or closed if they do not meet accrediting standards. All facilities should have copies of their latest accreditations available for the public to view. The licensing organizations may be called and queried with respect to licensing, complaints and problems with specific facilities. Note that different parts of facilities may fall under separate accreditation standards, e.g., assisted living, nursing home, or alzheimer's standards. The State Aging Society should also be able to tell the family if any complaints have been issued against the facilities of interest.

Questions to ask when considering facility care

1. What are the staffing ratios (# staff/resident) for the different levels of care?
2. What costs are included in the monthly fee and which costs are ancillary costs (e.g., laundry, housecleaning, medication assistance, etc.)?
3. Where will room be located and what distance is it to the dining hall, recreation center, library, laundry room, etc.? Some of these facilities are very large, and there may only be one or two rooms available. Ensure that reasonable access is available and that it will work for your loved one.
4. How available (within so many minutes) is a staff member if the emergency call button is pushed?

5. Types of care available
   a. Independent living (IL) only
   b. Independent and Assisted Living (AL) only
   c. Independent, Assisted Living, and Nursing Home – all venues

   If the facility does not offer nursing home care, what happens? Usually, this means that your loved one will be required to move to a different facility. Does the IL/AL facility have agreements with a specific Nursing Home? Check to see if the Nursing Home facility has an agreement with the IL/AL facility to be able to automatically return a person back to the IL/AL facility if nursing home care is no longer necessary.

6. Are different care types separated by wing or are the care types mixed together?
7. What happens if your loved one requires hospitalization?
8. What happens if a spouse dies? Is the other spouse able to stay in their two bedroom apartment, or is he/she required to downsize to a one bedroom apartment. If this is a requirement, over what time frame does the move occur?
9. What types of stimulation and activities are available, especially for the patient with dementia?
10. Can patients wander into other patient's rooms?
11. How are valuables protected?
12. What are the restraint practice rules? (Restraints are methods of tying a patient to the bed if combative or uncontrollable – these rules are governed by national accreditation agencies)
13. If dementia occurs following admission, how is it assessed? What happens to your loved one at that time?

© Copyright 2010, Janice Louise Long

Observations to make: are the staff friendly; do they talk to the patients in baby talk or do they address them as adults; are the bathrooms spacious enough to allow a wheelchair inside; what kind of safety equipment is available in the rooms, e.g., safety bars, call buttons; is the home easy to move around in – are the main centers easily accessible; is the home clean and cheerful or dull and drab; what temperature are the rooms and is it adjustable; what outdoor areas are available; what activities are available. The most important observation or thought to consider is whether or not you yourself would want to live there, and conversely, would you want your parent to live there.

Ombudsman – Both federally and state mandated, the Ombudsman program works as a health oversight agency and as an advocate for residents of long-term care facilities in all states. The ombudsman also conducts both overt and undercover investigations of long-term care facilities and has the authority to assess fines and to access medical records. The Ombudsman program also has links to Adult Protective Services, the Department of Health (DOH), and other community organizations.

Source: Lecture, New Mexico Long-Term Care Ombudsman Program, February 2009

Just to get a sense of the elderly population in the United States, the following information was released in a 2008 Press Release by the Census Bureau. These numbers become much larger when projected across all countries in our World.

> In 2030, when all of the baby boomers will be 65 and older, nearly one in five U.S. residents is expected to be 65 and older. This age group is projected to increase to 88.5 million in 2050, more than doubling the number in 2008 (38.7 million). Similarly, the 85 and older population is expected to more than triple, from 5.4 million to 19 million between 2008 and 2050.

Retrieved October 2009 from,
http://www.census.gov/Press-Release/www/releases/archives/population/012496.html

The main concern of the ombudsman program is to hear resident wishes and concerns, to resolve any complaints, and to empower the resident. The New Mexico ombudsman program conducts regular visits to over 300 licensed and unlicensed long-term care facilities, 70 of which are Nursing Homes. If any of the following concerns arise, contact the state Long-Term Care Ombudsman Program or the Department of Senior Affairs in your state. Residents in long-term care facilities are entitled to the Resident Rights in Table 4 below.

Table 4: Resident Rights	
Fairness	**Freedom**
Be treated with respect	Be free from physical and chemical restraints
Be free from discrimination	Be free from physical, emotional, and verbal abuse
Receive information about all services and their costs	Be free from financial exploitation
Receive a written description of your legal rights and responsibilities	Participate in activities
Live in a safe and clean facility	Participate in resident association
Be served appetizing and nutritious meals	Appeal any unjustified room changes
Be given help when you need it	Voice complaints and have them promptly resolved
Choice	**Privacy**
Decide to accept or refuse medical treatment	Keep and use your personal belongings without loss or damage
Understand and participate in your plan of care	Receive private and confidential medical care and records and have your records remain confidential
Choose your doctor, pharmacist or other health care professional	Privacy in your room, visits, phone conversations, and mail
Be given information about your medical condition and health	
Be given information about your eligibility for benefits	
Manage your own finances	

Retrieved February 2009 from, Lecture, New Mexico Long-Term Care Ombudsman Program

Hospice – The Best Beginning and the Best Ending

Hospice is my favorite type of care, primarily because it offers so much to the parent and to the family. When we first started receiving Hospice Care for my Mom, it was like a weight had been lifted from my shoulders. The level of care and frequency of the care given is dependent upon the Hospice assessment of your parent. Hospice offers a team based approach to care for the patient and also provides support for the family, whatever it might be. Several Hospice organizations may operate in the same city. Many are outpatient based and refer to an inpatient Hospice unit, should the family need respite care, or if the family chooses to have the patient moved to the inpatient unit. In larger cities, at least one or two hospitals in each area should offer Hospice care with an adjunct inpatient unit.

Hospice care is designed as comfort or palliative care for patients with terminal illnesses. The emphasis of Hospice care is that the natural course of the illness will most likely cause death within six months. However, the Hospice organization can recertify the patient after the initial six months for as many two month additional periods as is required. Palliative care encompasses the entire realm of pain management, depression care, blood pressure, pulse, weekly checks, instructions for home care, assistance with bathing/dressing and home needs. Palliative care is a team based approach to patient care that includes a physician assessment and oversight, a Registered Nurse (RN – college trained graduate), a social worker, a chaplain, healthcare aides, and volunteers. Palliative care encompasses the entire realm of care oversight of the illness, including pain management, depression care, instructions for home care, assistance with activities of daily living and home needs. The main goal is to ensure that the patient is comfortable and able to live to the highest quality of life possible during his/her remaining life. Palliative care becomes important when aggressive medical treatment is no longer helpful or when curative care (medical intervention designed to "cure") is no longer available.

Palliative care consults are beginning to be performed in hospitals. If palliative care consults are not available, ask for the medical staff to arrange for a visit from their affiliated Hospice or a local Hospice organization. A hospital chaplain may be able to assist in any intervention that is needed.

The duties of the Hospice team are shown below:

Physician: A licensed medical doctor that is responsible for directing and overseeing the patient's care; advises the team members with respect to the patient's condition. The physician may visit the patient occasionally, dependent upon team needs.

Registered Nurse (RN): a licensed, college degreed, healthcare professional with the ability to supervise all care. The RN leads the Hospice team under the direction of the physician, reviews the care of all Hospice patients with her team and the physician. The RN is responsible for visiting and assessing the patient as often as once a week, depending upon the patient's needs and the agency guidelines. The number of visits will be determined through the patient assessment and needs.

Social Worker: Supports the family in finding resources and information needed, e.g., shoppers, food service, aides to help with household needs, support groups, assisted living/nursing home placement.

Chaplain: A degreed and licensed pastor, hired by Hospice organizations to assist with counseling and spiritual needs. Pastors may be trained by different denominations. If the particular denomination of training, e.g., Catholic, Disciples of Christ, Jewish, Lutheran, Methodist, or Presbyterian is important to the family, this may be an important question to ask when selecting the Hospice organization to use. The family may use the Hospice chaplain as an adjunct to their own local pastor, priest, or rabbi.

Certified Nurse Assistant/Aide: The aides are usually licensed healthcare aides with the CNA certification, allowing them to give any care needed, including medications with the exception of intravenous care (IV). The CNA visits the patient 2-5 times per week, based upon the admission assessment. The aide helps with the Activities of Daily Living (ADLs) – bathing, dressing, toileting, ambulating, feeding – and often helps by starting the laundry or does small household chores. If the aide has not been certified, they may not dispense medications. If medications have been dispensed into a container, like a medication paper cup, they may then give only those medications to a patient.

Volunteer: Volunteers may be brought into the home for companionship, writing letters, reading to the patient, running errands, or other tasks needed. Volunteers do not generally provide nursing or medical care in the outpatient setting (but can if approved to do so), but may provide hands-on assistance to the caregivers/nurses in the inpatient Hospice unit.

Hospice care is comprised of four domains: physical, psychological/emotional, spiritual, and social. Their team support is directed towards the entire family. Support for the patient and family includes physical well-being and comfort care, e.g., medication prescriptions for the main diagnosis and for pain management, support for the current maintenance of care (e.g., dialysis or oxygen), assistance with acceptance of the disease and the dying process, to support the family through the dying process, respite care, to assist with spiritual care, to help with pre/post death grief, and bereavement counseling for a year afterwards.

To most people, admission to Hospice generally means that the patient is dying. Often, that is true. The patient will be admitted to Hospice with a specific medical diagnosis. Hospice pays for and delivers any medications pertinent to this primary diagnosis, which can greatly reduce medication costs for the family. A notebook will be placed inside the home, in which a record of daily and weekly notes is kept, along with any medication changes, assessments, or other requirements. At any time, a team member can be brought up-to-date on the patient's condition by reading this notebook. The Hospice team will request that copies of the Healthcare POA or the Five Wishes™ document – http://www.agingwithdignity.org, and the DNR paperwork be accessible to emergency personnel, should the need arise. Often, these documents will be stored in the notebook.

Many Hospice agencies, but not all, provide a Comfort Kit, which is placed in the refrigerator. The Comfort Kit may contain pain, nausea, and anxiety medications, including morphine, lorazepam, and ativan. Hospice is available 24 hours a day by telephone, so that if any kind of concern exists in the home, they may be contacted. The on-call nurse may advise the family to give one of the medications in the Comfort Kit to alleviate a situation. This system is much faster, easier on the patient and family, and relieves symptoms much quicker than a visit to the emergency room.

The Hospice team is just that – a team. Their goal is to help in any way they can, whether the help is for the patient or for the family. This team helps the family to understand what is happening, offers counseling to any member of the family, and also provides grief support for a year following the death of your loved one. Many Hospices provide memorial Christmas ornaments and an annual memorial service to honor our loved ones.

Acceptance to Hospice is based upon a needs assessment of the patient's physical/mental state and ability to care for him/herself. The needs assessment evaluates the Activities of Daily

Living and generally requires that the patient requires assistance with at least three of these ADLs. Once a patient is accepted into the Hospice program, the care team sets up a care plan to address the identified needs. A patient may be on Hospice for as long as needed – there is no time constraint, as long as the ADL criteria are met. The initial admission is for six months, with reevaluations every two months thereafter. An example of Hospice documentation, as given to our family, is shown below. These forms are inserted with author's permission.

Crossroads Hospice Care, Inc.
P.O. Box 3221
Albuquerque, NM 87109-3221

Phone: (505) 884-7532
Fax: (505) 884-7555

Worksheet for Determining Prognosis
PULMONARY DISEASE

Patient Name:_____ MR #:_____ Date:_____

The patient should meet the following criteria, clinical judgment is required in each case	YES	NO
Patient has severe lung disease as evidenced by:		
• Dyspnea at rest	✓	
• Dyspnea on exertion	✓	
• Housebound/chairbound	✓	
• Oxygen dependent	✓	
• Copious purulent sputum		✓
• Recurrent infections	✓	
• Severe cough		✓
• Cyanosis *Rare*		✓
• Pulmonary hyperinflation		
• Pursed lip breathing	✓	
• Using accessory muscles of respiration	✓	
• Wheezing *Periods*	✓	
• Diminished breath sounds	✓	
Poor response to bronchodilators	✓	
Presence of Cor Pulmonale/right heart failure ↑ *palpitations*	✓	
Unintentional weight loss of 10% of body weight in past 6 months *10% or less*		
Resting tachycardia *With SOB*	✓	
PO2 of 55 or less *unmeasured*	*NA*	
PCO2 of 50 or more *unmeasured x yr*	*NA*	
Decrease in Forced Expiratory Volume (FEV) of 40ml per year on serial testing	✓	

Narrative Summary
Of Prognosis Documentation

Documentation should be complete, consistent, concise, specific, measurable and descriptive.

Diagnosis/present underlying illness(es) and all other illness(es) affecting the terminal diagnosis:

[handwritten] ESCOPD — required steroid burst last cout period to present increasing drops in O₂ sats to 70s

Co-morbidity that affects the prognosis: *[handwritten] Dementia 2/s increased over last 6m. Now requires 5m doses Haldol for agitation periods. Periodic UTIs.*

History and Progression of the illness: *[handwritten] Long history of pulmonary disease. Over last 6mo has shown increased episodes SOB requires Morphine 15ER & Morphine liquid 3mg to 4mg for breakthrough dyspnea. She is chair, bed bound & has SOB with any activity, recently ↑ with eating.*

Physical Baseline(e.g. weight and weight change, vital signs, heart rhythms, rales, degree of edema): *[handwritten] Admit 132# has lost 7# probably in last 6mo. BP ranges 128/62 to 140/68. Pulse Range 74 to 90s only occ. irregular. Continues to have 1-2# pedal edema*

Physician's prognosis, stating why there is a life expectancy of six months or less(e.g. patient wishes to stop all treatment, patient has had optimal treatment for illness):

_____

_____

_____

_____

_____

_____

RN signature   Date   Physician signature   Date

As mentioned above, the goal of Hospice is palliative care – care to keep the patient comfortable and pain free. The goal of Hospice is not to make the patient well and not to provide proactive care or intervention to do so. If the patient improves to the point where the

ADL criteria are no longer met, then the patient will be discharged from Hospice. However, readmission can occur whenever the criteria again meet admission standards. Note that one agency may not be able to admit a patient based on the agency standards, but another agency might be able to. This happened with my Dad. When his blood clot was diagnosed, I called our initial Hospice agency – they came out and reassessed him and declined his readmission. I called another Hospice agency and they were able to admit him.

Certain medical situations may arise that require a physician's care or a hospitalization, e.g., a fall, broken bone or blood clot (see Dad's story), etc. Depending upon what the situation is, Hospice may discharge the patient until the medical issue is cleared up and the patient returns home. The reason for the discharge in this case is because once a patient is admitted to Hospice, the Hospice organization is responsible for all medical costs. Hospice is reimbursed by Medicare at a specific rate per day. This rate must cover all costs. Thus, if a patient is admitted to the hospital, the Hospice organization prefers to return the patient to their healthcare system and then readmit him/her upon return to the home.

Respite care is Hospice care given in an inpatient setting for a week at a time to give the family a break. The reason for the break may be a trip out-of-town or just to rest and recuperate from the energy draining twenty-four hour care. Inpatient respite care may be available at several local hospitals, but will be provided by the hospital your Hospice organization is affiliated with. Availability is based on the number of rooms in the unit and their current occupancy rates. Respite care may be available as often as once per month.

Interviewing Hospice organizations – Questions to ask:

1. How long has this organization been in existence? Is this organization certified? The Hospice movement is growing and new organizations begin or end constantly. Interview several organizations to assess their capabilities and ability to address the family needs.
2. How many staff does this organization employ? The number of staff may be an indication of stability.
3. Ask for references – this may be a difficult question in order to maintain confidentiality. However, families may have given their consent to be a reference for the organization.

4. Ask what conditions Hospice will allow medical treatment or hospitalization for your loved one. Hospice organizations qualify a patient under one main condition – if your loved one has several different conditions, medical treatment for those conditions may be necessary.

5. How many patients has this Hospice served; what is their current census?

6. How does this Hospice handle 24-hour on-call needs?

7. How long does it take a Hospice nurse to arrive at the home during the night?

8. Do they offer respite care or have respite care available through another agency?

9. What services do they offer to your loved one?

© Copyright 2010, Janice Louise Long

In addition, a questionnaire can be set up to address specific needs of the patient. Hospice will greatly benefit from having a copy of each patient's health history (see Chapter 6).

Health Plan Questions

Needs:

Internal Medicine Primary Care Manager (specify desired location); need someone that is good at managing overall care

Fill urgently needed medications at nearby location (specify location) Is 90 day mail order available?

Liquid Oxygen (require at least weekly fill)

Nebulizer machine and medications

Wheelchair & wheelchair consult (evaluate best options for safety)

Home health (Activities of Daily Living)

Specialist (list name and type of specialty) - Dr. X and location, telephone #

Specialist (list name and type of specialty) - Dr. X and location, telephone #

Safety evaluation

Hospice care? Nursing home care?

(Health Plan Questions, page 2)

Questions:

Transfer of medical records

See primary care before <u>insert date</u>? (How to pick?) (Can we pay for visit?)

Can we be referred to specialist (specify type) now?

Oxygen/Rx start immediately

We are worried about the cross-over of plans and need to ensure all parts of care transfers correctly

Pharmacy costs & savings

- Discontinue high plan for basic plan
- Enroll for Script savings
- Cost to us
- High deductible plan available??

If I need hospitalization, what hospital would I be going to? (Specify name and location of preferred hospital)

Current Medications and Monthly Cost:

Dad:		**Mom:**	
Aricept	$129.70	Norvasc	$ 43.13
Namenda	$114.50	Serevent	$ 89.15
Terazosin	$ 10.00	Albuterol inhaler	$ 10.00
HCTZ	$ 12.13	Albuterol nebulizer	$ 0.00
Folic acid	$ 7.36	Atrovent nebulizer	$ 0.00
Lovastatin	$ 10.00	Fosamax	$ 66.10
Levothroid	$ 10.00	Aricept	$129.70
Cimetidine	$ 10.00	Cimetidine	$ 10.00
		Lanoline	$ 10.00
		Rhinocort Aqua	$ 51.05
	$303.69		$409.13

Caregiving Form 40

Respite Care is available for Hospice patients at the inpatient units. The respite time of one week is to give the caregivers a break or to allow them to take a trip. Our particular Hospice program allowed this to occur one week per month (based upon room availability), although we had never used this resource. I suggest that Hospice resources in your area be checked to find out what amount of time is available. Some agencies, such as the Alzheimer's Association, also have funds or small annual stipends to assist families with caregiving, and may also provide avenues for respite care.

When to consider Hospice Care

When the prognosis of a chronic disease is no longer curative or when the loved one is losing capacity to perform his/her daily activities, hospice care should be considered. Do not wait until the patient and family are worn down by the disease and caregiving process to contact Hospice. A consult may be asked for at any time. In fact, the patient and family can "interview" different Hospices in the area to decide which Hospice would be the most appropriate for your family.

The national average length of stay (LOS) for Hospice in 2007 was 67.4 days with a median (50%) LOS of 20 days. However, 30.8% died or were discharged in less than seven days. On the other hand, 13.1% were on Hospice care for six months or longer. Our local average LOS is about 15 days. (Source: Private conversation with Physician from local Hospice unit) These numbers indicate that patients are not getting to Hospice soon enough. The most common diagnoses are ranked below in Table 5.

Table 5: Most Common Diagnoses for Hospice Admissions

Primary Diagnosis	2007
Cancer (malignant)	41.3%
Heart Disease	11.8%
Debility, Unspecified	11.2%
Dementia, including Alzheimer's Disease	10.1%
Lung disease, including COPD	7.9%
Stroke, Coma	3.8%
Kidney disease, including end stage renal disease	2.6%
Motor neuron disease, including ALS	2.3%
Liver disease	2.0%
HIV/AIDS disease	0.6%
Other diagnoses	6.5%

National Hospice and Palliative Care Organization, NHPCO Facts and Figures: Hospice Care in America. October 2008.

Approximately 80% of Hospice patients are 65 or greater. Research has shown that Hospice care reduces end of life costs to Medicare (hospital and doctor visits) by $2309 per Hospice patient. Medicare pays a daily rate to the specific Hospice organization for the care given to your loved one. Hospice may be given in any setting, e.g., hospital, home, assisted living, nursing home. Hospice care follows the patient even if he/she is already in an institutionalized care setting. Because of the hands-on team approach and pain management and control services, one's life is more comfortable and may even extend life. Hospice also receives funding from grants, donations (including in memory of a person), charity funds, and Medicaid.

National Hospice and Palliative Care Organization, NHPCO Facts and Figures: Hospice Care in America. October 2008

Specific services provided by the team include:

➢ Management of the patient's pain and symptoms
➢ Assisting the patient with emotional, psychosocial, and spiritual aspects of dying
➢ Provides needed drugs, medical supplies and equipment to support primary admission diagnosis
➢ Coaches family on how to care for patient
➢ Delivers special services like speech and physical therapy when needed
➢ Makes short-term inpatient care available when pain or symptoms become too difficult to treat at home, or the caregiver needs respite time
➢ Provides bereavement care and counseling to surviving family and friends.

National Hospice and Palliative Care Organization, NHPCO Facts and Figures: Hospice Care in America. October 2008

One of the important goals of the Hospice team is to give the patient a good "death" experience. Hospice will continue to offer grief support to the family for one year after the death. Most Hospice organizations have memorial services each year to honor those who have died under Hospice care that year and many organizations offer memorial Christmas ornaments as a remembrance and fundraiser for the particular organization.

Chapter 8:

Dying and Life Support

I did not ever come in contact with any medical personnel that would give information about how long Mom or Dad would live. This seemed to be a prevalent question for me – how long does either Mom or Dad have to live. It wasn't that I wanted them to die – of course I didn't. I am a planner and I tried to use the information I had to incorporate better care or to be ready for the next step. When Mom was in the hospital with her broken hip, the pulmonologist did tell me that about 75% of her lungs had deteriorated and that he estimated she would have about two years of lung capacity left. I think some of my family members were angry about that, but it gave me a good guideline of what to expect.

What is it to die? How does it feel? Do you or your loved one have explicit wishes with regards to how their death is managed? What kind of death experience do you or your loved one want? How should pain or feeding tubes be handled? Dying is very sad for the family. It is really hard to think about death and even harder to discuss this topic. I know my parents talked about it between the two of them. Other than expressing wishes to be cremated and not to be on terminal life support, we really didn't know what they wanted. Did they need to see or talk to a family member they hadn't seen in a long time? Did they have express wishes relating to their household goods? Did they have any idea about the environment that they wished to die in? Other than expressing wishes for specific household goods like Grandma's table, the Grandfather clock, Grandpa's antique dresser, or Mom's jewelry – not much was said.

Think about my Mom's pulmonary failure following her hip pinning. We knew she had emphysema, but in no way was she in respiratory failure before she broke her hip. Dad and Mom had always explicitly stated that they did not want extreme measures performed to keep them alive. Faced with her situation, it seemed like she might not survive and would die in the hospital. Initially, the doctors told us that they were keeping her sedated and on the ventilator to give her time to rest and to heal. But for them to put her on a ventilator in the first place meant that she would not have survived if the ventilator had not been put in.

The nurses would stop her morphine drip every few hours so that she would wake up and we could talk to her. Of course, she could not talk with the ventilator in place. But she could squeeze our hands and blink or nod her head in understanding. I would try to comfort her by rubbing her arm, stroking her head, or just holding her hand. Dad asked me, "Why do you do that?" I told him it lets her know we are here and our touch helps her relax and helps her healing. We were all devastated by her condition. Dad was beside himself. He just couldn't understand why she wasn't doing well, as her first two hip surgeries had no complications. Even when I explained to him that it was now 9-10 years later and that her lungs were not as strong, he just couldn't fathom why she didn't spring back like she did before and that she could possibly die.

What would we have done if she couldn't breathe when the doctor took out the ventilator? I just don't know. As one of the choices was to reinsert the ventilator, we would have allowed that to happen. Most likely, Mom's chances of survival would have dropped drastically at that point. Then, a reassessment of how long she could be kept on the ventilator would occur. Mom may have then lost her choice of free will.

What would the doctor have done? Due to managed care, hospitals no longer keep patients on a long term basis. But not too many facilities (especially a rehabilitation facility) would likely take Mom while she was on a respirator. Doctors are trained in medical school to cure, to provide interventions to insure that cure, and most likely do not enjoy this side of medicine. Doctors and nurses do not discuss the likelihood of death until it really is inevitable, within 1-3 days of death, and only then when lab results indicate the organ systems of the body are shutting down. Hospital procedures and care pathways require that a patient moves along a continuum, during which decisions may be made. Having a patient languish in a steady state does not help the cost system, nor the continuum of care. The task of the health care system is to maintain life and decrease suffering. A long passage of time equates to economic and clinical problems, requiring clinical or economic efficiencies to be put in place.

My mother-in-law suffered a ruptured brain aneurysm at home at age 61. She collapsed immediately, lapsing into a coma-like state, and was taken to the local hospital. When it was determined that she needed more specialized care, she was taken by ambulance to a regional hospital thirty miles away and put on life support. My husband was in the Navy and out on the ship, so it took us almost 24 hours to notify him, for him to arrive home, and for us to fly to New York to her bedside. That night the doctor "tested" her ability to breathe without the ventilator and she was not able to breathe on her own. He did tell us that he did not expect her to be able to come off life support and he anticipated that she also had no brain function. That is indeed what happened. He reinserted the ventilator until we came in the next day to say our goodbyes. Only knowing that the aneurysm had caused brain death made the removal of life support easier for us. But we knew it was the right thing to do, as she would never have agreed to live as a bedridden patient. She died about twenty minutes after being removed from the life support. The total time from the occurrence of the aneurysm to her death was about 3-1/2 days. Disconnecting her from life support was a very difficult decision, especially since she had been healthy up to that point and was only 61 years old.

Autonomy is described by Kaufman as:

> "Referring both to a psychological capacity to make decisions that reflect one's own goals and an ethical ideal of self-determination. The term is used in medicine to describe an evolving set of patient's rights, extending from rights to determine what happens to one's own body, to rights to informed consent and refusal of treatment, to rights to participate more fully in medical decision making. Many of these rights have emerged through lawsuits, and hence it is through a legalistic prism that physicians understand their obligations to respect autonomy."

Reprinted with the permission of Scribner, a Division of Simon & Schuster, Inc., from …AND A TIME TO DIE by Sharon R. Kaufman. Copyright © 2005 by Sharon R. Kaufman. All rights reserved.

The Patient Self-Determination Act (PSDA) of 1990 (federal law) mandates the "right" of all hospital patients to be informed about and to determine their own medical treatments, including the "refusal of treatments." This information is included here since a sudden pneumonia, a fall at home with a broken bone, a blood clot, or some new disease could cause your loved one to be admitted to a hospital in a critical condition. An explanation of the PSDA is shown below from the CDC website:

The 1990 Patient Self-Determination Act (PSDA) encourages everyone to decide now about the types and extent of medical care they want to accept or refuse if they become unable to make those decisions due to illness. The PSDA requires all health care agencies to recognize the living will and durable power of attorney for health care. The Act applies to hospitals, long-term care facilities, and home health agencies that get Medicare and Medicaid reimbursement. Under the PSDA, health care agencies must ask you whether you have an advance directive. They also must give you information about your rights under state law.

Everyone getting medical care in hospitals or extended care facilities (nursing homes), enrolling in Health Maintenance Organizations (HMOs), and entering into hospice or home care agreements must be given certain information in writing. This must include information on your state's laws about your rights to make decisions about medical care, such as your right to accept or refuse medical or surgical treatment. You are also entitled to receive information about your right to create an advance directive. They may even offer simple advance directive forms for you to use. But it may not be a good idea to wait until you are in the hospital to fill out a form. You might not be able to complete the form when you are admitted; and even if you are, these forms are very general and may not cover all of your wishes.

Retrieved October 2009, from http://www.cancer.org/docroot/MIT/ content/MIT_3_2X_The_Patient_Self-Determination_Act.asp

The family will be thrown into turmoil if your parent goes on life support. Your already stressed life and your loved one are now at the mercy of the doctors and the hospital system. Your primary care doctor may not even be involved. The specialist that is called in won't "know" your loved one or their wishes. Most likely, neither will "the hospitalist" – the doctor that will oversee the inpatient hospital care. Who will be the advocate for your loved one, especially if he/she cannot speak for him/herself? Who will help the family understand what is happening and how to advise the family on both the medical condition of your loved one and hospital procedures? What is your understanding of what is going on in the midst of being upset and scared? Yes, in another's situation, the scenario may be very clear, but when the patient is your own family member, things are not so clear cut. If your family member is 99 years old and was fairly active until she broke her hip two months ago, and is now at risk – do you want more "heroics" to preserve her "full" life? Or, do you accept the decline and limit what medical devices are used to maintain that life, even if the Quality of Life will not be good? How does one define Quality of Life at this point? How long does one wait before dying is defined or even suspected? What are the obstacles to the decisions that need to be made? How long will it take to make these decisions?

The doctor may be giving you hope through your discussions with him/her. Biomedical successes allow us to live longer through medications or technology. Ask yourself – What would my loved one want? Are there Health Care Advanced Directives at home or in the primary care chart? If the primary care doctor is on top of things, he would have made sure that Advanced Directives had been signed at some time along the care continuum, especially with an elderly person. How are the patient's wishes understood if they are silent, due to a stroke or some other disease process? Another question to consider is: when does the spouse or child take over the medical decisions from the loved one and when do they assert their opinions and rights over those of the hospital medical staff? Does the family blindly accept what is happening or does the family designate either a family spokesman or obtain an advocate from the hospital?

A patient/family advocate may be chosen from the hospital chaplaincy or perhaps one's own religious circle. Hospitals have bioethics committees that review medical care and the necessity for continued care. Ask to talk to someone from this committee or even the hospital chaplain. It is vitally important to find someone to review your loved one's condition and to explain the choices that the family has if you do not have a family member that can perform this function. I myself would wish for hope, but also for dignity, for compassionate interventions (including pain intervention), but also to have as high a quality of life possible. The hospital chaplain (or personal chaplain) can also offer prayers for the patient and the family on a daily basis, and can perform last rites or any other cultural ceremonial act that is required. The chaplain can also help both the patient and the family address any spiritual issues or concerns.

Example: Consider if you yourself were hospitalized on life-support and continued through the hospital system for three weeks –

    a.   Your organ systems begin to shut down OR

    b.   The hospital is considering moving you to a long term care facility

When would you want your options considered during this time period? When would you want your family to understand what could happen?

Your living will (Health Care Directives or Five Wishes™ – http://www.agingwithdignity.org) may fade into the background and become invisible as you progress along this path, if it was even incorporated into the medical chart at all. Health care systems are treatment oriented – not death oriented. Treatment comes first until there are no further available treatments or there is no response to the offered treatment.

Does the doctor know whether or not the person in the hospital bed will die? Absolutely not – at least, not until lab results show that the body's organ systems or nervous system are shutting down. If your loved one has cancer or a known "terminal" disease, then yes – death is inevitable, but may or may not occur during this hospitalization. Is the patient's condition reversible or irreversible? Doctors may eventually give a prognosis of death based upon their understanding of the patient's clinical condition. Even then, this prognosis will be based upon their "global" experience of all prior patients treated by that physician. When does curative or proactive care become palliative or comfort care? Is proactive care given until there is absolutely no hope or is the patient moved to a hospice setting and made comfortable for their remaining life? Is the condition reversible or irreversible? The nursing staff (especially those in intensive care settings) face these situations daily. The nursing staff is compassionate and try to keep suffering to a minimum and the quality of life to a maximum wherever possible. They try to maintain the highest dignity for the patient, and try to maintain hope.

Somewhere in the middle of this drastic hospitalization, someone needs to determine <u>what care is appropriate</u>, whether or not the patient needs to be moved to comfort care, and even if it is safe to move the patient.

The voice of the patient needs to be heard as well. Has the person told anyone – a chaplain, a spouse, a family member, a nurse or primary care physician that he/she is ready to die? Has the patient previously signed advanced health care directives or the Five Wishes? What is comfort care to the patient? Decision making has its obstacles and decisions take time. Perhaps the care team has been trying to give messages to the family, but nothing has happened. A new question then becomes: How well is the family able to "hear" what the care team is saying? The messages being given may need to be repeated over and over to be sure the family has a full understanding of the situation.

Language barriers may exist that require management. Cultural needs may exist that need to be addressed once it is known that your loved one may not live through this hospitalization. What does one do if there is a list of questions to ask and the doctor comes in for five minutes and is looking at his watch during that five minutes? Do you accept that he has other patients or time constraints and let your questions remain unanswered? Or, do you insist that he stay to answer your questions or make a specific appointment for later in the day?

One question to ask when the patient is in a coma is: How does he/she score on the Glasgow Coma Scale? The total score may be as high as 15. If the score falls between 3-8, then the person is considered to be "in a coma." Please visit the websites: http://www.bt.cdc.gov/masscasualties/gscale.asp to view information about the Glasgow Coma Scale. Other websites are also available by searching on Glasgow Coma Scale. Brain death and loss of cognitive function is a key to settling some of the above issues. Will the patient be in a persistive vegetative state when taken off the life support? What then? Another term to be familiar with is medical futility. Medical personnel may refer to this term, which means that further medical intervention is futile and will not make any difference in the patient's length of life or quality of life.

Kaufman cites the SUPPORT study: a study to understand prognosis and preferences for outcomes and risks of treatment. Over 4,300 patients with life-threatening illnesses were enrolled (average age = 65) in this study. The results show that prolonged deaths occur as a result of life-support technologies. The study found that 47% of physicians knew when their patients wanted to avoid cardiopulmonary resuscitation (CPR); that 38% of patients who died spent ten or more days in an intensive care unit immediately preceding death; that 46% of Do Not Resuscitate (DNR) orders were written within two days of death even though 79% of the patients had a DNR request somewhere in the medical record; and that in 50% of conscious patients, families reported moderate to severe pain at least half of the time in the three days preceding death. The study also found that dying in the hospital was not considered comfortable or supportive.

To resuscitate or not to resuscitate?

My grandmother was resuscitated following a heart attack at the age of 89. She was never the same again. My aunt had to admit her into a long term care facility, where she lived for another two years. For those two years, my grandmother did not know who my aunt was, and really had acquired "dementia" from the resuscitation.

Kaufman writes, "While in the popular view CPR "can bring the dead back to life," this is not actually the case. In cardiac arrest, the heart is unable to effectively maintain the blood flow and blood pressure necessary to sustain life. In respiratory arrest, the patient is unable to move enough air to oxygenate the blood supply and tissues and thus to sustain life. In both situations, at the moment of arrest, *the patient is in danger of imminent death* unless something is done to reverse the problem." "To override the default action (Code status = do not code), patients must decide at some point prior to or during a hospitalization whether, during an emergency that threatens their survival, they would want medical personnel to thrust a breathing tube down their windpipe, perform chest compressions (possibly breaking ribs), and electrically shock the heart *in the hope* that a life-sustaining heart rhythm would be restored." "It (CPR) may restore patients to *some kind of life* following a cardiac or respiratory arrest, but alternatively, it may be the most violent, "undignified" activity prior to death." She also states, "Studies have found that, depending on the patient's age, type of cardiac problem, number and type of other medical conditions, the physiological details of the arrest, and how soon the procedure was initiated after the person stopped breathing, 8 to 15 percent of hospitalized patients survive CPR to be discharged from the hospital." This survival rate could be lower for patients with extensive disease processes.

Caring for a loved one with a long-term illness is like riding on a roller coaster. Declines are of varying seriousness, and may be followed by several months of stability. The periods of stability may be at a lower level of functioning than was previously experienced. Note that a serious or rapid decline may be enough to throw the family into chaos, wondering how serious this decline is, whether or not the loved one will continue to decline, and that this decline may be the "beginning of the end." Then a week or a month or two later, some stability may again occur.

Giving your loved one permission to let go is also an important concept. He/she also needs to know that their spouse or the family caregiver understands and is prepared. Try and keep an open mind about what the dying person is experiencing. My Mom had been in a different time of her life for a couple of months prior to her death, even though her major stroke was the precipitating factor in her actual death. Ask the person who or what she is seeing and if seeing a person, what is that person saying. I am sure my Mom was talking to her mother. She was also experiencing a younger time of her life, thinking that she had to pick up my younger brothers from school and that she was going to be late.

The last two days of Dad's life, his breathing was labored and oxygen was used to allow him to breathe more easily. A few hours before he died, he became somewhat agitated. One of the caregivers explained that this could mean he had some unfinished business with someone in his life and he needed to hear that person's voice. The only person I could imagine that that could be was his sister. They had not seen each other in probably fifteen years and talked on birthdays or holidays before his illness. The phone calls between them had become less frequent, as his Alzheimer's progressed. I had kept my aunt up-to-date on his condition, so she was well aware of what was happening with him. Amazingly, I had just put her telephone number in my cell phone two weeks before. I called and asked her if she wanted to talk to him. I explained to her he would not be able to respond to her. I held the phone up to his ear, and she began talking. He immediately became calmer and remained calm for the five minutes of the conversation. When I took the phone away from his ear, I asked her what she had said. She had reminded him who he was, that they had grown up together in Iowa, that she loved him, recited The Lord's Prayer, and continued praying for him. He died while I was talking to her, only a few minutes after she had spoken to him.

Arizona told me to resolve any issues or say anything to Mom that I needed to say – but I could not do that. It was too hard to talk to them about what was going to happen. Even when my Mom told me she was worried about Dad and I reassured her he would be all right, I didn't talk to her because there were other people around. But I tell you – I did not understand the importance of that statement until it was too late. That may sound silly. Of course, I knew that she was going to die, but the true realization of this concept hit me afterwards. Once they die, you no longer have the ability to talk to them any more – at least, not face-to-face. Be sure and talk to your parent about any unresolved issues from either your side or your parents. Let them know you love them.

The Dying Trajectory

Dying has its own trajectory. Tasks have been attributed to the dying path that needs to be completed by the person that is undergoing this process. If the person is in too much pain, all their energy is spent trying to get through the pain. The patient may need to redefine their role or purpose in life or may feel they have lost their sense of self-worth. Questions or thoughts the dying person may have are listed below:

➤ Weakness and dependence diminish my worth. Because a terminal illness results in increasing weakness and dependence, my worth will continue to diminish as I become sicker, weaker, and more dependent.

➤ People love me because of the things I do. As I become sicker, people will cease to love me because the illness will interfere with my ability to perform certain roles.

➤ Who am I now that I can no longer do all of the things I used to do?

➤ Will people still love me and care for me when I smell bad, look bad, and must depend on them for everything, including all of my personal needs?

➤ Who am I after I sustain such terrible losses?

➤ What is happening to me and why is it happening to me?

➢ How is this going to affect me now and in the future?

➢ How can I go on in the face of such terrible losses?

➢ Am I to blame? Did I deserve to have this terrible thing happen to me?

➢ Am I being punished by God for something I did?

➢ Will my life ever again contain moments of joy or happiness?

➢ Will I be abandoned, or will people help me endure and find meaning in the current situation?

Holmes HM, Stein R, and Knight CF. UNIPAC 2: Alleviating Psychological and Spiritual Pain in Patients with Life-Limiting Illness. American Academy of Hospice and Palliative Medicine, Glenview, IL, 2008. Storey CP, Levine S, Shega JW, eds., Hospice and Palliative Care Training for Physicians: A Self-Study Program. Adapted with permission.

The UNIPAC 2 research document published by the American Academy of Hospice and Palliative Medicine also shows four levels of developmental tasks of dying patient.

1. Develop a Renewed Sense of Personhood and Meaning
   ➢ Find meanings in life through life review and personal narrative
   ➢ Develop a sense of worthiness, both in the past and in the current situation
   ➢ Learn to accept love and caring from other people

2. Bring Closure to Personal and Community Relationships
   ➢ Say good-by to family members and friends with expressions of regret, gratitude, appreciation, and affection
   ➢ Ask for and grant forgiveness to estranged friends and family members so that reconciliation can occur.
   ➢ Say good-by to community relationships (employment, civic, and religious organizations) with expressions of regret, gratitude, forgiveness, and appreciation.

3. Bring Closure to Worldly Affairs
   ➢ Arrange for the transfer of fiscal, legal, and social responsibilities.

4. Accept the finality of Life and Surrender to the Transcendent
   ➢ Express the depth of personal tragedy that dying may represent and acknowledge the totality of personal loss.

➤ Withdraw from the world and accept increased dependency.

➤ Develop a sense of awe and accept the seeming chaos that can prefigure transcendence.

Holmes HM, Stein R, and Knight CF. UNIPAC 2: Alleviating Psychological and Spiritual Pain in Patients with Life-Limiting Illness. American Academy of Hospice and Palliative Medicine, Glenview, IL, 2008. Storey CP, Levine S, Shega JW, eds., Hospice and Palliative Care Training for Physicians: A Self-Study Program. Adapted with permission.

Emanuel, Bennett and Richardson group these tasks under the categories of Practical, Relational, and Personal Tasks in their article, "The Dying Role." Table 6 below is taken from this article, describing these tasks somewhat differently.

Table 6: Key Features of the Dying Role

Practical Tasks	Relational Tasks	Personal Tasks
Financial legacy	Coexistence with other roles	Adjustment to loss
End-of-life planning	Teaching the dying role	Reaching closure
Caring for dependents	Passing the mantle	Existential tasks
Last good-byes	Giving permission	Final growth phase
	Placing a legacy capstone	Last rites of passage

Emanuel L, M.D., Ph.D., Bennett Katherine, M.D., and Richardson Virginia E., Ph.D. "The Dying Role," Journal of Palliative Medicine, Volume 10, Number 1, 2007.

Two of the most important of these tasks are the life review and reaching closure with family members or friends, including those with whom they have unfinished business. The person may ask to see certain people. These requests should be honored. The family can help by notifying friends and family members that they should come by and visit.

Organ Donation

Donate Life America is a non-profit organization that campaigns and educates about organ donation. The decision to donate internal organs or tissues should be relayed to the care staff as soon as possible. Donating is an important decision – one person can save many lives through this process. Thousands of people in the United States wait for transplants every year. Donate Life America cites the following statistics:

- More than 100,000 men, women and children currently need life-saving organ transplants.

- Every 11 minutes another name is added to the national organ transplant waiting list.

- An average of 18 people die each day from the lack of available organs for transplant.

- In 2008, there were 7,984 deceased organ donors and 6,218 living organ donors resulting in 27,961 organ transplants.

- In 2007, approximately 30,000 grafts were made available for transplant by eye banks within the United States.

- According to research, 98% of all adults have heard about organ donation and 86% have heard of tissue donation.

- 90% of Americans say they support donation, but only 30% know the essential steps to take to be a donor.

Retrieved September 2009, from
http://www.donatelife.net/UnderstandingDonation/Statistics.php

Readers may go to http://www.donatelife.net/CommitToDonation/ to indicate the wish to be a donor. Individual states also have their own websites. For example, the website for New Mexico (nm = New Mexico) is: http://www.donatelifenm.org. A designation for organ donation on a driver's license is also available in many states. Table 7 shows organs and tissues of the body, the function of each, and how this type of donation will help those receiving the donation. Information about how the donor process works in New Mexico is available at: http://www.nmdonor.com/donor/(X(1)S(wi2anxfcx00etgroje12fz55))/DonationProcess.aspx. This link will at least introduce one to the process and allow time for questions and thoughts to be compiled before calling your specific state donor system.

Table 7: Types of Organ Donations

Organ/Tissue	Function	Who It Will Help
Heart	Pumps blood to all body systems	Patients suffering from cardiomyopathy, coronary artery disease or infants born with defective hearts.
Liver	Energy regulation, makes protein, removes waste from blood	Patients suffering from Wilson's disease, cirrhosis, other life-threatening liver disease, or infants born with biliary atresia.
Kidney	Filters waste from blood	Patients suffering from severe kidney failure caused by conditions such as high blood pressure, diabetes, or polycystic kidney disease. A transplant eliminates the need for dialysis.
Lung	Organs of respiration	Patients suffering from emphysema, cystic fibrosis, or other life-threatening lung diseases.
Pancreas	Makes enzymes needed for digestion, makes insulin to regulate blood sugars	Insulin dependent Type I diabetic patients. A transplant eliminates the need for insulin injections and reduces the risk of losing sight or limbs.
Intestine	Processes food ingested	Patients suffering from short-gut syndrome and other life-threatening intestine diseases.
Corneas	Allows light to enter the eye	Patients suffering from corneal blindness caused by disease or injury.
Skin	Protects body from infection, dehydration and injury	Patients with severe burns. Skin grafts provide a temporary bandage to decrease pain, infection, scarring and dehydration.

Organ/Tissue	Function	Who It Will Help
Bone	Supports the body, protects vital organs	Patients requiring facial reconstruction, limb salvage, correction of birth defects, cancer treatment, oral surgery, or spinal surgery.
Heart Valves	Directs blood flow through the heart	Patients requiring replacement of a malfunctioning heart valve. A donated valve is preferred over a mechanical or pig valve.
Tendons	Attaches muscles to bone	Patients requiring reconstructive surgery, commonly used in the treatment of sports injuries.
Veins	Transports blood	Patients requiring coronary artery by-pass surgery. The donated veins are used to replace the patient's blocked arteries.

Retrieved July 2009, from http://www.donatelifenm.org

A person may decide to donate all of the above organs/tissues or may also donate specified organs/tissues. The patient must still be alive for donation to work. Therefore, prior to death, a patient must be transported to a donation center (usually a tertiary care hospital or medical center). The hospital and medical staff will be supportive of the patient and the family and will not do anything to hasten the death. If brain death occurs, the patient will be put on life support mechanisms to keep oxygen flowing to the organs and tissues. Patients who die from a cardiac death will still be able to donate tissues or corneas, and may be able to donate organs, depending upon the specific circumstances. The family will not bear any cost for the donation. Costs are absorbed by the organ donation society or by the research institute involved.

Notification of the state donor service organization will occur. The donor service organization has the responsibility for notifying the United Network for Organ Donation, which is in charge of the national computer matching service. The patient's blood type, size and tissue matching information will be input into the matching service. The transplant patients with the greatest need will be matched with the patient's characteristics. The organ transplant centers for these patients will be notified of the potential transplant.

Upon death, transplant teams from each center will converge upon the tertiary care hospital to receive the organs/tissues. The specific organs/tissues are retrieved through surgery, and each transplant team will transport them back to their transplant center.

The above explanation is an extreme simplification of what actually occurs. Organ/tissue donations are vitally important and occur many times from sudden or traumatic events, such as automobile accidents, aneurysm, gunshot wound, etc. Many man-hours go into the matching process and the actual donation/transplant of the organs/tissues. Generally, the organs/tissues are required to be transplanted within either 24 or 48 hours after the donation, depending upon the organ system involved.

A person may become a donor through their local Motor Vehicles Department. A red heart will be pictured on the driver's license to indicate the intent to donate. This intent may also be stated in Advanced Directives (Health Care Power of Attorney) or Five Wishes documents. The family should be aware of this intent, which should be relayed to the health care team, so that proper arrangements may be made at the appropriate time.

A person may also wish to donate specific organs or their entire bodies toward medical research. The International Institute for the Advancement of Medicine (IIAM) links donors with scientific research and education programs. Again, costs are absorbed by the medical school or research program, including cost of cremation following the cost of the research. The IIAM may be contacted at 1-800-486-IIAM or through their website: http://www.iiam.org. A donor card will be issued to the person, which may be placed in their wallet. A donor card (Figure 6) is shown below.

Figure 6: IIAM Donor Card

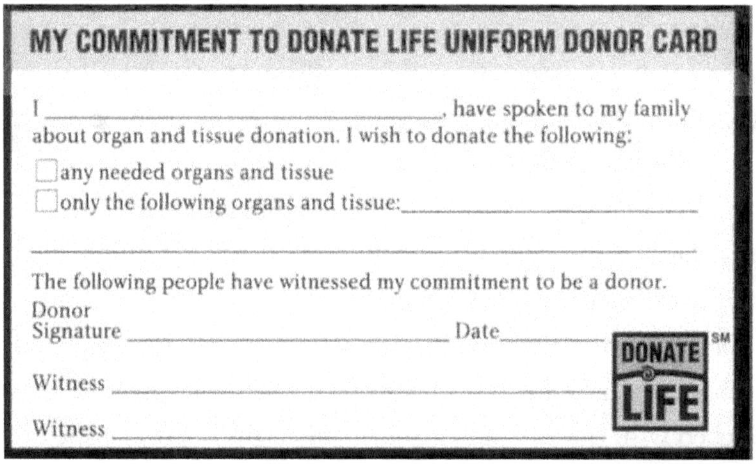

MY COMMITMENT TO DONATE LIFE UNIFORM DONOR CARD

I _____, have spoken to my family about organ and tissue donation. I wish to donate the following:

☐ any needed organs and tissue
☐ only the following organs and tissue:_____

_____

The following people have witnessed my commitment to be a donor.

Donor
Signature _____ Date_____

Witness _____

Witness _____

DONATE LIFE ˢᴹ

Image courtesy of International Institute for the Advancement of Medicine, http://www.iiam.org/

Funeral arrangements may be made without delays and open casket funerals are still permissible following the donation process. The hospital will notify the funeral home of choice when the patient's body is ready for transport to the funeral home.

Each state has its own donation system. The website http://www.donatelife.net/Commit ToDonation/ shows a map of the United States. Each particular state may be selected to find out the correct organization to contact to begin this process.

Embalming or Cremation:

The decision to embalm is entirely dependent on the needs of the family with relationship to the funeral service. Embalming removes the blood from the arterial system of the body and injects preservation fluids to replace the blood. This is done to prevent gasses from building up inside the body. If a visitation or the funeral service will be held with the body present, embalming will be required. If the loved one desired to be cremated and a memorial service will be held, the family can work with the funeral director to release the body for cremation without performing the embalming (usually an extra charge). Cremation will need to be performed within 1-2 days of death and takes about 3 hours.

Chapter 9:

The Dying Process

About three to four months before Mom died, she began talking like she was living in a prior time. The main theme seemed to be that she didn't want to be late to pick up "the boys" from school. This would mean that my younger two brothers were either in grade school or even junior high, approximately 35 or so years prior to this time. She would become agitated and we would reassure her that the boys were no longer in school, but working at their jobs. We let her know they were both fine and didn't need a ride. Above all, she wasn't even late! Mom had not driven in ten years!

Dad went through this same process; he thought he was supposed to be at work and was continually worrying about being at a meeting. He wanted paper and pencil so he could work on the problem at hand. Prior to this period, he did not remember that he owned his own company or what his profession had been. He really couldn't explain it during this process either, but he surely knew he had to complete a project. Kind of amazing, since his Alzheimer's was advanced enough that he would not be able to tell anyone what his career had been.

I would always try to get a feeling from the Hospice nurse during her weekly visits or from Arizona if they thought changes were occurring. The answer would always be – when they are ready, and when it is time, they will go. The death experience was explained to me as a transition period. It takes time for the person to prepare for death – they have to go through a period of reliving their lives, they visit their past, and they get ready to transition to the spiritual world. They have to be ready for the actual time of the death experience and any unresolved issues need to be solved internally, externally, or both.

This is important work that must be done. Obviously, if a person dies suddenly, this transition period may not occur. But, again, one never knows. A friend of mine died suddenly from a heart attack at the age of 50. Her husband, upon reflection of the six months prior to her heart attack thought that she had actually been going through her life review and that she knew she was going to die. The day before, she actually thanked him for taking care of her as well as he had for all the years they had been married.

As time went on, I believe Mom and Dad knew that they would not live much longer, but neither would talk about dying. The only statement Mom made to me (perhaps nine months before she died) was that she didn't want to lose Dad first and she didn't want to be a widow. When Mom expressed this feeling, Dad had been in a decline and we were extremely worried about him.

A couple of weeks before Dad died, he looked up at me and said, "There just isn't any reason to live anymore." I just feebly answered, "I know, Dad, I know," trying to give him some support that it was OK. Giving them permission to die is an extremely important concept. They need to know you will be OK – you will be, but it just doesn't seem like you can be.

The Hospice organization gave me a booklet called, "Gone From My Sight: The Dying Experience" by Barbara Karnes. This booklet helped me tremendously. This booklet explains what some of the physical changes are that might be seen in the last three weeks of life. Other reading has portrayed stages that accompany the transition period as one becomes closer to death. Some of these stages did not occur with my Mom and Dad, as they both had episodes that hastened their death.

➢ Withdrawal – a separation from the live world; perhaps a decrease in interest in television or news, not wanting family members to visit, staying in bed, an increase in naps, or appearance of sleep.

➢ Eating – decrease in appetite, no interest in food, decreased taste. Dad would spit out his food or even refuse to eat. Thoughout his last six months, food would taste funny or have no taste – even his favorite foods would not taste good. Once he decided he did not need to live any longer, he didn't eat more than a couple of bites at a time. We gave him Ensure, or milk shakes, anything to get liquids down him. He still loved sweet foods.

➢ Transition – Mom appeared to have conversations with her mother, and once I thought she was actually looking at her mother.

➤ Physical Changes during last week – In bed, not much interest in food, decrease in blood pressure, changes in body temperature from too hot to too cold, clamminess of the skin, skin changes (more blue due to less circulation), rapid or difficulty in breathing (may appear as restlessness), a congestion may seem to be present. Pneumonia is common at this stage and may be undetectible.

➤ Last Meal – A surge in alertness or increased appetite may occur. This definitely happened with Mom. She ate two fairly large bowls of homemade, pureed vegetable soup about 14-15 hours before she died. Supposedly the last meal gives them enough energy for the transition to the spiritual world.

➤ Breathing – the loved one's breathing may become slower. Their eyes may become less focused and restlessness may occur. With Dad, some of his restlessness calmed down with oxygen treatment. The blood pressure will decrease, but generally it will be obvious what is going on. There is really no need to take their blood pressure or temperature. The most important act is to ensure there is no pain and to keep them as comfortable as possible.

➤ Last few hours – a rattling or gurgling can occur in the throat – this is known as the "death rattle"; a decrease in urine output may occur. The most imminent sign is called "mottling" – the legs and feet begin to have purplish red blotches on them, particularly on the lower side. This process is the pooling of the blood. This mottling moves up to the knees, buttocks, and arms. Death can occur at any time once this mottling begins, from an hour or two or longer. (Note that this mottling can occur much longer, even for months, with specific health conditions and may not be a sign of imminent death.)

➤ Once death occurs, bodily fluids (urine, feces) will be released from the body. If the patient has not been eating or drinking, this may seem like a small urinary or bowel episode. Most people die with their eyes partially open, and it may be necessary to close their eyes. If a pacemaker is in place, the pacemaker will need to be turned off. Turning off the pacemaker may be done with a small magnet. If a pacemaker check kit is available, a small round magnet with a hole in the middle will be in the kit. The magnet should be placed over the pacemaker, with the hole directly over the pacemaker device. It may take 1-2 minutes for the pacemaker to turn off. We knew it was off when the nurse listened to Dad's chest with her stethoscope. Note that some of the newer pacemakers do not require this step.

Karnes, Barbara, R.N. Gone From My Sight. See also http://www.gonefrommysight.com

Barbara Karnes has additional booklets on her website relating to grief, living with life-threatening illnesses, dying, and reflections as a Hospice nurse. Additional information on end of life care is also available at http://www.cancer.gov/cancertopics/factsheet/support/end-of-life-care or http://www.hospicepatients.org/hospic60.html and endoflifecare.tripod.com/Caregiving/id89.html.

If the immediate family is not already present, phone calls may be made throughout the last few hours to give updates. Once mottling occurs, any family member desiring to be present should be notified immediately, if they are not already on their way. If the Hospice nurse is not there, she should also be notified. This entire process will not be as quick as you may wish it to be. It may take 30-60 minutes for the Hospice nurse to arrive, to pronounce the death, and to fill out the required paperwork.

Once death has been pronounced, the funeral home may be called to come and take your loved one to the mortuary. Even this step may take up to several hours, depending upon other calls that have come in or the time of the day. When death occurs, any remaining bodily fluids that are in the body are released and the person will require bathing. We felt that bathing our parents ourselves was a personal service to them and something further we could do, rather than having the funeral personnel do this. We actually had our caregivers give them their final baths and dress them in the clothes we had picked out for them. We felt this was a way to honor our parents.

Chapter 10:

Grief

Grief takes its own form for everyone. Whether or not there is an outward show of grieving or not, everyone has to grieve somehow and sometime, in some form. The time it takes to grieve is different for each person. And, the intensity of the grief can be much more difficult for the ones that perform the caregiving.

I cried a lot throughout those four years I cared for my parents and still occasionally tear up now. Grief doesn't stop, it just becomes more manageable. If something happened during the care day that upset me, I would be as brave as I could in front of my parents. I would then retreat to my office and cry. Not only was I afraid of losing my parents, even though I knew that this was inevitable, it was very hard to watch their decline day by day. They had been there my entire life – I could always pick up the telephone and call just to say "Hi."

Grieving started during these care years, especially for my Dad, as we were losing a piece of him all the time. Just recently, I went to a baby shower for Arizona's daughter. I was calmly sitting in the living room in a chair and glanced over to talk to someone. There was my Mom's couch next to me. I had forgotten that we had given it to Arizona. The surprise and shock of seeing it there was so abrupt, I had to leave the room. I burst into tears, but was able to calm down after a few minutes and return to the baby shower. This occurrence happened 3 years after Mom's death and 1-1/2 years after Dad's death.

The first year is the toughest – going through birthdays, holidays, Mother's Day and Father's Day. I can still get choked up on a moment's notice, if a phrase or comment triggers a memory. This process is entirely normal. Treasure it as a remembrance and don't feel like you are abnormal or a bad person.

It seems as though I grieved more for my Mom than for my Dad. I think now the grieving was as deep for each, but in different ways. Mom was the central figure in our lives. She was there everyday – so was Dad, but Dad was mainly there at night after work. Mom was there in the morning: helping us with breakfast, telling us what we could put in our sack lunches, in the afternoon: baking cookies, in the evening: fixing the dinner meal, shepherding homework, ensuring we did our household chores, or cleaned up the living room before Dad came home. She was the main enforcer, with Dad as backup, if we had really done something bad. We always knew when he arrived home, because we could hear him open the hall closet door to put his hat away.

Mom and Dad were very close and usually the only time we had to spend with Dad was on the weekends or on summer evenings. Dad also helped with homework. They were both task masters – I know I was never late with homework, but I remember several high school nights when I had to stay up late to finish a paper or two. Mom always baked – there were usually cookies or cake for dessert and plenty of goodies in the house at Christmas time. In summary, Mom and Dad had always been there. They might not always approve of what we did or how we did it, but they were always there. And, soon, they wouldn't be there anymore.

The first two years that I was at home taking care of them, I would help Mom bathe, get dressed and do her hair. This was our time to talk. One morning she told me she was very afraid of being a widow – she did not want Dad to die first. Usually, the women outlive the men, unless the woman marries someone ten years younger. I couldn't tell her that Dad would die first – but at the time, he was declining faster than she was. I just had to assure her that I understood and that if he did die first, I would be there to help her. She did not like for me to cry. She always said there wasn't anything I could do about whatever situation we were talking about anyway. But, I did. It is OK to grieve. Grieving helps to release some of the stress that is being felt. I must have a really transparent face, because Dad always knew when I was upset about something, even if I wasn't trying to show it. He would always ask me what was wrong, even up to the last few weeks.

My grief for Mom was more immediate. Even though she had some dimension of dementia, her mind was still intact and Mom was still Mom. I think the grieving seemed different for each of them because I was grieving for Dad throughout his Alzheimer's, and by the time he died, the grief entered a different stage. Mom ended up dying nineteen months before Dad, so she got her wish to not be a widow. She had a large stroke a week before she died. We made sure she was bathed every day, that she was turned at least every two hours if she was sleeping, and more often while she was awake. Arizona would tell me, "if you have something to say, you had better say it now." The absolute hardest part to hit you immediately when death occurs is that you can not ever talk to that person again and get a response. It is hard to know this or be able to voice this thought beforehand.

Grief is difficult to explain. The form that grief takes and the process one goes through to resolve grief is different for each person. The time that it takes to resolve grief is different for each person as well. The role that each person took with relation to the patient will also have its own ramifications on the grieving process. The family caretaker may grieve much harder and longer than other family members. Grief is a natural and normal response to the loss of a loved one. Each person will have to identify their own process for resolving grief. However, books, websites, grief support groups, and friends can help one through this process. It is very possible for a person to become so depressed from the burden of grief that professional assistance or even medication is required to combat the grief. A primary care physician is a good place to begin inquiring into assistance with this type of depression. But, please seek help if depression is suspected before the depressive state becomes too severe.

After the death of my mother, I went to a grief support group. About 8-10 people attended each week. Some people had been attending only a few weeks, others had been attending for over four years. I suppose the support group had become not only a support group for the grieving process but for their lives as well. A support group is definitely a way to release the pent-up emotions in a safe environment. The group is very supportive and understanding. It did seem though that a few people were using the group as a crutch – their lives had changed, but they still attended the grief support group each week. I attended for a few weeks, but eventually had to go through the grieving process on my own.

Going through the process of arranging and holding a funeral gets one over the first large hurdle in accepting the death. Over time, little thoughts or comments from others will bring the grief to the forefront, but for shorter moments as time goes on. I think I grieved more for my mother when she died, as her mind was mostly intact and she was aware of what was happening. Dad may have been subliminally aware that he was dying, but he was not vocal about it. My grief for him occurred throughout the four years of care, as we lost small pieces of him day by day. My Mom has now been deceased for almost four years and my Dad, two years. Getting through the first year for each person is another hurdle to conquer, as are the birthdays and holidays. I don't think I really let go of the bulk of my grief until after Dad had been gone for a year. But, I still have my moments. Well-meaning friends may come up and ask how your parent is doing, not knowing that they have died. This situation is difficult to respond to.

Hospice organizations are equipped to help the family deal with their grief for one year following the death of their loved one. Funeral homes often offer monthly grief bulletins to anyone in the family for a year. Subscriptions for these free bulletins may be signed up for during the time of the funeral arrangements.

The cancer survivors website and other websites cite five stages of grief for the survivor. Grief not only includes the loss of the person, but the reaction to this loss. Note that the patient may also go through some of these stages of grief, once they realize they have a terminal illness or the realization that he/she is going to die is known. These stages are:

Denial – this isn't happening to me!
Anger – Why is this happening to me?
Bargaining – I promise I'll be a better person if …
Depression – I don't care anymore
Acceptance – I'm ready for whatever comes

Retrieved September 2009 from:
http://www.cancersurvivors.org/Coping/end%20term/stages.htm

Along with denial comes shock, protest, numbness, alarm, and a feeling of being disconnected. Once the shock is dealt with, common feelings include reliving the loss, aimless wandering and restlessness, being unable to start or finish activities, feeling lost or disorganized, being confused and disoriented. Eventually mental and physical well-being are regained, along with an ability to enjoy life again. The poem below expresses the feelings of grief very well.

Grief

Grief is hard, diamond-hard, pointed and dazzling in its intensity,

Grief begins when someone dies,
    the moment when you realize you will never hear that voice again, except in dreams,
    or see that face again except in pictures,
    or along the dying journey, when changes occur in those you love.

Grief is huge,
    it consumes your life,
    it drags you down into sadness,
    it weighs you down, so that nothing can be accomplished,
    so that it is hard to know if you will ever feel joy or laughter again.

Grief is timeless,
    grief pops up suddenly during the day, at night, or in speaking,
    the tears come unexpectedly without relief,
    grief is neverending,
    time for grieving is different for each person and for each relationship lost –
        was the person a friend, a relative, a spouse, a child, a parent?

The loss is always there – even in anecdotes told later.
    Yet, grief somehow turns to joy of good memories,
        of times long ago,
        of special moments,
                And, then, grief softens and becomes easier to bear.

© Copyright 2010, Janice Louise Long

The psychiatrist, Elisabeth Kübler-Ross, published her now famous work on grief in 1969 in a book titled "On Death and Dying." She later published another book titled "On Grief and Grieving: Finding the Meaning of Grief Through the Five Stages of Loss." In this book, she writes:

> "The stages have evolved since their introduction, and they have been very misunderstood over the past three decades. They were never meant to help tuck messy emotions into neat packages. They are responses to loss that many people have, but there is not a typical response to loss, as there is no typical loss.
>
> Our grief is as individual as our lives. Not everyone goes through all of them or goes in a prescribed order."

Permission for use granted from Ken Ross, www.EKRFoundation.org.

More information about Dr. Kübler-Ross's work is available at http://www.EKRFoundation.org. Articles relating to grief topics are available at: http://www.grief.net/ArticleIndex.html. The site http://www.grief.net also offers books and workshops for those who grieve.

Chapter 11:

Legal Forms and Checklist for Seniors

Once you or your parent begins to decline, the legal and financial aspects of their lives need to be put in order, if these issues have not already been taken care of. A checklist of items to review is shown below. Parents, bear in mind that your children may not know much, if any, of your personal business. My parents never disclosed any of their financial or personal business with the kids, so when it came time to take care of their financial concerns, it was a big deal. Fortunately, Dad kept important papers in the safe in the garage. However, he could no longer answer specifics about any account or what stocks he had sold, etc. I went through two file cabinets of records to find out what were the current records, what were closed, and set up a spreadsheet of current accounts. At this point, he certainly did not mind my doing so, and was glad that I was able to understand what had transpired and could give him updates as we went along. At any rate, things would have been much easier if old records had either been destroyed or put in a different location and if important documents would have been in the same location.

Document Checklist

	Location/Account #/Name of Institution

Legal:
Will _____
Durable Power of Attorney _____
Healthcare Power of Attorney _____
Five Wishes _____
Funeral plans/obituary _____

Personal Identification:
Birth Certificate _____
Social Security Card _____
Medicare Card _____
Health insurance cards (including Medigap) _____
Driver's License _____
Passport _____

Policies/Pensions/Deeds/Taxes:
Insurance policies and numbers _____
IRA, 401k _____
Retirement pension _____
Stock Certificates _____
Deeds - car, home, funeral plot _____
Taxes - filed federal and state taxes for past 7 years

Banking:
Mortgage _____
Credit card accounts _____
Checking account _____
Savings account _____
Safe deposit box _____
Loan - car, other

Other investments/certificates of deposit:
_____ _____
_____ _____

Miscellaneous:
Computer passwords _____
Bank Card PINs _____
Safe combination _____

If documents are kept in a safety deposit box or safe, be sure and list where keys are or what the combinations are
Locate as many current documents as possible in the same location
Copies of identification cards and credit cards may be made and put with important documents

Caregiving Form 41
© Copyright 2010, Janice Louise Long

Documents to begin with are the Durable Power of Attorney (DPOA), the Healthcare Power of Attorney (HCPOA), the will, and the Do Not Resuscitate (DNR) form. If your parents have had the foresight to establish these forms, BRAVO for them!!

It is important to accomplish this while your parent is still able to make sound decisions, and that the documents can attest to such. All existing legal documents should be reviewed (especially if drawn up some time before the health decline) to ensure that the decisions made in the original documents are still valid and respect your parents' wishes. Different people may be named as the DPOA and the HCPOA, but the same person may perform both jobs. The will should name an executor that becomes the primary representative of the estate upon the parent's death. At death, the DPOA becomes invalid.

Do Not Resuscitate (DNR) Form

The DNR form (Figure 7) is designed to limit the amount of care an emergency medical team may deliver, whether the team is an ambulance team or a hospital team. Most of us might be familiar with this form when having a surgical procedure. Even if we are having a minor surgery, we may be requested by the surgeon to sign a DNR form, in the event that an emergency occurs during surgery.

However, a DNR form should also be signed by anyone that is experiencing a terminal illness or by the elderly. The DNR form is specific to restoring breathing or heart functions. The DNR form is signed by the parent and the primary doctor. The DNR should be displayed in a known and accessible place in the home. If an emergency situation arose and ambulance personnel called, the ambulance personnel could make the decision to perform cardiopulmonary resuscitation (CPR) if the DNR form was not seen. If the DNR form is present and signed, the Emergency Medical Response or hospital team will be required to assess the patient's situation and decide what the benefits and risks of resuscitation are. CPR can include heavy compressions to the chest (which may cause internal organ damage or broken ribs) or even electric shock therapy.

A picture of the New Mexico Department of Health Form (Figure 7) and its envelope that the form goes into are shown on the next two pages.

Figure 7: New Mexico Department of Health DNR Form and Envelope

EMERGENCY MEDICAL SERVICES (EMS)
DO NOT RESUSCITATE (DNR) FORM

AN ADVANCE DIRECTIVE TO LIMIT THE SCOPE OF EMS CARE

NOTE: THIS ORDER TAKES PRECEDENCE OVER A DURABLE HEALTH CARE POWER OF ATTORNEY FOR EMS TREATMENT ONLY

I, _____, request limited EMS care as described in this document. If my heart stops beating or if I stop breathing, no medical procedure to restore breathing or heart functioning will be instituted, by any health care provider, including but not limited to EMS personnel.

I understand that this decision will not prevent me from receiving other EMS care, such as oxygen and other comfort care measures.

I understand that I may revoke this Order at any time.

I give permission for this information to be given to EMS personnel, doctors, nurses and other health care professionals. I hereby agree to this DNR Order.

_____   OR   _____
Signature   Signature/Authorized
                                                                  Health Care Decision Maker

                                                                  _____
                                                                  Relationship

I affirm that this patient/authorized health care decision maker is making an informed decision and that this is the expressed directive of the patient. I hereby certify that I or my designee have explained to the patient the full meaning of the Order, available alternatives, and how the Order may be revoked. I or my designee have provided an opportunity for the patient/authorized health care decision maker to ask and have answered any questions regarding the execution of this form. A copy of this Order has been placed in the medical record. In the event of cardiopulmonary arrest, no chest compressions, artificial ventilations, intubation, defibrillation, or cardiac medications are to be initiated.

_____   _____
Physician's Signature / Date   Physician's Name - PRINT

_____
Physician's Address / Phone

White Copy: To be kept by patient in white envelope and immediately available to Emergency Responders
Yellow Copy: To be kept in patient's permanent medical record
Pink Copy: If DNR Bracelet/Medallion is desired send to MedicAlert with enrollment form.   2/95

The DNR form is usually state mandated as to its content and recognizability. Even though my parents had signed individual DNR's at the primary care office (which were in the primary care medical record and not linked to the hospital), Hospice had us sign another set at home during the individual Hospice admissions for Mom and Dad. The Hospice DNR's were placed in the kitchen where they were visible and easily located in case of emergency.

The acceptance of Hospice care in the home means that the patient (and the family) is agreeing to palliative comfort care with no heroics or life support measures. The DNR form states that the patient does not want to be resuscitated, even on an emergency basis. During my caregiving period, I was informed by a home health nurse, that the ambulance personnel would be required to resuscitate and that the coroner would be called in to pronounce a death if we did not have a DNR form. I subsequently found out that there are circumstances in which CPR is not required by the ambulance team without a DNR.

However, I did not want one of my parents to die at home without the DNR form, and have the other parent sitting there watching the ambulance team perform CPR, and wait any number of hours for the coroner to come and pronounce a death. Most likely, your parent will be under Hospice care or in a hospital setting and the above scenario will not occur. Hospice nurses are qualified to pronounce a death in the home, following which a funeral home team will lovingly come to take your loved one to the mortuary. (See further information under Office of the Medical Examiner and Hospice)

A doctor is required to certify the cause of death for the death certificate. Without Hospice, this determination is made by the county coroner. The coroner will determine whether or not an autopsy will be required to determine the diagnosis. Do not be afraid of the potential of the autopsy. The body is not harmed in a way that a viewing is not possible. An autopsy most likely will be required in any sudden or suspicious death, including a potential of suicide. The autopsy is performed by the Office of the Medical Investigator (OMI) at the County Coroner's office.

Early on in the caregiving process, I had been told that if Mom and Dad did not have a Do Not Resuscitate order, the possibility existed that an emergency response team would be required to attempt to resuscitate either of them should they die at home. A private telephone conversation with the Administrator of our local OMI office revealed the following information. The OMI investigation team will be called to the home or site of the death. The team will perform a scene investigation and interview the family and witnesses. They will also contact the primary care physician, review the deceased's medical history, see if there is a possibility of a natural death occurring, and ask the physician if he is comfortable in signing the deceased person's death certificate.

All of these findings are factored into the OMI decision of whether or not to do an autopsy. The Administrator also stated that the Emergency Medical Response (EMR) teams are trained to view heart attacks as a natural death. Also, if obvious signs of death have already occurred, they will not resuscitate. However, the EMR team will resuscitate if they feel the circumstances indicate a possibility of survival. Note that it takes several hours for rigor mortis or pooling of the blood in the body to occur.

Source: Personal telephone consultation with OMI, New Mexico office, February 2009

Durable Power of Attorney (DPOA)

The Durable Power of Attorney governs the person to whom control of the financial and other assets is given. The DPOA expires at time of death, upon which time the executor of the estate takes over. The DPOA allows the designated person to make any financial decisions, to pay bills, and to make decisions regarding personal property. This person also becomes responsible for these decisions when the designator becomes unable to do so. Generally, it would be better for the loved one to familiarize the designee with these financial affairs as soon as the DPOA is written. The designee should be discreet, and be empowered to act in good faith, along the designators guidelines and expectations.

To be on the safe side, take a copy of the DPOA to the bank and ask that a note is attached to these accounts stating that no one is allowed to perform any transactions except for the DPOA. The DPOA must have identification to perform transactions as well. Doing so will prevent any person from taking undue advantage of the ill person.

Advanced Directive or Health Care/Medical Power of Attorney (HCPOA, MPOA)

The advanced directive is a legal document which addresses future medical care of the person who signed the advanced directives. Two types of advanced directives exist: the Health Care Power of Attorney (HCPOA) or Medical Power of Attorney (MPOA). The premise behind these documents is that your directions will be specified during any time that you cannot communicate or act for yourself. The living will specifies end-of-life care and the HCPOA or MPOA appoints a person(s) to act on your behalf at any time, not just for end-of-life care. The HCPOA or MPOA must be able to put aside his/her own wishes or feelings to "do everything" to keep you alive, and be able to understand the medical situation to make the appropriate decisions, based upon your stated wishes.

Saying that you want "no life support" is too broad. The question to think about is: do the statements you make in an advanced directive pertain only to a terminal illness or life threatening situation? What if you were in a car accident and unconscious? Where do you want to die: at home, in a hospital, in another location? Do you want hospice care? Do you want your family around you? Do you want pain meds? Do you want artificial nutrition and fluids? Do you want to be resuscitated? It is almost impossible to imagine all possible scenarios and what might happen.

Questions to think about and to discuss with your spouse and/or children, HCPOA appointee and your primary care physician: What care would you want under the following situations (e.g., feeding tubes, oxygen, full life support, pain medications, blood transfusions)?

1. If condition is the result of a long-term illness
2. If your illness is terminal
3. If brain activity is present or absent
4. How serious is your condition
5. Can your condition be cured
6. What issues are bothering you – express your concerns now – what bothers you the most about being in a terminal situation – do any of these concerns affect what life saving measures are picked for you?

Specify what types of tubes you will accept, e.g., feeding, intravenous (IV) antibiotics, etc. if an infection becomes active and requires antibiotics. Will you allow prolongation of your life with the placement of an IV? Life-threatening and life prolonging are the key terms. Only when lab chemistries indicate organ system failure will a person's classification be changed from "life-threatening" to "fatal." Obviously, a urinary tract infection would not normally be life-threatening (unless the person is on kidney dialysis) but a pneumonia could be, especially in an elderly person. Pneumonia can sneak up quietly and may not even be detectable. Dad's death diagnosis was pneumonia and we didn't even know he had it, even though his lungs had been listened to several times a day for weeks. Perhaps life support could be specified for a lung or bronchial episode and tested for continued need after a specified number of days – 3, 4, or 5 – based upon the recommendations of the medical staff.

It is heart wrenching for a family to make the decision to discontinue life support without knowing the loved one's specific wishes. Discuss your "draft" living will or HCPOA with your physician to check if the language is clear and your wishes are able to be understood from a physician/medical staff point of view. In the actual setting of decision making, the answer may not be very clear. The decision will need to fit the circumstances, based upon your wishes.

The Five Wishes™

Another way for the wishes of the loved one to be heard is through a document called Five Wishes™ – http://www.agingwithdignity.org. The Five Wishes™ document was created by the Aging with Dignity non-profit organization.

> "Aging with Dignity is a national non-profit organization with a mission to affirm and safeguard the human dignity of individuals as they age and to promote better care for those near the end of life. The life and work of Mother Teresa of Calcutta served as the inspirational foundation of Aging with Dignity."

> Retrieved July 2009, from http://www.agingwithdignity.org

This document allows one to determine the quality of life that he/she wants to have at the end of their life and may be filled out at any time in one's life AND can supercede the HCPOA. The Aging with Dignity organization has addressed many scenarios and issues related to aging and final wishes in this document. This document addresses five areas:

1. Which person you want to make health care decisions for you when you cannot make them
2. The kind of medical treatment you want or don't want
3. How comfortable you want to be
4. How you want people to treat you
5. What you want your loved ones to know

The Five Wishes™ is accepted in forty-three states as a viable document, is available in 23 languages or in Braille, and offers a pediatric version. The Five Wishes™ replaces the HCPOA or MPOA. It may be attached to the HCPOA or POA in the other seven states (Alabama, Indiana, Kansas, New Hampshire, Ohio, Oregon, and Texas). Keep in mind that what one wishes for in their advanced directives or Five Wishes™ planning can change once the dying trajectory becomes active, both for the patient and for the family. We really do not want our loved one to die. Sometimes the patient himself may have an awareness that death is coming, but if the patient is in the hospital on life-support mechanisms and cannot make their own decisions, consider the following questions.

1. Is the treatment being given too aggressive for the medical condition?
2. Are the life-support mechanisms artificially prolonging life, essentially putting death "on hold?"
3. What is the function of the medications being given? Is the blood pressure being medically stabilized?
4. Are heroic steps being taken to preserve the life because of who the person is or the fullness of their life? Does the patient still have the chance to have a decent quality of life or are you looking for more quantity (length) of life?
5. How would your loved one perceive this situation? What would he/she want?
6. How much pain is your loved one in?
7. Do you really want your loved one to undergo CPR, if necessary? CPR can be life threatening in and of itself; ribs may be broken from the constant compressions or damage done to the internal organs.
8. If the patient has asked to have everything possible done to save his life, when can you, the family, say "no more." The doctors will abide by your wishes in this case, as their job is to save and prolong life. But even the doctor may come to the point where he knows it is useless to offer further treatment.
9. Is it time for palliative or comfort care? If so, is the loved one stable enough to be moved to an inpatient Hospice unit or to their home, under Hospice care? If the patient wants to go home, are there enough family members available that are capable

enough and willing to care for your loved one? This may mean that several persons need to be available to move the person or to meet all bodily care required.

10. Do the hospital procedures support palliative care? The answer to this question will depend on the physical state of your loved one. If a possibility exists to move her, the hospital will probably want to have her moved. Again, this goes back to reimbursement issues and the possibility of payment from Medicare or the health insurance company.

11. Has your loved one expressed any particular desire of where to die? Does he want to die at home or in a hospital (including Hospice care)? Sometimes one may feel that it would be too hard for the family for them to die at home. My parents wanted to die at home. I chose to bring in an hospital bed for Mom due to the ease of care issues and to hopefully prevent Dad from a further decline of his Alzheimer's disease when Mom did pass away. A friend of mine recently lost her husband from cancer. He did not want to die at home. He and his family had decided to move him to Respite Care for a week to give the family a break. He was being transported to Respite Care when he died in the ambulance. His death was not unexpected, but it was unexpected for him to die in the ambulance. Everyone had been prepared for him to return home from Respite Care.

The Five Wishes™ plan even includes the loved one's intent towards the "setting" during the dying process. Consider what would make your loved one comfortable – a particular type of music (classical, jazz, blues, rock & roll, hymns), or text (a favorite book on tape, favorite religious passages like the 23rd Psalm, I Corinthians 13, or other familiar verses, or memories of their life, or a favorite sports happening replayed in the background. Does the loved one want friends and family surrounding him, or does he want quiet? Should the lighting be bright or dim? Does your loved one love the sunshine and warmth? Be cognizant that the hearing is the last sense to leave the body. Conversation should be respectful, especially when talking/comforting the loved one. Are there religious/cultural beliefs that need to be adhered to upon the actual death with respect to the spirit or to the body?

A family member should be designated to discuss any particular issues with the hospital staff. Even if the person has not been actually religious or faithful in their latter years, their upbringing and childhood beliefs may be of importance at this time and may be comforting to them. Know what their spirituality is or isn't. Listening and silence are also gifts at this time – listening to those around you (spouse or child), reflection of your loved one's life and the sharing of that life with yourself, or silence towards your loved one with the comfort of your presence.

The Five Wishes™ document (proprietary and watermarked) may be viewed in Appendix III. It may be changed over time. Any previous versions should be destroyed or have the word "REVOKED" written across all pages. The Five Wishes™ includes a wallet card that will show hospital personnel that you have this document, who your HCPOA is, who your primary care doctor is, and where the document is located.

Retrieved July 2009, from http://www.agingwithdignity.org/contact.php

Finances

Once we knew Dad had Alzheimer's Disease, I stepped into the picture to take care of Mom and Dad's finances. Dad had an IRA and investment accounts at many different firms. Several accounts were earning the lowest amount of interest possible or actually losing money. I won't go into details of how I finalized his financial positions, but I will tell you what worked for us.

We initially had a long-distance financial advisor, which managed several of the accounts. I quickly realized that although he seemed to have good intentions, he was still trying to make as much money as possible by moving stocks around, calling to ask me to agree to different options, etc. This advisor changed companies, and then I had both he and his successor calling me. My goal as the steward of Dad's money was to optimize our returns, and ensure that we did indeed have enough money to cover any expenses that might occur over an unknown number of years of caregiving. I also was not comfortable having long-distance representation.

After spending many hours gleaning information from these stockbrokers and studying, I set up a scenario and asked both of these advisors to come up with a solution to best optimize our needs. During this time, I had also contacted Mom and Dad's long-term care (LTC) insurance representative to find out about the benefits they were entitled to. This LTC representative was a local financial advisor for a leading company, which held a portfolio of stocks and bonds. I also asked this local advisor to create a third solution. One of the requirements was the provision of a monthly income to meet monthly caregiving expenses. As one might imagine, the local advisor won out. He set up exactly the plan that I needed, without causing Dad extra expenses. We also consolidated about 90% of all the assets into two accounts (IRA and non-IRA monies). Even though this was a time-intensive process, the time was well worth the effort. The consolidation also facilitated the estate business processes.

Estate Rule

The link to the IRS document that explains the estate rule and the forms associated may be found at: http://www.irs.gov/pub/irs-pdf/i706.pdf.

Trusts

My parents initially had an AB Trust, in which the assets of the couple are equally split into two parts, A and B. Each was the beneficiary of the other. When their AB Trust was set up, their assets were higher than allowed for estate tax purposes. Splitting the assets into two parts allowed the estate tax to become zero. When the Economic Growth and Tax Relief Reconciliation Act of 2001 (see Chapter 13) was enacted, the AB Trust was no longer needed, as their total assets met the requirements for this Act. Many different types of trusts are available and are generally used to transfer assets and property or to maximize the amount of assets and property that are available to beneficiaries.

IRS Tax Return Form

"The executor of a decedent's estate uses Form 706 to figure the estate tax imposed by Chapter 11 of the Internal Revenue Code. This tax is levied on the entire taxable estate, not just on the share received by a particular beneficiary. Form 706 is also used to compute the generation-skipping transfer (GST) tax imposed by Chapter 13 on direct skips (transfers to skip persons of interests in property included in the decedent's gross estate)."

Veteran's Administration (VA)

Military veterans are eligible for death and burial veteran's benefits including: $300 towards the burial; the possibility of burial in a Veteran's Administration cemetery; a memorial marker; and a flag for the casket. Information about these benefits may be found at the http://www.cem.va.gov/ website. The discharge paperwork or DD Form 214 and a copy of the death certificate will be required. Veterans may also have a $10,000 life insurance policy filed with the VA. Benefits will be paid equally to all joint beneficiaries.

Chapter 12:

The Funeral - The Final Goodbye

We chose to give Mom and Dad their final baths and to dress them. We picked out the final outfits – a beautiful lavender pantsuit for Mom and the red shirt Dad wore to my brother's wedding, with a favorite bolo tie for him. He had made the bolo tie and had about twenty of them in his drawer. We would have taken off their wedding rings and watches, but both of them had removed them prior to their deaths because they were too loose. We designated a family member to stay with them until the mortuary came to the house to take them away.

Mom and Dad had always wanted to be cremated. I had always had a particular aversion to cremation, but also had one about being buried in the ground. But, I knew it was important to honor their wishes. When we were kids, Dad had handmade a coffee table to fit the couch in the living room. It was rectangular, had decorative framed wooden blocks around the middle, with a dark green and black marble tabletop. They had always joked about this table being the receptacle for their ashes. Somewhere along the way, the table had been given to one of my brothers.

It was still a surprise when I found out at the funeral home that they had only paid for the cardboard box that they would be cremated in. What happened? Evidently, at the time they made their arrangements, there was a state law that only allowed the process to be finalized up to and including cremation. So, there I was – finding out that they had bought the typical cardboard box for cremation and nothing else. Essentially, the ashes would be sitting on the crematory table the next day and I had to figure out what to do and pay for any further actions. This was a real surprise and about the last thing I had the wherewithal to do at that minute.

I decided upon a memorial service at the funeral home and picked out an urn for Mom's ashes. I found a beautiful rose carved rosewood urn that would fit their likes perfectly. They both loved roses and always had them in the garden and in the house. I visited the cemetery to figure out where the best place would be to place the urns. Choices for the urn placement were inside – in a decorative room with glass panels (behind which one can see the urn), outside – numerous walls were available, most were of plain metal coverings of different colors (to me – these did not look very inviting), but finally, I was shown a mosaic wall.

The mosaic wall depicted the entrance to Albuquerque's "Old Town" with the church behind the gates. Roses were blooming around the gates. Above the church were the mountains, the clouds, and the blue sky. The mosaic wall faces east toward our mountains and would have sunlight a great portion of the day. This was the most perfect choice. I wanted them to be happy with my choices, so my decisions were based upon my reflections of what they loved. Mom and Dad had high picture windows in their living room, through which they would watch the clouds go by. They also sat on their back patio, facing the pine trees, watching the clouds, wind, and birds. Their urns are in the clouds of the mosaic wall, where they can look out and see the mountains, the clouds, and the sky.

My advice is to decide what you (the future patient) want and let your wishes be known. Do you want to be in a wooden box, buried underground (even though the box may be put in a sealed crypt) or in a drawer, where the cemetery caretaker can pull open the drawer for your loved ones to see your casket? I thought the plain niches in cement walls were impersonal. Actually, I never personally liked any of the choices. So, for me, finding this mosaic wall was perfect for them. In fact, I also finalized Dad's arrangements, as well as my own at this time. I don't want my daughters to have to make these decisions. I reserved a spot next to Mom and Dad. I never wanted to be cremated, but prefer this solution to others, and want to be close to them when I die.

The processes of this day (when Mom died) took the entire day. My mind kept running through details and somehow I had the energy to continue until everything was set in place. It was like I couldn't stop until I was done. Thus, I had contacted the minister, arranged for the music, fleshed out the program for the service, had the flowers picked out and ordered, and of course, made all the appropriate telephone calls to family members and friends. I really couldn't stop until all that was done. My daughter hung in there with me until these things were done – she was 21 at that time and a great source of comfort. The next few days were spent taking care of Dad and finalizing any other necessary details.

Mom's Memorial Service

We made a Memory Board of pictures of Mom, of which many were of both she and Dad. She was hardly ever in any pictures without him. We had family pictures as well – as a child with her brothers and parents, her college photos, their wedding pictures, our family growing up, and recent pictures. Mom was an expert counted cross stitch artist. Her favorite subject was angels. Some of these pictures were 8" x 10", but some were 17" x 24". We took several of these and placed them in front of the sanctuary to honor her talent.

The minister came to the house the day after Mom died to get family impressions of Mom as a person and what our memories of her were. She then crafted Mom's life story as her eulogy and incorporated our memories and Mom's cross-stitching ability as well. When Dad died, the same minister took Mom's story and pieced it together with Dad's story. It was beautifully done.

Dad and his Memorial Service

Dad was an engineer and an architect. He owned his own company from the time he was about 44 until he retired. Dad was very successful and fortunately for us, had saved up the resources to ensure that we could care for them in the manner in which they wanted us to.

Mom was the serious one – but Dad could bring her out of the seriousness and get her to have fun. Dad was always the "Life of the Party." He always had plenty of energy, was always telling jokes, and was famous for being direct, caring, and unscrupulously honest. We were not allowed to call him at work, but I think I did twice – both times during or after college. I also went to see him once at his office. I was able to do that as I had worked for him in high school when he first started his company.

The two biggest lessons I learned from him were honesty and to show you care for others. One time I called him at his office, and he answered the telephone himself. I asked him, "Dad, how come you answered the phone and not your secretary?" Dad replied, "If someone cares enough to take the time to call me, then I have the time to talk with them. I am not so important that I can't answer the phone myself." Dad loved to dance and sing as well. He was always telling stories or ditties – as he called them. His Christmas party poems depicting the office personnel were legendary. This was the persona I wanted to impart at his service.

Dad's business partner told two stories about him. One was that whenever it was payday, Dad would take everyone out to eat or have food brought in. The other was that when they had a big deadline, everyone was working late or had worked long hours, Dad would go out to the drafting room and call everyone together for a break. They would have a contest of pitching pennies to see who could pitch them the closest to a door threshold. Dad kept a box of pennies in his desk for this purpose. I didn't hear about this story until I was talking to his partner about the eulogy. I found Dad's box of pennies in his dresser drawer, even after a retirement of twenty years.

An example of Dad's humor: He had appendicitis while he was serving in the Navy during World War II. He was stationed in the Solomon Islands in the Pacific. The story was that the only doctor available was an obstetrician (doctor that delivers babies). The punch line was: Dad was the only Lieutenant Junior Grade in the Navy with a bikini scar. The other story he loved to tell: He was in his stateroom on the ship. The phone rang. It was the Admiral asking for Lt. Short. My Dad replied, "Sir, Lt. Short is not here right now. This is Lt. Long, may I help you?" He always ended this story by saying he was almost court-martialed by being a smart aleck!!

Dad loved jazz and blues and had blue suede dancing shoes from the 1940's that he could still wear. I had visited New Orleans some time previously, which is famous for their street funerals. For some reason, I bought a CD of one of these jazz funerals. I had never listened to it, but when Dad died, I dug it out, opened it, and listened to it. It was perfect! We had jazz from this CD played before and after the service. At the close of the scripture and eulogy, we played the version of "Taps" that was on this CD to honor Dad's military service.

At the front of the chapel, there were two tables. A small table at the center had his blue suede shoes, his hat, his harmonica, and the flag commemorating his WWII service. Another table to the side showed a piece of his artwork (painted on both sides – he never wasted his canvases. If he didn't like a painting, he just turned it over and painted it on the other side.) As the funeral attendees left the service, each was given a penny at the doorway. Each pitched the penny across the threshold into the lobby. In the lobby were mementos of Dad's Navy life, his work life, and his pictoral life with Mom. We had german chocolate cake in honor of my mother and cherry pie in honor of my Dad at the reception. The reception was followed by the interment of his ashes (in the rosewood urn) next to Mom in the mosaic wall.

Preparations for the Service

Even though Mom and Dad had already arranged for the funeral home to cremate them, the final arrangements still involved time and expense. If initial or complete final arrangements have not been made, documents may be required to make these arrangements. Documents may include the birth certificate, driver's license or picture identification, social security number, Veteran's Administration discharge papers (if parent was a veteran).

Step 1: Decide upon the funeral home

Step 2: Call the funeral home to let them know your parent has passed away (anytime of day or night). Hospice can also notify them if you wish.

Once the parent has passed away, the funeral home should be contacted to come and move the parent to the mortuary.

Step 3: Transporting the loved one

A transportation team will come and pick up your loved one. They will bring a stretcher with a body bag into the house. The team will transfer your loved one onto their own sheet, wrap the body in this sheet, allow you to say your goodbyes, and seal the body bag closed with identification tags on the outside. These steps are performed with care, in accordance with State Law, and protect your loved one.

Step 3a: Questionable death circumstances

If the death is questionable, either by accident, suicide, or homicide, an autopsy may be required. If one of these circumstances occurs, the State Medical Examiner's office must be notified. The Hospice team or the funeral home will be able to assist in this notification for you. The State Medical Examination Transport Team will then be the correct team to come and transport your loved one. The autopsy will usually be done the same day. Following the autopsy, the funeral home will be notified to transport your loved one from the Medical Examiner's office to the mortuary. (See Office of the Medical Investigator, Chapter One)

Step 4: Meet with the Funeral Director at the funeral home

Sometime during that day or the next day, an appointment may be made with a funeral planner to make service arrangements. The funeral home will set the appointment so that the parent may be viewed while the family is making the funeral arrangements (if this viewing is desired). This appointment may take up to two hours. Be prepared to take information relating to the date of birth, place of birth, parent's names (including mother's maiden name), and Social Security number.

When I went to the funeral home, the planner explained the choices Mom and Dad had made. That is when I found out there was no urn or burial plot decided upon. I made the arrangements for Mom the day she died, and went back a few days later to ensure that Dad had identical arrangements. I wanted him to be placed next to her when he died. All of this entails paperwork and choices that are extremely difficult to make so soon after the final passing of the loved one. The funeral personnel are well trained and very sympathetic. As much time as is needed will be given to you to make these arrangements.

The appropriate paperwork will be filled out and decisions made with regards to the type of disposition (casket burial or cremation), traditional service (body present in casket (open or closed)), or memorial service with urn, whether or not viewing sessions will be held, where the burial will take place (locally or in other location), whether or not the urn will be taken home or placed in a solumbarium. Arrangements for the service may also be made through the mortuary. Many mortuaries have their own chapels with either organs or piped in music. Funeral homes may also be able to provide flower service, and will provide memorial items, such as guest book and thank you cards.

Transportation of the family to the church and/or burial service may be arranged. Be prepared to answer questions about your Mom or Dad's body, e.g., do they have dentures, glasses (if not on them), any type of medical device or prosthesis, etc. Dad had a partial dental plate, but we hadn't been able to get it in his mouth the last week of his life; he also had a pacemaker; Mom had glasses which were returned prior to cremation; Mom also had a hip replacement on one side and hip screws on the other side.

During this visit, the obituary for the newspaper will be prepared. In my mind, I would have preferred that I took the time to think about what to write ahead of time. It was very difficult to sit there and recite family member names and the person's life experiences to someone who didn't know my Mom or Dad. Spellings of names are asked for and repetition occurs to ensure that the obituary is correct. The obituary is printed for your review. If misspellings are not caught, the obituary will go in the newspaper incorrectly. The funeral home sends the obituary to the newspaper. The first printing of the obituary should be checked. If any mistakes occur, the newspaper should be notified for correction. There is a daily cost for the obituary printing.

Note any potential differences of opinion among the family members while preparing for the funeral. My two younger brothers were 10 and 11 years younger than I was. When my oldest brother and I were children, we went to Sunday School and church every week. Mom and Dad had both been brought up in their respective churches. During my childhood, Dad was active in the Deacons, ushered every Sunday at church, and was Pack Master for the Boy Scout Troop at the church. During my junior high years, Mom and Dad quit going to church for various reasons. Thus, my two younger brothers did not associate Mom and Dad as being particularly religious. One of them was pretty vocal in his opinion that the funeral service did not need to occur in a church.

Thus, a compromise was made to have a church type service at the funeral home. When our family met with the minister to recount memories for the eulogy, we found out that even dinnertime was different for them than it was for the two older siblings. It truly was like having two different families!! This points again to ensure that if one has specific wishes, to be sure these wishes are vocalized or written down, and understood by the family. If not, the family members will have to figure out the best way to honor the memory of the loved one, in accordance to what they know in their hearts.

Step 5: Ashes

State and/or National laws govern where ashes may be buried or scattered. If the deceased's home will be sold, part of the home inspection includes a check of whether or not ashes have been buried on the property.

Step 6: Death Certificate

The funeral home will receive the formal state certified death certificate and will call the family when they are available for pick up. This may take 2-3 weeks. The number of copies needed by the family is specified during the funeral home planning visit. Usually, the maximum number of copies offered is 20, but a reasonable number is 10. There may be a cost associated with copies over the minimum supplied by the funeral home. An assessment of the financial concerns of the loved one will be an indicator of the number of copies needed. Some institutions require original, certified copies, some will accept a copy of the original, and others will accept a scanned/emailed copy of the original. Each original is individually numbered. I kept one copy aside and used it to send copies without designating that number to any particular organization. The funeral home gave me an instruction book of financial details to investigate, and recommended that I make a list of each death certificate serial number, to whom it was sent, and on what date.

Step 7: Costs

In my area, funeral arrangements range from $7000-9000. This price is dependent upon location, the services provided by the funeral home, and the cost of the land at the cemetery. These prices will be area dependent.

Step 8: Cemetery

Following the funeral home visit, a visit to the cemetery will be required, if the ashes are not to be taken home or there is a casket burial. Again, choices will be made at this step. The main choice is location. Various types of walls (at various prices) are available for cremated remains in urns, and in-ground or inside locations are available for caskets. The costs associated with an urn interment include the niche, the inscription on the outside of the niche, and the opening/closing of the niche during the service. The costs associated with casket burial include the grave, the vault (the container that the casket is placed in), the headstone, and the opening/closing of the grave. Bear in mind that one of the choices here will be to have the casket placed inside a drawer inside a memorial building. The cemetery in which my parents are placed issues deeds for every burial. This deed is a lifetime deed and is protected by law. This is not a nationwide practice. Another possibility is that the deed could expire after 100 years. I can't imagine what happens at the 100 year point, but the deed particulars should be investigated before deciding upon a burial location. The average costs in my location for a niche burial is about $2000, and $3000 for a casket burial.

Chapter 13:

After Death

Responsibilities of the Executor/Personal Representative

At the time of death, the Durable Power of Attorney and Healthcare Power of Attorney forms become invalid. The will should appoint an executor/executrix (female) or personal representative for the estate. The executor or personal representative (PR) is an individual (or company) designated by the will to preside over the distribution of the estate. The individual is usually a spouse, child, or other close family member. However, a financial institution, attorney or Certified Public Accountant may be named as executor/executrix for particularly large estates. Contents of the estate include everything owned by the deceased person: homes, land, vehicles, bank accounts, investments, etc.

Duties of the Personal Representative:

1. Plan the funeral, place the obituary, and pay any related expenses from the estate
2. Request death certificates (10-20 copies) from the funeral home
3. Notify Social Security at 1-800-772-1213; see www.ssa.gov – Click on "Survivors"
4. Notify Life Insurance companies which hold policies for the deceased
5. Notify any agencies from which retirement check benefits are received
6. Contact insurance agencies which hold policies for the home, automobiles, personal property, etc.
7. Notify Internal Revenue Service (IRS) – set up estate Tax Identification Number
8. Handle estate assets
   a. Pay debts/obligations
   b. Make distributions to the beneficiaries
   c. Handle tax returns

    i.   Personal taxes for year of death up to the date of death

    ii. Estate taxes from date of death to end of year and any tax year thereafter in which the estate remains open (until all issues are settled and all proceeds paid to the beneficiaries)

    iii. K-1's should be declared to show beneficiary distributions from the estate

        1. K-1's will be required by each beneficiary to file on their personal returns to show distributions received from the estate. Due to the length of time it may take to get the estate tax returns filed, extensions may be requested. Beneficiaries will be required to file amended tax returns, showing the K-1 distributions, if they have already filed their tax return for that year.

9. Open the estate:

    The executor should petition the court, providing proof that he/she is the legally appointed executor. The petition includes a request for "letters testamentary". The court returns a certified document, naming the petitioner as the Personal Representative for the names person's estate. (Some institutions will require an original of this form, others will accept a copy, or an emailed version of a scanned original.) Request as many copies of the certified document that you expect to need; I suggest a minimum of 3-5 copies.

10. Retitle any assets, e.g., house, land, vehicles, or loans. If possible, do this prior to the death. If the loved one is diagnosed with dementia, do this as soon as possible after the diagnosis. The executor/personal representative has the right to be reimbursed for expenses associated with the settling of the estate. The state can determine this fee, which may be from 1-5% of the estate's value. Beneficiaries who are personal representatives can choose to waive this fee.

11. Manage/sell investments

12. Record Keeping

    a. Amounts paid/Received by the estate

        i.   Debtors, including medical, funeral, ambulance

        ii. Certified Public Accountant or Attorney

        iii. Beneficiaries

        iv. Dividends

    v.   Tax Refunds

    vi. Life Insurance Benefits

    vii. 401K, IRA, or other Retirement Accounts

13. Keep beneficiaries informed of progress on a monthly basis, even if no activity has occurred

14. Close the estate: Formal or informal closing

Once all the liabilities of the estate have been paid and all the beneficiary distributions have been made, a petition may be made to the state court to close the estate. Two types of closing are possible: formal and informal. Establish with the family attorney which type he would prefer. One option is to just wait for the judge to close the case based upon inaction.

    a.   The informal closing is less expensive. The informal closing involved the filing of a signed certificate stipulating that all matters of the estate have been dealt with. Specifically, all debts of the estate have been paid for or provisions have been made for the payment of the debts. Secondly, all beneficiary distributions have been paid or provisions have been made to do so. The informal closing petition is registered with the court and the estate will be closed one year after the petition. A court document will be issued at the end of the year recording the closing of the estate.

    b.   The formal closing of the estate involves a court hearing, petitioning the court to close the estate. The stipulation is made that all of the debts and beneficiary distributions have been made (including all tax returns filed and accepted). The personal representative will be present at the court hearing and may be queried by the judge of the actions that have occurred within the estate. It would be wise to have a list of estate proceedings at this hearing so that any questions may be readily answered. The hearing results in a formal order of the court that the estate is closed.

    c.   Court closing - If there is no legal activity on the estate over a period of time, the court may close the estate itself. The judge that signed the order designating the personal representative may review these cases from time to time, as his calendar and docket permits. The judge may decree that an estate is closed without a petition for an informal or formal closing. If one wishes to do so, with the agreement of the estate's attorney, the personal representative then needs to do nothing but wait.

Caveat: When making final cash distributions to the beneficiaries, a wise move is to keep $5000-10,000 remaining in the trust account, in case the IRS writes to demand a penalty on a prior tax return. If all the monies in the estate are disbursed, it may be difficult to retrieve money back from the beneficiaries, and the personal representative could be entirely liable for the cost. This concern may not be an issue if the tax returns have been properly filed through an accountant. Dad's 2001 tax return was sent back in 2004, with an extra amount due. This tax return would have been completed before we knew we had any problems.

15. Inheritance and Estate Tax

These taxes are government imposed. An Estate/Tax Attorney or Certified Public Accountant should be contacted to advise the family on this matter.

In the United States, inheritance tax is levied by the state. In recent years, however, many states have repealed or phased out their inheritance taxes. Inheritance tax is a tax on the money and assets received by a beneficiary (also called a transferee or heir) from the estate of the decedent (the person who died). The estate is the grand total of everything the decedent owned and had interests in (business investments, for example) at the time of death. Beneficiaries must pay taxes on the value of whatever they inherit, though they can claim a number of exemptions to reduce these taxes. The inheritance tax rate depends primarily on the type of property being inherited and the relationship of the heir to the decedent.

The U.S. federal government levies the estate tax. However, the Economic Growth and Tax Relief Reconciliation Act of 2001 is phasing out the estate tax, and is set to repeal it in 2010. It will be interesting to see what happens to this tax in 2011. The U.S. Congress continues to debate the final fate of the estate tax.

Estate tax is a tax on the total value of the money and assets left behind by a decedent. Whereas heirs are responsible for paying inheritance taxes, the estate's executor or administrator (the person responsible for handling the affairs of the estate, as directed in the decedent's **will**) must pay the estate tax. After various exemptions are applied, the executor uses money from the estate itself to pay the tax. The estate tax rate depends on the overall value of the estate. Usually, appraisers assess the fair market value of the estate's assets and interests to come up with the overall value of the estate.

Reprinted courtesy of HowStuffWorks.com from the article "How Inheritance Tax Works."

16. Economic Growth and Tax Relief Reconciliation Act of 2001

At the current time, assets of an individual may be given to beneficiaries during the lifetime up to $11,000 per individual per year. Thus, if both parents are still living, an amount of $22,000 could be given to each beneficiary each year. This amount may change over time, but this is a way to distribute assets prior to death, even over time. A unified estate tax credit and exclusion amount is set by the Economic Growth and Tax Relief Reconciliation Act, which repeals December 31, 2010. The gift tax exclusion was set at $1,000,000 in 2002. This meant that estates with assets falling under $1,000,000 were excluded from paying estate taxes. The chart below shows the change in assets through 2009. Following the repeal in 2010, the exclusion amount is expected to remain at $1,000,000 from then forward with estate taxes being reenacted. From 2001 through 2009, estates under the amount set for each year are excluded from estate taxes. An estate and tax attorney or a qualified certified public accountant will be able give advice about changes.

Year of Death	Unified Estate Tax Credit/Exclusion
2002-2003	$1,000,000
2004-2005	$1,500,000
2006-2008	$2,000,000
2009	$3,500,000
2010	And thereafter, $1,000,000 – unknown as law repeals end of year 2010

Retrieved August 2009, from http://www.gpo.gov/fdsys/pkg/PLAW-107publ16/pdf/PLAW-107publ16.pdfIRS Pub 559, Survivors, Executors & Administrators, 800-829-3676 http://www.irs.gov/publications/p559/index.html

Legal/Financial Concerns

1. Cancel any existing credit cards

2. Check the banks for safety deposit boxes or for $1000 life insurance benefit; banks have offered this benefit over the past few years; your loved one may have signed up for this benefit. Contents of safety deposit boxes become part of the estate.

3. If the deceased's spouse is still living, check that joint custody is in force on all accounts. If your loved one's beneficiaries are the children, ensure that the Durable Power of Attorney sets a joint representative on each account <u>prior to the death</u> of the loved one.

4. Before death, check beneficiary listings on all accounts (bank, life insurance, IRAs, trust accounts, investment accounts) to ensure that beneficiary listings are correct or if any beneficiaries need to be added. If the two spouses are the only beneficiaries, problems may arise when settling the final estate.

Co-beneficiary versus primary beneficiary: The executor/executrix of the estate may be listed as the next beneficiary in line once both spouses die. It is the responsibility of the executor/executrix to ensure all property/monies are divided equally among any named beneficiaries (or as specified by the will). The court designates this person as the Personal Representative (PR) of the estate. Thus, the PR is answerable to the court.

Bank Accounts:

It is not necessary to close the bank accounts immediately. The bank does desire to have a death certificate presented to it, however, the PR can be a cosigner on the accounts prior to death. I was a cosigner on Mom and Dad's accounts for four years prior to Dad's death. I was taking care of their financial affairs for the entire time. I kept the personal account open to pay bills and house expenses until the house sold. I also opened up a trust account for the estate to deposit all dividends, tax returns, life insurance returns, etc. into. Disbursements to the beneficiaries were made from the trust account. Once the main account was closed, any remaining monies were also transferred to the trust account. Note that deposits of estate monies could be deposited into an interest bearing money market account until all the distributions are ready to be made.

The trust account should remain open with some funds available until all assets are cleared and all tax returns are final. This process may take two-three years.

Social Security Check:

The current month's check will need to be refunded to the Social Security Administration (SSA), even if the person dies on the last day of the month. This process was automated by the time Dad died, and the SSA requested the transfer directly from the bank. When Mom died, I actually had to send them a check. The procedure in place will be explained to you when you contact them to report the death.

Investments:

If specific instructions have not been left in the wills about trusts or continuation of the estate funds, all investment houses will require a copy of the death certificate and the PR appointment letter. A letter should accompany the death certificate (see example below) specifying your instructions. For example, the letter should state that the deceased died on (list the date) and that you are the PR of the deceased. The letter should request that the stock be sold and distributed to the Estate (list the Estate Name). Request that any uncashed dividends also be paid to the estate. Request that the 1099 form for the sale be attributed to the estate Tax Identification Number (TIN). List the name and address that the estate check should be sent to (e.g., the PR). Set up an estate TIN with the Internal Revenue Service. Each investment copy will have specific forms that need to be filled out and they will send them to you. This may be a confusing process and sometimes it is difficult to get accurate information over the telephone. Repeated telephone calls should be made to follow-up on the process to ensure that all forms are received, that the assets are sold, and that the distribution check is sent. Note that income tax prior to death is filed under the person's social security number and that income tax after death is filed under the TIN. It is extremely important that asset changes be tracked separately following death.

Notification of Death Letter

<u>Date of letter</u>

Stock Name
Address
City, State Zip Code

RE: Name on account, Account # _____, SSN _____
    Address:
    City:

Dear Sir:

This letter is to inform your company of my father's death on <u>List Date</u>. My father held shares in at least two of your stock holdings, <u>Name of Stocks</u>.

I am enclosing a copy of my father's death certificate, as well as a copy of the probate document, showing that I have been designated his "Personal Representative." Please advise how I may liquidate these holdings. If these documents are sufficient, please use this documentation and this letter as authorization to liquidate my father's holdings, and forward the funds to the address below. Please advise of any other procedures required to perform this liquidation, if necessary. Specific instructions are:

1. Please transfer the shares to the **estate or trust** (give full legal name of estate or trust) and then liquidate them, so that I may disburse the proceedings to the heirs of the estate.
2. Please also reissue any uncashed dividends, if any exist.
3. Please issue any tax forms related to dividends or to this liquidation to the estate tax ID# (list tax ID #).

Please note that there are four children involved, so proceeds will be divided equally among the four. Any tax documentation should be addressed to the "<u>Estate or Trust Name</u>," in care of <u>Personal Representative Name</u>, Trustee.

Sincerely,

Personal Representative
Address:
City:
Telephone:

Caregiving Form 42
© Copyright 2010, Janice Louise Long

Disposal of Household Goods

Professional companies exist to perform estate sales of the household goods. Hopefully, your loved one has set aside a list of belongings and the person to whom each belonging is to belong. Some of the household goods may already have been designated. Another issue is that the understandings may be different among the family members. I had thought that I was to receive my grandmother's china, only to find out that Mom had already given both sets to my nieces. That was fine, but it took me a long time to find out what had happened to it. One of my brothers was to receive our grandfather's antique dresser, but he didn't want it. I had assumed some of these things would be automatic, but they weren't. I know what Mom and Dad had told me, but did not check with my brothers as to what their understandings were. We each set up a wish list, and for the most part, everything worked out well. The four of us got together twice to take our pick of household items. The two of us that remained in town packed up the house for donation, as none of us wished to have an estate sale. We donated any worthwhile goods to the local Battered Women's shelter.

Selling the Residence

When putting the household residence up for sale, the seller is required to fill out a Seller's Disclosure form. Most likely, not all aspects of the house condition and needed repairs will be known. Take the time to have the disclosure form reviewed by an attorney, even if the real estate representative is pushing to have this completed quickly.

Documents to Locate:

Any document that might affect the estate should be located, such as: letters of instruction, living trust, will, pre-arranged funeral plans and plot/niche deeds, Driver's License, SSN, Birth Certificate, Passport, stock certificates, bank accounts, safety deposit boxes, Veteran's Administration discharge paperwork, past year's income tax returns, insurance companies (auto, home, personal property). See also the document checklist at the beginning of Chapter 11.

Attorney:

If the family does not already have an attorney, find an attorney specializing in Tax and Estate Law to assist in handling the Personal Representative Court Order, Opening/Closing the estate, and any further estate business required. If property is involved, be sure to have the attorney review the Seller's Disclosure Report prior to turning it over to the realtor.

IRS:

The form to establish a Tax Identification Number may be printed from the IRS website, http://www.irs.gov. Fill out the form and telephone the IRS to obtain an estate TIN (equivalent to a social security number). The new TIN should be used on all estate transactions, rather than the original SSN.

Tax returns:

The final tax return for the deceased person is filed for the year up to the date of death in the year of the death. Any tax returns filed for income or disbursements to the estate are filed under the TIN from the date of death forward.

Appendix I – Keeping Mom and Dad From Going Down

Check for Safety:
A Home Prevention Fall Checklist For Older Adults

Check for Safety: A Home Fall Prevention Checklist for Older Adults

FALLS AT HOME

Each year, thousands of older Americans fall at home. Many of them are seriously injured, and some are disabled. In 2002, more than 12,800 people over age 65 died and 1.6 million were treated in emergency departments because of falls.

Falls are often due to hazards that are easy to overlook but easy to fix. This checklist will help you find and fix those hazards in your home.

The checklist asks about hazards found in each room of your home. For each hazard, the checklist tells you how to fix the problem. At the end of the checklist, you'll find other tips for preventing falls.

FLOORS: Look at the floor in each room.

Q: When you walk through a room, do you have to walk around furniture?

Ask someone to move the furniture so your path is clear.

Q: Do you have throw rugs on the floor?

Remove the rugs or use double-sided tape or a non-slip backing so the rugs won't slip.

Q: Are there papers, books, towels, shoes, magazines, boxes, blankets, or other objects on the floor?

Pick up things that are on the floor. Always keep objects off the floor.

Q: Do you have to walk over or around wires or cords (like lamp, telephone, or extension cords)?

Coil or tape cords and wires next to the wall so you can't trip over them. If needed, have an electrician put in another outlet.

STAIRS AND STEPS: Look at the stairs you use both inside and outside your home.

Q: Are there papers, shoes, books, or other objects on the stairs?

Pick up things on the stairs. Always keep objects off stairs.

Q: Are some steps broken or uneven?

Fix loose or uneven steps.

Q: Are you missing a light over the stairway?

Have an electrician put in an overhead light at the top and bottom of the stairs.

Q: Do you have only one light switch for your stairs (only at the top or at the bottom of the stairs)?

Have an electrician put in a light switch at the top and bottom of the stairs. You can get light switches that glow.

Q: Has the stairway light bulb burned out?

Have a friend or family member change the light bulb.

Q: Is the carpet on the steps loose or torn?

Make sure the carpet is firmly attached to every step, or remove the carpet and attach non-slip rubber treads to the stairs.

Q: Are the handrails loose or broken? Is there a handrail on only one side of the stairs?

Fix loose handrails or put in new ones. Make sure handrails are on both sides of the stairs and are as long as the stairs.

KITCHEN: Look at your kitchen and eating area.

Q: Are the things you use often on high shelves?

Move items in your cabinets. Keep things you use often on the lower shelves (about waist level).

Q: Is your step stool unsteady?

If you must use a step stool, get one with a bar to hold on to. Never use a chair as a step stool.

BATHROOMS: Look at all your bathrooms.

Q: Is the tub or shower floor slippery?

Put a non-slip rubber mat or self-stick strips on the floor of the tub or shower.

Q: Do you need some support when you get in and out of the tub or up from the toilet?

Have a carpenter put grab bars inside the tub and next to the toilet.

BEDROOMS: Look at all your bedrooms.

Q: Is the light near the bed hard to reach?

Place a lamp close to the bed where it's easy to reach.

Q: Is the path from your bed to the bathroom dark?

Put in a night-light so you can see where you're walking. Some night-lights go on by themselves after dark.

Other Things You Can Do to Prevent Falls

1. Exercise regularly. Exercise makes you stronger and improves your balance and coordination.
2. Have your doctor or pharmacist look at all the medicines you take, even over-the-counter medicines. Some medicines can make you sleepy or dizzy.
3. Have your vision checked at least once a year by an eye doctor. Poor vision can increase your risk of falling.
4. Get up slowly after you sit or lie down.
5. Wear shoes both inside and outside the house. Avoid going barefoot or wearing slippers.
6. Improve the lighting in your home. Put in brighter light bulbs. Florescent bulbs are bright and cost less to use.
7. It's safest to have uniform lighting in a room. Add lighting to dark areas. Hang lightweight curtains or shades to reduce glare.
8. Paint a contrasting color on the top edge of all steps so you can see the stairs better. For example, use a light color paint on dark wood.

Other Safety Tips

Keep emergency numbers in large print near each phone.

Put a phone near the floor in case you fall and can't get up.

Think about wearing an alarm device that will bring help in case you fall and can't get up.

Retrieved August 2009, from

http://www.cdc.gov/ncipc/pub-res/toolkit/CheckListForSafety.htm

Appendix II

Diagnosing Alzheimer's:
The Mini Mental State Examination

Marshal Folstein developed the MMSE in 1975, to assist in diagnosing mental status in elderly patients. The MMSE is a short screening test for cognitive impairment. The test takes approximately 5-10 minutes to administer and covers a variety of intellectual functions, such as reading, writing, recall, and comprehension. An achievement score takes very little time to obtain and allows a neurologist or primary care physician to obtain a sense of cognitive function. The Mini Mental State Examination is shown below for informational purposes only.

Proper diagnosis must be made by a licensed practitioner educated to do so, preferably a neurologist. When the MMSE is administered, it is important that Folstein's instructions are followed in order that mutual comparisons are possible. The eleven question boxes measure different cognitive functions and a specific sub-division within a question can measure more than one cognitive function. Four questions from the actual Mini-Mental State Examination are shown below:

MMSE Sample Items

Orientation to Time
"What is the date?"

Registration
"Listen carefully. I am going to say three words. You say them back after I stop.
Ready? Here they are…
APPLE (pause), PENNY (pause), TABLE (pause). Now repeat those words back to me."
[Repeat up to 5 times, but score only the first trial.]

Naming
"What is this?" [Point to a pencil or pen.]

Reading
"Please read this and do what it says." [Show examinee the words on the stimulus form.]
CLOSE YOUR EYES

Interpretation

A normal MMSE score for adults is considered to be at least 24 and may be as high as 29 or 30. Scoring can decrease after the age of 80. <u>The results are considered in conjunction with education, age, and clinical indications of the patient.</u> A score of less than 24 (of the 30 total) indicates some type of global cognitive impairment. Thus, it is imperative for a licensed practitioner to administer the test and determine the diagnosis.

Scoring

Normal	24-30
Abnormal	24
Mild cognitive function	18-23
Severe cognitive function	0-17

Appendix III

The Five Wishes – The Best Healthcare Power of Attorney

The *Five Wishes* document helps you express how you want to be treated if you are seriously ill and unable to speak for yourself. It is unique among all other living will and health agent forms because it looks at all of a person's needs: medical, personal, emotional and spiritual. *Five Wishes* also encourages discussing your wishes with your family and physician. *Five Wishes* lets your family and doctors know:

1. **Which person you want to make health care decisions for you when you can't make them.** (Note: Be sure the person designated is one that you trust to carry out your wishes)

2. **The kind of medical treatment you want or don't want.**

3. **How comfortable you want to be.**

4. **How you want people to treat you.**

5. **What you want your loved ones to know.**

Five Wishes is changing the way America talks about and plans for care at the end of life. More than twelve million copies of the document are circulating throughout the nation. In addition, more than 15,000 organizations are distributing this revolutionary document, including churches, synagogues, hospices, hospitals, doctor and law offices, and social service agencies. Many employers are providing *Five Wishes* to their employees to help them plan for themselves and have those delicate discussions with their aging parents.

The document speaks to people in their own language, not in "doctor speak" or "lawyer talk." It can be used in the living room instead of the emergency room. And it helps families talk with their physician about a difficult subject.

There are a few states (Alabama, Indiana, Kansas, New Hampshire, Ohio, Oregon, and Texas) in which *Five Wishes* does not yet meet the legal requirements. These states either require a specific state form or that the person completing an advance directive be read a mandatory notice or "warning." Residents of these states can still use *Five Wishes* to put their wishes in writing and communicate their wishes with their family and physician. Most health care professionals understand they have a duty to listen to the wishes of their patients no matter how they are expressed.

Five Wishes was introduced and originally distributed with support from a generous grant by The Robert Wood Johnson Foundation, the nation's largest philanthropy devoted exclusively to health and health care.

The following states (including the District of Columbia) accept the Five Wishes as a legal document: Alaska, Arizona, Arkansas, California, Colorado, Connecticut, Delaware, District of Columbia, Florida, Georgia, Hawaii, Idaho, Illinois, Iowa, Kentucky, Louisiana, Maine, Maryland, Massachusetts, Michigan, Minnesota, Mississippi, Missouri, Montana, Nebraska, Nevada, New Jersey, New Mexico, New York, North Carolina, North Dakota, Oklahoma, Pennsylvania, Rhode Island, South Carolina, South Dakota, Tennessee, Utah, Vermont, Virginia, Washington, West Virginia, Wisconsin, and Wyoming.

Aging with Dignity

PO Box 1661
Tallahassee, FL 32302-1661
Phone: (850) 681-2010

Orders with payment by credit card are welcome online, by phone or by mail. Checks may be made payable to *Aging with Dignity*, and should be mailed along with the order form.

If you have questions, or would like to place your order by phone, call toll-free 1-888-5WISHES (1-888-594-7437).

Five Wishes:

Individual copies are $5 each. Bulk orders of 25 or more copies are only $1 each. (Shipping and handling charges apply to bulk orders).
Retrieved July 2009, from http://www.agingwithdignity.org/5wishes.html

The document below is a watermarked, copyrighted copy of the Five Wishes, used with permission from the Aging With Dignity organization. This document is not to be copied and used by readers. Please use the order information above to obtain an original document.

FIVE
WISHES®

MY WISH FOR:

The Person I Want to Make Care Decisions for Me When I Can't

The Kind of Medical Treatment I Want or Don't Want

How Comfortable I Want to Be

How I Want People to Treat Me

What I Want My Loved Ones to Know

print your name

birthdate

Five Wishes

*T**here are many things in life that are out of our hands. This
Five Wishes booklet gives you a way to control something very
important—how you are treated if you get seriously ill. It is an easy-to-
complete form that lets you say exactly what you want. Once it is filled out
and properly signed it is valid under the laws of most states.*

What Is Five Wishes?

Five Wishes is the first living will that talks about your personal, emotional and spiritual needs as well as your medical wishes. It lets you choose the person you want to make health care decisions for you if you are not able to make them for yourself. Five Wishes lets you say exactly how you wish to be treated if you get seriously ill. It was written with the help of The American Bar Association's Commission on Law and Aging, and the nation's leading experts in end-of-life care. It's also easy to use. All you have to do is check a box, circle a direction, or write a few sentences.

How Five Wishes Can Help You And Your Family

- It lets you talk with your family, friends and doctor about how you want to be treated if you become seriously ill.

- Your family members will not have to guess what you want. It protects them if you become seriously ill, because they won't have to make hard choices without knowing your wishes.

- You can know what your mom, dad, spouse, or friend wants through a Five Wishes living will. You can be there for them when they need you most. You will understand what they really want.

How Five Wishes Began

For 12 years, a man named Jim Towey worked closely with Mother Teresa, and, for one year, he lived in a hospice she ran in Washington, DC. Inspired by this first-hand experience, Mr. Towey sought a way for patients and their families to plan ahead and to cope with serious illness. The result is Five Wishes and the response to it has been overwhelming. It has been featured on CNN and NBC's Today Show and in the pages of *Time* and *Money* magazines. Newspapers have called Five Wishes the first "living will with a heart."

Who Should Use Five Wishes

Five Wishes is for anyone 18 or older — married, single, parents, adult children, and friends. Over eight million Americans of all ages have already used it. Because it works so well, lawyers, doctors, hospitals and hospices, faith communities, employers, and retiree groups are handing out this document.

Five Wishes States

If you live in the **District of Columbia** or one of the **40 states** listed below, you can use Five Wishes and have the peace of mind to know that it substantially meets your state's requirements under the law:

Alaska	Idaho	Missouri	Rhode Island
Arizona	Illinois	Montana	South Carolina
Arkansas	Iowa	Nebraska	South Dakota
California	Louisiana	New Jersey	Tennessee
Colorado	Maine	New Mexico	Vermont
Connecticut	Maryland	New York	Virginia
Delaware	Massachusetts	North Carolina	Washington
Florida	Michigan	North Dakota	West Virginia
Georgia	Minnesota	Oklahoma	Wisconsin
Hawaii	Mississippi	Pennsylvania	Wyoming

If your state is not one of the 40 states listed here, Five Wishes does not meet the technical requirements in the statutes of your state. So some doctors in your state may be reluctant to honor Five Wishes. However, many people from states not on this list do complete Five Wishes along with their state's legal form. They find that Five Wishes helps them express all that they want and provides a helpful guide to family members, friends, care givers and doctors. Most doctors and health care professionals know they need to listen to your wishes no matter how you express them.

How Do I Change To Five Wishes?

You may already have a living will or a durable power of attorney for health care. If you want to use Five Wishes instead, all you need to do is fill out and sign a new Five Wishes as directed. As soon as you sign it, it takes away any advance directive you had before. To make sure the right form is used, please do the following:

- Destroy all copies of your old living will or durable power of attorney for health care. Or you can write "revoked" in large letters across the copy you have. Tell your lawyer if he or she helped prepare those old forms for you. *AND*

- Tell your Health Care Agent, family members, and doctor that you have filled out the new Five Wishes. Make sure they know about your new wishes.

WISH 1

The Person I Want To Make Health Care Decisions For Me When I Can't Make Them For Myself.

If I am no longer able to make my own health care decisions, this form names the person I choose to make these choices for me. This person will be my Health Care Agent (or other term that may be used in my state, such as proxy, representative, or surrogate). This person will make my health care choices if both of these things happen:

- *My attending or treating doctor finds I am no longer able to make health care choices, AND*
- *Another health care professional agrees that this is true.*

If my state has a different way of finding that I am not able to make health care choices, then my state's way should be followed.

The Person I Choose As My Health Care Agent Is:

First Choice Name _____

Phone _____

Address _____

City/State/Zip _____

If this person is not able or willing to make these choices for me, *OR* is divorced or legally separated from me, *OR* this person has died, then these people are my next choices:

Second Choice Name _____

Third Choice Name _____

Address _____

Address _____

City/State/Zip _____

City/State/Zip _____

Phone _____

Phone _____

Picking The Right Person To Be Your Health Care Agent

Choose someone who knows you very well, cares about you, and who can make difficult decisions. A spouse or family member may not be the best choice because they are too emotionally involved. Sometimes they **are** the best choice. You know best. Choose someone who is able to stand up for you so that your wishes are followed. Also, choose someone who is likely to be nearby so that they can help when you need them. Whether you choose a spouse, family member, or friend as your Health Care Agent, make sure you talk about these wishes and be sure that this person agrees to respect and follow your wishes. Your Health Care Agent should be **at least 18 years or older** (in Colorado, 21 years or older) and should **not** be:

- Your health care provider, including the owner or operator of a health or residential or community care facility serving you.
- An employee or spouse of an employee of your health care provider.
- Serving as an agent or proxy for 10 or more people unless he or she is your spouse or close relative.

I understand that my Health Care Agent can make health care decisions for me. I want my Agent to be able to do the following: **(Please cross out anything you don't want your Agent to do that is listed below.)**

- Make choices for me about my medical care or services, like tests, medicine, or surgery. This care or service could be to find out what my health problem is, or how to treat it. It can also include care to keep me alive. If the treatment or care has already started, my Health Care Agent can keep it going or have it stopped.

- Interpret any instructions I have given in this form or given in other discussions, according to my Health Care Agent's understanding of my wishes and values.

- Consent to admission to an assisted living facility, hospital, hospice, or nursing home for me. My Health Care Agent can hire any kind of health care worker I may need to help me or take care of me. My Agent may also fire a health care worker, if needed.

- Make the decision to request, take away or not give medical treatments, including artificially-provided food and water, and any other treatments to keep me alive.

- See and approve release of my medical records and personal files. If I need to sign my name to get any of these files, my Health Care Agent can sign it for me.

- Move me to another state to get the care I need or to carry out my wishes.

- Authorize or refuse to authorize any medication or procedure needed to help with pain.

- Take any legal action needed to carry out my wishes.

- Donate useable organs or tissues of mine as allowed by law.

- Apply for Medicare, Medicaid, or other programs or insurance benefits for me. My Health Care Agent can see my personal files, like bank records, to find out what is needed to fill out these forms.

- Listed below are any changes, additions, or limitations on my Health Care Agent's powers.

_____
_____
_____
_____
_____
_____

If I Change My Mind About Having A Health Care Agent, I Will

- Destroy all copies of this part of the Five Wishes form. *OR*

- Tell someone, such as my doctor or family, that I want to cancel or change my Health Care Agent. *OR*

- Write the word "Revoked" in large letters across the name of each agent whose authority I want to cancel. Sign my name on that page.

WISH 2

My Wish For The Kind Of Medical Treatment I Want Or Don't Want.

I believe that my life is precious and I deserve to be treated with dignity. When the time comes that I am very sick and am not able to speak for myself, I want the following wishes, and any other directions I have given to my Health Care Agent, to be respected and followed.

What You Should Keep In Mind As My Caregiver

- I do not want to be in pain. I want my doctor to give me enough medicine to relieve my pain, even if that means that I will be drowsy or sleep more than I would otherwise.

- I do not want anything done or omitted by my doctors or nurses with the intention of taking my life.

- I want to be offered food and fluids by mouth, and kept clean and warm.

What "Life-Support Treatment" Means To Me

Life-support treatment means any medical procedure, device or medication to keep me alive. Life-support treatment includes: medical devices put in me to help me breathe; food and water supplied by medical device (tube feeding); cardiopulmonary resuscitation (CPR); major surgery; blood transfusions; dialysis; antibiotics; and anything else meant to keep me alive. If I wish to limit the meaning of life-support treatment because of my religious or personal beliefs, I write this limitation in the space below. I do this to make very clear what I want and under what conditions.

_____

_____

_____

_____

_____

In Case Of An Emergency

If you have a medical emergency and ambulance personnel arrive, they may look to see if you have a **Do Not Resuscitate** form or bracelet. Many states require a person to have a **Do Not Resuscitate** form filled out and signed by a doctor. This form lets ambulance personnel know that you don't want them to use life-support treatment when you are dying. Please check with your doctor to see if you need to have a **Do Not Resuscitate** form filled out.

Here is the kind of medical treatment that I want or don't want in the four situations listed below. I want my Health Care Agent, my family, my doctors and other health care providers, my friends and all others to know these directions.

Close to death:

If my doctor and another health care professional both decide that I am likely to die within a short period of time, and life-support treatment would only delay the moment of my death (Choose *one* of the following):

- ❏ I want to have life-support treatment.
- ❏ I do not want life-support treatment. If it has been started, I want it stopped.
- ❏ I want to have life-support treatment if my doctor believes it could help. But I want my doctor to stop giving me life-support treatment if it is not helping my health condition or symptoms.

In A Coma And Not Expected To Wake Up Or Recover:

If my doctor and another health care professional both decide that I am in a coma from which I am not expected to wake up or recover, and I have brain damage, and life-support treatment would only delay the moment of my death (Choose *one* of the following):

- ❏ I want to have life-support treatment.
- ❏ I do not want life-support treatment. If it has been started, I want it stopped.
- ❏ I want to have life-support treatment if my doctor believes it could help. But I want my doctor to stop giving me life-support treatment if it is not helping my health condition or symptoms.

Permanent And Severe Brain Damage And Not Expected To Recover:

If my doctor and another health care professional both decide that I have permanent and severe brain damage, (for example, I can open my eyes, but I can not speak or understand) and I am not expected to get better, and life-support treatment would only delay the moment of my death (Choose *one* of the following):

- ❏ I want to have life-support treatment.
- ❏ I do not want life-support treatment. If it has been started, I want it stopped.
- ❏ I want to have life-support treatment if my doctor believes it could help. But I want my doctor to stop giving me life-support treatment if it is not helping my health condition or symptoms.

In Another Condition Under Which I Do Not Wish To Be Kept Alive:

If there is another condition under which I do not wish to have life-support treatment, I describe it below. In this condition, I believe that the costs and burdens of life-support treatment are too much and not worth the benefits to me. Therefore, in this condition, I do not want life-support treatment. (For example, you may write "end-stage condition." That means that your health has gotten worse. You are not able to take care of yourself in any way, mentally or physically. Life-support treatment will not help you recover. Please leave the space blank if you have no other condition to describe.)

_____

_____

_____

_____

_____

The next three wishes deal with my personal, spiritual and emotional wishes. They are important to me. I want to be treated with dignity near the end of my life, so I would like people to do the things written in Wishes 3, 4, and 5 when they can be done. I understand that my family, my doctors and other health care providers, my friends, and others may not be able to do these things or are not required by law to do these things. I do not expect the following wishes to place new or added legal duties on my doctors or other health care providers. I also do not expect these wishes to excuse my doctor or other health care providers from giving me the proper care asked for by law.

WISH 3

My Wish For How Comfortable I Want To Be.

(Please cross out anything that you don't agree with.)

- I do not want to be in pain. I want my doctor to give me enough medicine to relieve my pain, even if that means I will be drowsy or sleep more than I would otherwise.

- If I show signs of depression, nausea, shortness of breath, or hallucinations, I want my care givers to do whatever they can to help me.

- I wish to have a cool moist cloth put on my head if I have a fever.

- I want my lips and mouth kept moist to stop dryness.

- I wish to have warm baths often. I wish to be kept fresh and clean at all times.

- I wish to be massaged with warm oils as often as I can be.

- I wish to have my favorite music played when possible until my time of death.

- I wish to have personal care like shaving, nail clipping, hair brushing, and teeth brushing, as long as they do not cause me pain or discomfort.

- I wish to have religious readings and well-loved poems read aloud when I am near death.

- I wish to know about options for hospice care to provide medical, emotional and spiritual care for me and my loved ones.

WISH 4

My Wish For How I Want People To Treat Me.

(Please cross out anything that you don't agree with.)

- I wish to have people with me when possible. I want someone to be with me when it seems that death may come at any time.

- I wish to have my hand held and to be talked to when possible, even if I don't seem to respond to the voice or touch of others.

- I wish to have others by my side praying for me when possible.

- I wish to have the members of my faith community told that I am sick and asked to pray for me and visit me.

- I wish to be cared for with kindness and cheerfulness, and not sadness.

- I wish to have pictures of my loved ones in my room, near my bed.

- If I am not able to control my bowel or bladder functions, I wish for my clothes and bed linens to be kept clean, and for them to be changed as soon as they can be if they have been soiled.

- I want to die in my home, if that can be done.

WISH 5
My Wish For What I Want My Loved Ones To Know.
(Please cross out anything that you don't agree with.)

- I wish to have my family and friends know that I love them.

- I wish to be forgiven for the times I have hurt my family, friends, and others.

- I wish to have my family, friends and others know that I forgive them for when they may have hurt me in my life.

- I wish for my family and friends to know that I do not fear death itself. I think it is not the end, but a new beginning for me.

- I wish for all of my family members to make peace with each other before my death, if they can.

- I wish for my family and friends to think about what I was like before I became seriously ill. I want them to remember me in this way after my death.

- I wish for my family and friends and caregivers to respect my wishes even if they don't agree with them.

- I wish for my family and friends to look at my dying as a time of personal growth for everyone, including me. This will help me live a meaningful life in my final days.

- I wish for my family and friends to get counseling if they have trouble with my death. I want memories of my life to give them joy and not sorrow.

- After my death, I would like my body to be (circle one): buried   or   cremated.

- My body or remains should be put in the following location_____.

- The following person knows my funeral wishes: _____.

If anyone asks how I want to be remembered, please say the following about me:

_____

_____

_____

If there is to be a memorial service for me, I wish for this service to include the following
(list music, songs, readings or other specific requests that you have):

_____

_____

_____

(Please use the space below for any other wishes. For example, you may want to donate any or all parts of your body when you die. Please attach a separate sheet of paper if you need more space.)

_____

_____

_____

Signing The Five Wishes Form

Please make sure you sign your Five Wishes form in the presence of the two witnesses.

I, _____, ask that my family, my doctors, and other health care providers, my friends, and all others, follow my wishes as communicated by my Health Care Agent (if I have one and he or she is available), or as otherwise expressed in this form. This form becomes valid when I am unable to make decisions or speak for myself. If any part of this form cannot be legally followed, I ask that all other parts of this form be followed. I also revoke any health care advance directives I have made before.

Signature:_____

Address:_____

Phone:_____ Date:_____

Witness Statement · (2 witnesses needed):

I, the witness, declare that the person who signed or acknowledged this form (hereafter "person") is personally known to me, that he/she signed or acknowledged this [Health Care Agent and/or Living Will form(s)] in my presence, and that he/she appears to be of sound mind and under no duress, fraud, or undue influence.

I also declare that I am over 18 years of age and am NOT:

- The individual appointed as (agent/proxy/ surrogate/patient advocate/representative) by this document or his/her successor,
- The person's health care provider, including owner or operator of a health, long-term care, or other residential or community care facility serving the person,
- An employee of the person's health care provider,

- Financially responsible for the person's health care,
- An employee of a life or health insurance provider for the person,
- Related to the person by blood, marriage, or adoption, and,
- To the best of my knowledge, a creditor of the person or entitled to any part of his/her estate under a will or codicil, by operation of law.

(Some states may have fewer rules about who may be a witness. Unless you know your state's rules, please follow the above.)

_____
Signature of Witness #1

_____
Printed Name of Witness

_____
Address

_____
Phone

_____
Signature of Witness #2

_____
Printed Name of Witness

_____
Address

_____
Phone

Notarization · Only required for residents of Missouri, North Carolina, South Carolina and West Virginia

If you live in Missouri, only your signature should be notarized.

- If you live in North Carolina, South Carolina or West Virginia, you should have your signature, and the signatures of your witnesses, notarized.

STATE OF_____ COUNTY OF_____

On this _____ day of _____, 20_____, the said _____,
_____, and _____, known to me (or satisfactorily proven) to be the person named in the foregoing instrument and witnesses, respectively, personally appeared before me, a Notary Public, within and for the State and County aforesaid, and acknowledged that they freely and voluntarily executed the same for the purposes stated therein.

My Commission Expires: _____   _____
                                              Notary Public

What To Do After You Complete Five Wishes

- Make sure you sign and witness the form just the way it says in the directions. Then your Five Wishes will be legal and valid.

- Talk about your wishes with your health care agent, family members and others who care about you. Give them copies of your completed Five Wishes.

- Keep the original copy you signed in a special place in your home. Do NOT put it in a safe deposit box. Keep it nearby so that someone can find it when you need it.

- Fill out the wallet card below. Carry it with you. That way people will know where you keep your Five Wishes.

- Talk to your doctor during your next office visit. Give your doctor a copy of your Five Wishes. Make sure it is put in your medical record. Be sure your doctor understands your wishes and is willing to follow them. Ask him or her to tell other doctors who treat you to honor them.

- If you are admitted to a hospital or nursing home, take a copy of your Five Wishes with you. Ask that it be put in your medical record.

- I have given the following people copies of my completed Five Wishes:

  _____

  _____

  _____

Residents of WISCONSIN must attach the WISCONSIN notice statement to Five Wishes.
More information and the notice statement are available at www.agingwithdignity.org or 1-888-594-7437.

Residents of Institutions In CALIFORNIA, CONNECTICUT, DELAWARE, GEORGIA, NEW YORK, NORTH DAKOTA, SOUTH CAROLINA, and VERMONT Must Follow Special Witnessing Rules.

If you live in certain institutions (a nursing home, other licensed long term care facility, a home for the mentally retarded or developmentally disabled, or a mental health institution) in one of the states listed above, you may have to follow special "witnessing requirements" for your Five Wishes to be valid. For further information, please contact a social worker or patient advocate at your institution.

Five Wishes is meant to help you plan for the future. It is not meant to give you legal advice. It does not try to answer all questions about anything that could come up. Every person is different, and every situation is different. Laws change from time to time. If you have a specific question or problem, talk to a medical or legal professional for advice.

Five Wishes Wallet Card

Important Notice to Medical Personnel:
I have a Five Wishes Advance Directive.

_____
Signature

Please consult this document and/or my Health Care Agent in an emergency. My Agent is:

_____
Name
_____
Address   City/State/Zip
_____
Phone

My primary care physician is:

_____
Name
_____
Address   City/State/Zip
_____
Phone

My document is located at:

_____
_____
_____

Cut Out Card, Fold and Laminate for Safekeeping

Here's What People Are Saying About Five Wishes:

"It will be a year since my mother passed on. We knew what she wanted because she had the Five Wishes living will. When it came down to the end, my brother and I had no questions on what we needed to do. We had peace of mind."

Cheryl K.
Longwood, Florida

"I must say I love your Five Wishes. It's clear, easy to understand, and doesn't dwell on the concrete issues of medical care, but on the issues of real importance—human care. I used it for myself and my husband."

Susan W.
Flagstaff, Arizona

"I don't want my children to have to make the decisions I am having to make for my mother. I never knew that there were so many medical options to be considered. Thank you for such a sensitive and caring form. I can simply fill it out and have it on file for my children."

Diana W.
Hanover, Illinois

To Order:

Call 1-888-5-WISHES to purchase more copies of Five Wishes, the Five Wishes Video, or Next Steps guides. Ask about the "Family Package" that includes 10 Five Wishes, 2 Next Steps guides and 1 video at a savings of more than 50%. For more information visit Aging with Dignity's web site, or call for details.

1-888-5-WISHES (1-888-594-7437)

Aging with Dignity
P.O. Box 1661
Tallahassee, Florida 32302-1661
www.agingwithdignity.org
1-888-594-7437

Appendix IV

Aaahhh – Comforting Oil Treatment Recipes and Their Uses

Oil Recipes and Uses

Essential oils have been used by herbalists worldwide for centuries. Essential oils were used in early Egypt and have been recorded in Egyptian hieroglyphics. The Bible refers to frankincense, myrrh, rosemary, hyssop, and spikenard as healing or anointing oils.

Our primary caregiver, Arizona, was well-versed in the use of essential oils and blends of essential oils for healing purposes. She purchased her oils and oil blends through Young Living® Essential Oils (http://www.youngliving.us/). Her recipes for healing purposes were gleaned from the book "Reference Guide for Essential Oils" compiled by Connie and Alan Higley. The Higleys reference Young Living Essential Oils in this amazing reference guide. (See footnote at bottom of this Appendix.)

Included in the "Reference Guide for Essential Oils" is information about the science of oils, their use, blends of oil, how to make personal care products, massage oils, supplements and vitamins, and a personal guide to health related topics.

The oils that Arizona uses are picked based upon the need of the patient. For my Mom, she used a breathing recipe to help my Mom utilize her oxygen better. She used five oil recipes for my Dad's Alzheimer's disease, one oil recipe for his bruises, and one recipe for his circulatory system. The circulatory oil recipe kept my Dad walking, even when ultrasound testing showed no arterial blood flow to his lower leg. These recipes are shown below. Particular techniques for more extensive use of essential oils are available from the Reference Guide and the Young Living website.

Any natural oil may be used to blend the recipes, like fractionated coconut oil, grape seed oil, wheat germ oil, sweet almond oil, olive oil, or vitamin E oil. Oil mixing blends are also available from Young Living Essential Oils. In a six ounce bottle, use about 6-10 drops of each essential oil, with the remaining volume of the bottle filled with the mixing oil. Add a small amount of the mixing oil into the bottle, then the essential oils, filling the remaining volume with the mixing oil.

Note: Arizona generally used a total of 20 drops of essential oils per 6 ounce vial and divided the essential oils equally into the twenty drops. The exception to this is the circulatory blend shown below.

Awaken the Mind, Spirit

10 drops Awaken™ essential oil blend

10 drops Myrrh

Olive oil

Awaken the Past

20 drops Cypress essential oil

Awareness: Greater Awareness of One's Potential

7 drops Believe™ essential oil blend

7 drops Into the Future™ essential oil blend

7 drops White Angelica™ essential oil blend

Olive oil

Awareness: Increases Sensory System

7 drops Awaken™ essential oil blend

7 drops Birch essential oil

7 drops Wintergreen essential oil

Olive oil

Awareness: Opens Sensory System

7 drops Birch essential oil

7 drops Peppermint essential oil

7 drops Wintergreen essential oil

Olive oil

The above five recipes may be massaged onto the forehead, the right and left temples, the middle of the back of the neck, and the crown of the head.

Breathing (Oxygen)

7 drops Cedarwood essential oil

7 drops Frankincense essential oil

7 drops Sandalwood essential oil

Olive oil

This recipe should be massaged onto the upper chest (front) area, where the lungs are located.

Bruises

2 drops White Angelica™ essential oil

2 drops Fennel essential oil

2 drops Geranium essential oil

2 drops Helichrysum essential oil

2 drops Hyssop essential oil

2 drops Lavender essential oil

2 drops Melrose™ essential oil blend

2 drops PanAway® essential oil blend

2 drops Thieves®[1] essential oil blend

Olive oil

Circulation

10 drops Geranium essential oil

10 drops Cypress essential oil

10 drops Rosemary essential oil

10 drops Marjarom essential oil

Olive oil

This mixture was rubbed on Dad's arms and legs to improve the circulation after each shower. If his legs were hurting, the mixture was massaged onto his legs.

---

1   All trademarks and registered trademarks are the property of Young Living Essential Oils, LC, Lehi, UT, and are used by permission. Young Living is not responsible for and is not the author of this work.

Appendix V

Food for the Soul

The recipes included in this chapter are personal recipes either gathered over time or recipes I have altered. I hope you enjoy them. J. L. Long

Balsamic Chicken

4-6 chicken breasts, cut into small sections

1 small jar Paul Newman's Balsamic Vinegar dressing, regular or light

Italian Seasoning

Garlic salt

Place cut-up chicken breasts into baking dish. Pour entire bottle of Balsamic Vinegar dressing over chicken. Season with Italian Seasoning and garlic salt, making sure to sprinkle all pieces of chicken. Marinate 1 hour. Bake at 350°F for one hour.

Black Forest Ice Cream Cake

½ cup sliced or chopped almonds (optional)

24 bite-sized, muffin shaped brownies, halfed crosswise

1 21-ounce can cherry pie filling

3 Tablespoons almond-flavored liqueur, such as amaretto

1 pint premium vanilla ice cream, softened

½ cup (about 3 ounces) chopped semisweet chocolate (or chocolate chips)

1 pint premium chocolate ice cream, softened

Vegetable cooking spray

Toast almonds in a 350 degree oven for 6-8 minutes until golden. Coat a 9-inch loaf pan with cooking spray, then line with plastic wrap; spray again. Line the bottom and sides of the loaf pan with half of the brownies, with the cut sides facing the pan.

Remove ½ cup of the smooth cherry filling (not the fruit) from the can of filling and discard. Stir liqueur into cherries; set aside.

Soften the ice creams enough so that folding in the almonds and chocolate is just doable. This can be done by microwaving the cartons on high for about 20 seconds. Using a rubber spatula, fold almonds into vanilla ice cream, then spread it evenly over the bottom of the pan. Top with cherries.

Fold chopped chocolate into chocolate ice cream, then scrape it into the loaf pan, spreading it evenly over the cherries. Top with the remaining brownie halves. Cover with plastic wrap and freeze at least 3 hours (may be made up to one month ahead).

Turn out onto a cutting board and peel off plastic wrap. Slice and serve immediately.

Cheese Quesadillas

Slice cheddar cheese and place between two flour tortillas (or use one tortilla and fold in half). The quesadilla may be served with just cheese or with added ingredients, such as: ground beef, small chicken chunks, salsa, green chile, olives, or other favorites. The quesadilla may be heated in a frying pan over the stove or in a toaster oven.

Chile con Queso (cheese)

½ block Velveeta cheese
1 can diced green chilies, medium or hot
1 can cream of mushroom soup

Melt cheese carefully in microwave oven. When melted, add chilies and soup. Mix and heat until warm. Serve with tortilla chips. (May be put into small containers, frozen, and reheated)

Crescent Beef Bites

1 pound ground beef
2 Tablespoons dried onion flakes or diced onion
½ teaspoon garlic salt
½ cup minced fresh mushrooms (optional)
3 ounces cream cheese, softened
2 packages (8 in each package) crescent rolls
Preheat oven to 350° F.

Cook beef in a medium skillet over medium-high heat until browned and crumbly. Drain fat. Add onion and garlic salt. Add mushrooms and cream cheese. Mix well. Separate crescent rolls into 8 rectangles. Spoon beef mixture over each piece of dough. Roll to enclose filling. Press ends of rolls to seal. Place on ungreased baking sheets. Bake until golden brown, about 15 minutes. Cut each into four pieces. Serve immediately.

Fajitas

3 chicken breasts, cut into 2-3 inch strips

1 green bell pepper, sliced

1 red bell pepper, sliced

1 small yellow onion, cut into strips

Fajita seasoning (McCormick)

Italian Seasoning

Frank's Red Hot Sauce

Flour tortillas

Stir fry chicken until white on outside. Add bell pepper and onion. Add about ½ cup water. Sprinkle fajita seasoning and Italian seasoning over mixture (fairly heavy). Simmer for about twenty minutes. Add ¼ to ½ cup Frank's Red Hot Sauce (same taste as a buffalo wing hot sauce). Simmer for another ten minutes. Heat a flour tortilla in a toaster oven or in a saucepan. Fill tortilla with fajita mixture. Cut into small bites if necessary.

Greek Lemon Soup

1 Tablespoon Chicken base

4-5 large chicken breasts

4-5 lemons

½ cup rice

2 eggs

Fill large stock pot or soup pot with 6-8 cups of water. Add chicken breasts and cook until done. Remove chicken from pot and dice – easier when slightly cool. Add 1 Tablespoon chicken base (available from grocery store) and stir. Add rice and cook until rice is done. Add juice of 4-5 lemons (to taste). Let simmer 2-3 hours or overnight on a low heat setting (can be made in crockpot). Just before serving, take some soup stock from pot and cool. Add beaten eggs to cooled soup stock. Stir. Add mixture to soup pot. Serve immediately.

Ham Pinwheels

1 pkg Danish Ham

1 pkg cream cheese or spreadable cream cheese

1 tsp crushed garlic

Dash of worchestershire sauce

Mix garlic and worchestershire sauce into the cream cheese. Spread on slices of ham and roll up. Cut across roll to make bite size pieces. Chill.

Linguine with Chicken and Mushrooms

1 pound linguine

4 Tablespoons olive oil

1 pound chicken breasts, boned and cut in strips

1-1/2 pounds plum or any fresh tomatoes, peeled, seeded and chopped

6 ounces shitake or other exotic mushrooms sliced

¼ cup cilantro, chopped (optional)

¼ teaspoon cumin (optional)

Salt and pepper to taste

4 ounces grated Parmesan cheese

1 serrano chile seeded and minced (optional)

Heat oil in a sauté pan. Stir-fry chicken strips until translucent. Add scallions, mushrooms and Serrano chile. Saute by stirring 5 minutes longer. Add tomatoes, cumin, cilantro and salt and pepper. Partly covering the pan, simmer over a low heat for 15 to 20 minutes, stirring occasionally. Just before serving, cook linguine in a large pot of salted boiling water until al dente (cooked enough to be firm but not soft). Toss the cooked pasta with the chicken sauce and serve at once with Parmesan cheese. The sauce may be cooked ahead of time and reheated.

Meatloaf

3 Tablespoons butter

¾ cup each finely chopped onion and scallion

½ cup finely chopped carrots

¼ cup finely chopped celery

¼ cup chopped green bell pepper

¼ cup chopped red bell pepper

2 teaspoons minced garlic

3 eggs, well beaten

½ cup ketchup

½ cup half-and-half

1 teaspoon ground cumin

½ teaspoon ground nutmeg

¼ teaspoon cayenne pepper

Salt and pepper, to taste

2 pounds lean ground beef chuck

12 ounces ground sausage

(can substitute ground lean veal or ground pork)

¾ cup fine fresh bread crumbs, toasted

Melt the butter in a heavy skillet, adding onion, scallion, carrots, celery, bell peppers, and garlic. Cook, stirring often, until the moisture from the vegetables has evaporated (about 10 minutes). Set aside to cool; then cover and refrigerate until chilled, about 1 hour

In a mixing bowl, beat together the eggs, ketchup, half-and-half, cumin, nutmeg, cayenne, salt and pepper. Add the ground beef, sausage and bread crumbs. Then add the chilled vegetables and mix thoroughly with your hands, kneading for 5 minutes.

Preheat the oven to 350 degrees. Form the mixture into a loaf, approximately 12 x 5 x 2-1/2 inches, on a baking sheet. Bake until cooked through, about 1 hour. Let rest 20 minutes before slicing.

Pulled BBQ Pork

Pork shoulder roast or good pork chops (without bone)

1-1/2 cups Apple cider vinegar

1 cup Ketchup

2-3 Tablespoons Yellow mustard

2-3 Tablespoons crushed or chopped Garlic

½ chopped yellow onion

1-2 dashes Worchestershire sauce

Salt to taste

Boil pork until tender or cook in crock pot. Cook sauce in pan while pork is cooking. Amount of ingredients will depend on amount of meat cooked. Enough sauce should be made to cover meat. Shred meat – can cut strings of meat in half to make bite-size pieces. Cover meat with warm sauce and stir – serve immediately.

Sandwiches

Consider sandwiches with the crusts cut off with soft fillings, e.g., egg salad, ham salad, peanut butter (with honey, jam, or banana slices), pimento cheese.

Sloppy Joes

1 pound lean hamburger (90-10)

1 onion, diced

¾ to 1 cup ketchup

2 Tablespoons yellow mustard

2 Tablespoons cider vinegar

Brown hamburger and scramble into small bits. Drain fat and add diced onion. Add ketchup, mustard, and vinegar to desired taste (amounts are estimates). Simmer about 20 minutes. Serve on hamburger bun or plain on plate.

Tortilla Roll-ups

1 pkg flour tortillas

8 oz sour cream

8 oz cream cheese

1 can chopped green chilies (or fresh)

Optional: green onion, bell pepper, shredded cheddar cheese

Mix all ingredients. Spread on tortillas. Roll-up and chill. Cut into bite-size pieces.

Vegetable Chowder

3 slices diced bacon

1 diced onion

2 diced carrots

1 diced turnip

1 diced potato

¼ diced green pepper

2 stalks diced celery and leaves

2-1/2 cups boiling water

1 tsp salt

Dash pepper

2T minced parsley, basil, oregano

1 large can cut green beans

1 16 ounce can tomatoes

Prepare vegetables. Saute onion and bacon until soft and until onions are clear, but not brown. Add onion and bacon to boiling water in large pot, and add all vegetables except canned tomatoes. Bring to a boil. Cover and reduce heat to low, and cook until vegetables are fork tender (about 20 minutes). Add canned tomatoes and heat to boiling. Serve hot with crackers or toasted cheese sandwiches.

Variations:

1. At step 2, sauté ½ lb ground beef instead of bacon.

2. Omit bacon and use 3 chicken or beef bouillon cubes when adding tomatoes. Add 1 cup of sour cream or evaporated milk and 1 can clams if desired.

Appendix VI

Website Resources

The websites listed here are selected websites related to topics in this book, such as caregiving, seniors, aging, health issues of seniors, senior research, and informational sites. All websites have been tested and reviewed and by all means, do not include all websites available. The websites are organized alphabetically by topic. Topics include Advanced Directives, Adult Protective Services, Advocacy, Aging/Senior Citizens, Alzheimer's, Assisted Living, Cancer, Caregiving, Driving Safety, Dying, Facilities, Funeral, Grief Support, Health/Disease, Home Care, Hospice, Incontinence, Law, Medical Alert Systems, Mobility, Nursing Homes, Pain, Pastoral Care, Physicians, Prescription Drugs, Senior Help Agencies, Social Security, Tax Information, Wills, and Veteran's Administration.

Advanced Directives

Agency for Health Care Research and Quality (AHRQ) – http://www.ahcpr.gov/research/endliferia/endria.htm - research results of advanced directives, their use, and patient preferences for end of life care.

Aging with Dignity (Five Wishes) – http://www.agingwithdignity.org – goal is to protect the rights of the sick, aging, and dying; promotes the Five Wishes document over the Health Care Power of Attorney

American Association for Retired Persons (AARP) – http://www.aarp.org/research/endoflife/issues - research reports about end of life issues; also leads to other topics related to end of life

American Medical Association (AMA) – http://www.ama-assn.org/ama/pub/patients/patients.shtml; http://www.medem.com/medlib/384 - the first website is a link for patients to find information on various medical issues (click on Patient Medical Library) – the second is a specific link to end of life care and associated concerns.

The Center for Practical Bioethics - http://caringcommunity.org/links/midbiolinks - a 20 year history of raising and responding to ethical issues in health and healthcare and works specifically in Clinical and Organizational Ethics, Aging and End of Life care, Life Science and Research Ethics, Disparities in Health and Healthcare.

Last Acts Partnership – http://www.caringinfo.org - Caring Connections, a program of the <u>National Hospice and Palliative Care Organization (NHPCO)</u>, is a national consumer and community engagement initiative to improve care at the end of life, supported by a grant from The Robert Wood Johnson Foundation; includes information about advanced directives, dying, grief, caregiving, legal issues, and planning, etc.

The President's Council on Bioethics - http://www.bioethics.gov/topics/end_of_life_index.html (home page = http://www.bioethics.gov/ - reports on issues relating to advanced directives, end of life, human dignity, death, bioethics, and other topics of health interest.

Adult Protective Services (example)

New Mexico Adult Protective Services - http://www.nmaging.state.nm.us/Adult_Protective_Services_Division.html - Each state has its own website related to Adult Protective Services, who investigate elder abuse or neglect and protect seniors through placement. In New Mexico, this service falls under the New Mexico Aging and Long-Term Care Services department. Other included departments on this website are aging network, consumer and elder rights, elderly and disability services, Indian elder affairs, and links to related websites. Other state websites may be found by searching for "adult protective services," "aging," "aging and adult services," "elder services," elder rights."

Advocacy

Center for Medicare Advocacy – http://www.medicareadvocacy.org - The Center for Medicare Advocacy works to advance fair access to comprehensive Medicare coverage and quality health care for older people and people with disabilities by providing the highest quality analysis, education and advocacy. Offers news items, articles on health topics, and publications related to Medicare issues. Weekly newsletter available.

Families USA – http://www.familiesusa.org - Families USA is a national nonprofit, non-partisan organization dedicated to the achievement of high-quality, affordable health care for all Americans. Working at the national, state, and community levels, Families USA has earned a national reputation as an effective voice for health care consumers for 25 years. Offers information about health insurance issues and articles related to insurance issues.

Aging/Senior Citizens Websites

Alliance for Aging Research – http://www.agingresearch.org – The Alliance for Aging Research is "dedicated to supporting and accelerating the pace of medical discoveries to vastly improve the universal human experience of aging and health." Website contains news, topics and publications relating to aging, as well as tools and education for healthy aging.

American Association for Retired Persons (AARP) – http://www.aarp.org – website addresses health, money, leisure, family, and community issues for the retired person. Their magazine may be found at http://www.aarpmagazine.org and lists a search feature to see prior articles relating to any issue.

Americans for Better Care of the Dying – http://www.abcd-caring.org This organization focuses efforts on fundamental reforms related to dying such as, improved pain management, better financial reimbursement systems, enhanced continuity of care, support for family caregivers, and changes in public policy.

American Medical Association Patient Page - http://www.ama-assn.org/ama/pub/patients/patients.shtml - health care resource and patient library for consumers resourced by the AMA.

American Society on Aging – http://www.asaging.org - Resources, publications, and educational opportunities are geared to enhance the knowledge and skills of people working with older adults and their families.

The Center for Aging Services Technologies (CAST) http://www.agingtech.org/index.aspx Working to expedite the development, evaluation and adoption of emerging technologies that can improve the aging experience.

Children of Aging Parents – http://www.caps4caregivers.org - Children of Aging Parents is a nonprofit, charitable organization whose mission is to assist the nation's nearly 54 million caregivers of the elderly or chronically ill with reliable information, referrals and support, and to heighten public awareness that the health of the family caregivers is essential to ensure quality care of the nation's growing elderly population. Includes links to a few state support group meetings and information about caregiving.

ElderNet – http://www.eldernet.com - A seniors' guide to health, housing, legal, financial, retirement, lifestyles, news and entertainment information on the World Wide Web. Their health site http://www.eldernet.com/health.htm contains specific information about health, caregiving, long term care, specific illnesses, and other topics.

ElderWeb – http://www.elderweb.com – a website for seniors including information on aging, diseases, end-of-life, long term care, elder law, and other topics.

Help Guide – http://www.helpguide.org – Help Guide is a website dedicated to helping people understand life's challenges by providing helpful information. In addition to seniors and aging, other sections include mental and emotional health, family and relationships, and healthy living.

Journey to Wellness - http://www.journeytowellness.com - JourneyToWellness.com is an award winning, online health magazine for African-Americans, providing current and credible information about Black health and wellness, including topics such as diabetes, heart disease, HIV/AIDS, cancer, asthma, obesity and high blood pressure. Journey to Wellness recognizes the importance of the relationship between a healthy mind and body and the need to focus on faith and wellness. The articles and webcasts on this website are interesting for all readers.

National Institute on Aging (http://www.nia.nih.gov) – National government website with information on elder health and research.

SeniorNet – http://www.seniornet.org - SeniorNet's mission is to provide older adults education for and access to computer technologies to enhance their lives and enable them to share their knowledge and wisdom. Requires membership.

United States Administration on Aging – http://www.aoa.gov - Site contains a wide array of information on older persons and services for the elderly. Several resource rooms focusing on such topics as Alzheimer's Disease and caregiving are available.

United States Government for Seniors – http://www.usa.gov/topics/seniors.shtml - This site helps users access all government sites that provide services for senior citizens.

Alzheimer's

The Alzheimer Disease Research Center – http://www.alzheimer.wustl.edu – links to the Alzheimer's and dementia research center at Washington University School of Medicine in St. Louis, Missouri. Offers newsletters and fact sheets related to alzheimer's and dementia.

Alzheimer's Disease Education and Referral Center (ADEAR Center) – http://www.alzheimers. org - a current, comprehensive, unbiased source of information about Alzheimer's Disease. The ADEAR Center is operated as a service of the National Institute on Aging.

Alzheimer's Organization - http://www.alz.org – the National Site for alzheimer's disease

WebMD - http://www.webmd.com/alzheimers/default.htm - An alzheimer's disease center with news, videos, symptoms, diagnosis, treatment, living with and managing the disease, support and resource links. Also has information about related issues including caregiving, dementia, long-term care, has question and answer section, and offers the ability to talk with others about alzheimer's disease.

Assisted Living

Assisted Living Federation of America – http://www.alfa.org - The Assisted Living Federation of America (ALFA) is the largest national association exclusively dedicated to professionally operated assisted living communities for seniors. ALFA's member-driven programs promote business and operational excellence through national conferences, research, publications, and executive networks. ALFA works to influence public policy by advocating for informed choice, quality care, and accessibility for all Americans. Visitors to the website may sign up for their Friends and Family newsletter, related to assisted living issues.

Cancer

American Cancer Society – http://www.cancer.org – National cancer site – includes information about caregiving, specific cancer topics, and resources

Cancer Information Service – http://www.cis.nci.nih.gov – a program of the National Cancer Institute (NCI), provides the latest and most accurate cancer information to patients, their families, the public, and health professionals.

Cancer Care, Inc. – http://www.cancercare.org - Cancer*Care* is a national nonprofit organization that provides free, professional support services for anyone affected by cancer.

Caregiving

Empowering Caregivers - http://www.care-givers.com - The Empowering Caregivers site is under the umbrella of National Organization For Empowering Caregivers

Caregivers - http://www.nofec.org - a 501(c)(3) Charitable Non Profit Organization. The site provides an opportunity to look at many of the issues you, as a caregiver may experience or are already experiencing in your time of need.

CareGivers Directory – www.caregiversdirectory.com – a resource center for caregivers or prospective caregivers.

http://www.caregiving.com – Stories about caregiving, including personal stories; offers links for caregiving information.

Caring Road – http://www.caringroad.com - The CaringRoad Support Network is an online caregiving support website that will help you meet other family caregivers who understand and empathize with how difficult it is to sustain this important role. You can base your search on the illness that you are dealing with, your relationship to the person that you are caring for or your geographical location. Based on the information you provide, this unique database will generate a list of other family caregivers in similar situations.

Elder Independence of Maine – www.elderindependence.org – a Home Care coordination agency for Maine that also offers information about long term care and caregiving.

Eldercare Locator - http://www.eldercare.gov - a public service of the U.S. Administration on Aging. The Eldercare Locator assists in finding local agencies, in every U.S. community, that can help older persons and their families access home and community-based services like transportation, meals, home care, and caregiver support services. Offers links to fact sheets and federal websites.

National Alliance for Caregiving - http://www.caregiver.org - a non-profit coalition of national organizations focusing on issues of family caregiving. Alliance members include grassroots organizations, professional associations, service organizations, disease-specific organizations, a government agency, and corporations.

National Council on the Aging, Inc. – http://www.ncoa.org - NCOA is a national voice for older adults – especially those who are vulnerable and disadvantaged -- and the community organizations that serve them. NCOA brings together non-profit organizations, businesses and government to develop creative solutions that improve the lives of all older adults. NCOA works with thousands of organizations across the country to help seniors live independently, find jobs and benefits, improve their health, live independently and remain active in their communities

National Family Caregivers Association – http://www.nfcacares.org - The National Family Caregivers Association educates, supports, empowers and speaks up for the more than 50 million Americans who care for loved ones with a chronic illness or disability or the frailties of old age. NFCA reaches across the boundaries of diagnoses, relationships and life stages to help transform family caregivers' lives by removing barriers to health and well being.

Rosalynn Carter Institute for Caregiving – http://www.rosalynncarter.org - The Rosalynn Carter Institute establishes local, state and national partnerships committed to building quality long-term, home and community- based services. The Institute believes in supporting caregiver health, skills and resilience. The Institute also believes in recognition and support for professional and family caregivers. The Rosalynn Carter Institute offers audio library training sessions for caregivers and their families.

Tad Publishing Company – 847-823-0639 – Monthly newsletter for caregivers

Utah coalition for Caregiver Support - http://www.caregivers.utah.gov/index.htm - provides statewide support for caregivers including finding a caregiver, caregiver support, and other topics. This website is the source of the caregiver contract shown in the book at http://www.caregivers.utah.gov/sample_contract.htm.

Driving Safety

American Society on Aging - http://www.asaging.org/cdc/index.cfm - a health promotion and disease prevention site for seniors – also includes modules on driving - http://www.asaging.org/cdc/module4/home.cfm

Dying

Compassion and Choices - http://www.compassionandchoices.org - Compassion & Choices, a nonprofit organization, improves care and expands choice at the end of life through support, education, and advocacy.

Elisabeth Kübler-Ross Foundation – http://www.EKRFoundation.org – education about death, dying, and end-of-life care to continue Dr. Kübler-Ross's teachings.

Growth House, Inc. – http://www.growthhouse.org – Their primary mission is to improve the quality of compassionate care for people who are dying through public education and global professional collaboration.

National Cancer Institute - http://www.cancer.gov/cancertopics/factsheet/support/end-of-life-care - Fact Sheet about dying and the end of life.

National Institutes of Health - http://www.nlm.nih.gov/medlineplus/endoflifeissues.html - issues and links associated with end of life.

Emergency Care

Emergency Care For You – www.emergencycareforyou.org – sponsored by the American College of Emergency Physicians – offers information about emergency care and how to be prepared.

Facilities

American Association for Homes and Services for the Aging – http://www.aahsa.org – provides a consumer page with fact sheets about aging; offers a search site for professional care settings (independent living, assisted living, long-term-care etc. that are members of AAHSA by name, city, state, zip code.

Funeral

Funeral Consumers Alliance – http://www.funerals.org – Funeral Consumers Alliance is a nonprofit organization dedicated to protecting a consumer's right to choose a meaningful, dignified, affordable funeral. Offers information and articles to consumers about funeral planning.

Funerals: A Consumer's Guide – http://www.ftc.gov/bcp/conline/pubs/services/funeral.htm

Federal Trade Commission - http://www.ftc.gov/bcp/conline/edcams/funerals/ - lists consumer rights related to funerals. http://www.ftc.gov/bcp/edu/pubs/consumer/products/pro26.pdf - a document produced by the FTC that discusses consumer rights when buying funeral products.

Grief Support

AARP – http://www.aarp.org/griefandloss - a subsite of AARP – discusses grief issues, legal and financial planning issues related to life after the loss of a loved one.

ElderHope, LLC – http://www.elderhope.com – a website offering support for caregivers; requires a log in ID and password.

Hospice Foundation of America – http://www.hospicefoundation.org – exists to help those who cope personally or professionally with terminal illness, death, and the process of grief and bereavement.

Health/Disease

Food & Drug Administration for Seniors – http://www.fda.gov/oc/seniors - FDA has numerous articles, brochures and other publications with information for older people on a wide range of health issues, including arthritis, cancer, health fraud, and nutrition.

Healthfinder – http://www.healthfinder.gov - Provides links to selected online publications, clearinghouses, databases, websites and support and self-help groups, as well as government agencies and nonprofit organizations for seniors and others.

National Institutes of Health for Seniors – http://www.nihseniorhealth.gov - Site provides aging-related health information easily accessible for adults 60 and over.

NetWellness – http://www.netwellness.org – offers consumer health information sponsored by three Ohio universities.

Rxlist – http://www.rxlist.com – website that offers information by drug name; information includes the chemical description of the drug, indications and dosage, side effects and drug interactions, warnings and precautions, overdosage and contraindications, clinical pharmacology, patient and consumer information

Home Care

Visiting Angels - http://www.visitingangels.com/ - A care network of non-medical, private duty home care agencies providing senior care, elder care, personal care, respite care and companion care to help the elderly and adults continue to live in their homes across America. Provides in-home alternatives to institutional care.

Hospice

American Academy of Hospice and Palliative Medicine – http://www.aahpm.org/education/patienteducation.html - patient education about hospice, palliative care, pain, end of life issues.

American Hospice Foundation – http://www.americanhospice.org – offers care and support for dying and grieving people of all ages; offers articles, publications, and workshops.

Hospice Foundation of America – http://www.hospicefoundation.org – exists to help those who cope personally or professionally with terminal illness, death, and the process of grief and bereavement.

Hospice Education Institute - http://www.hospiceworld.org/organization.htm - offers a computerized database and links to hospice and palliative care programs; also provides information for patients and caregivers as well as a forum to discuss personal situations (does not provide counseling).

National Hospice Foundation – http://www.hospiceinfo.org –

National Hospice and Palliative Care Organization – http://www.caringinfo.org – sponsored by NHPCO – national consumer and community initiative to improve care at the end of life; discusses planning, caregiving, being ill, and suffering a loss.

Incontinence

National Association for Continence – http://www.nafc.org – information about bladder and bowel health

Law

National Academy of Elder Law Attorneys, Inc. – http://www.naela.com - The National Academy of Elder Law Attorneys, Inc. is a non-profit association that assists lawyers, bar organizations and others who work with older clients and their families. The Academy provides a resource of information, education, networking and assistance to those who deal with the many specialized issues involved with legal services to seniors and people with special needs.

National Center for State Courts - http://www.ncsconline.org/ - provides a link to court web sites around the country, including state court structure sites. The New Mexico State Court website is: http://www.nmcourts.gov, which includes a case lookup link. Cases may be looked up by name.

National Senior Citizens Law Center – http://www.nsclc.org – a senior citizen advocacy group – offers publications about long term care, medicare, and Medicaid.

Senior Law – http://www.seniorlaw.com – offers information about elder law, Medicare, Medicaid, Medicaid planning, guardianship, estate planning, trusts and the rights of the elderly and disabled.

Medical Alert Systems

Lifeline - http://www.lifelinesystems.com – medical alert service for consumers

Medic Alert – http://www.medicalert.org – offers products including the well known medical alert bracelets and watches that alert emergency personnel to specific conditions; also offers a 24 hour emergency response service.

Mobility – Scooters, Wheelchairs – the websites below offer various solutions for patient transportation including scooters, wheelchairs, electric chairs, shower chairs, etc.

http://www.assistivelivingmobility.com

http://richardhernandez.vox.com/

http://www.thewheelchairsite.com/

http://www.thescooterstore.com/

Nursing Homes

National Citizens' Consumer Voice for Quality Long-Term Care – http://www.nccnhr.org – provides consumer education and fact sheets about long-term care: resources, insurance, getting quality care, patient rights, and family involvement; also lists state ombudsmen.

Nursing Home Compare – http://www.medicare.gov/nhcompare.home.asp - The primary purpose of this tool is to provide detailed information about the past performance of every Medicare and Medicaid certified nursing home in the country.

Organ Donation

Donate Life - www.donatelife.net – a national website dedicated to organ donation and increasing the number of organ and tissue donors in the United States. Gives links to state donation programs.

International Institute for the Advancement of Medicine – www.iiam.org – the recovery network for the acquisition of donated human tissue for research and education.

New Mexico - www.nmdonor.com – the organ donation site for New Mexico

Pain

American Academy of Pain Medicine - http://www.painmed.org/patient/index.html - professional organization dedicated to the diagnosis and management of pain patient webpage

American Pain Foundation – http://www.painfoundation.org/ - a resource center for patients with pain; offers publications, links for assistance and support, as well as specific topic information.

National Hospice and Palliative Care Organization – http://www.nhpco.org/i4a/pages/index.cfm?pageid=3254&openpage=3254 – patient resource website regarding hospice and end of life issues

Partners Against Pain - http://www.partnersagainstpain.com/ - a website for professionals, patients, and caregivers – shows information about pain standards, e.g., pain scales, information about pain advocacy, and pain resources.

Pastoral Care

American Association of Pastoral Counselors – http://www.aapc.org/content/find-counselor - find a pastoral care counselor.

Physicians

National Association of Professional Geriatric Care Managers – http://www.caremanager.org – dedicated to information for professionals who care for the elderly – has a search engine to find a geriatric care manager as well as pertinent articles.

Prescription Drugs

Medicare Prescription Drug Program – http://www.medicare.gov/assistanceprograms.home.asp - his section of the Medicare.gov website provides information on public and private programs that offer discounted or free medication, programs that provide assistance with other health care costs, and Medicare health plans that include prescription coverage.

Senior Help Agencies

Senior Corps – http://www.seniorcorps.org - Senior Corps is a network of programs that tap the experience, skills, and talents of older citizens to meet community challenges. Through its three programs – Foster Grandparents, Senior Companions, and RSVP (the Retired and Senior Volunteer Program).

Social Security

Social Security – http://www.ssa.gov - The Social Security Administration toll-free number operates from 7AM to 7PM, Monday to Friday. Recorded information and services are available 24 hours a day. The website contains a wealth of information and resources including on-line databases and publications.

Tax Information

Employer's Supplemental Tax Guide - http://www.irs.gov/pub/irs-pdf/p15a.pdf

Self-Employed Tax Information - http://www.irs.gov/businesses/small

Wills

Nolo - http://www.nolo.com/resource.cfm/catID/FD1795A9-8049-422C-9087838F86A2BC2B/309/ - information about all legal aspects of will and estate planning

Veterans Administration (VA)

Veterans Administration – http://www.va.gov – information about benefits and services provided by the VA

Glossary

Activities of Daily Living (ADLs) – Basic: normal everyday activities that we perform for ourselves, e.g., bathing, dressing, eating, moving from a bed to a chair, toileting, walking.
>   Instrumental ADLs: activities not necessary for daily functioning, but allow an adult to live independently – light housekeeping, meal preparation, dispensing and taking medications; shopping, managing money, using the telephone.

Adult Protective Services (APS) – a state organization that protects adults from abuse, exploitation, or neglect and investigates such cases. May offer Adult Day Care to assist elders with Activities of Daily Living.

Advanced directives – a legal document that states one's wishes for health care treatments if that person is unable to make medical directives. This document may also express health care treatments based upon the level of illness.

Alveoli – Balloon-like structures at the ends of bronchial tubes in the lungs; inflate and deflate with each breath; emphysema damages the alveoli and causes problems with breathing out so there is only a little room to breath in with the following breath.

Alzheimer's Disease – a progressive and fatal brain disease that destroys brain cells and linkages between neural pathways; the most common type of dementia; incidence is 50% after age 85; by 2010, the number of new cases is expected to increase to 454,000 per year.

Apraxia – a neurological disorder which affects the ability to execute or carry out learned purposeful movements, despite having the desire and ability to do so.

Anesthesia, general – Inhalation, injection or intravenous (IV) administration of anesthetic types of drugs (or a combination of these routes), which cause unconsciousness and absence of pain sensation over the entire body.

Anesthesia, local - Injection or intravenous (IV) administration of anesthetic types of drugs, which cause unconsciousness and absence of pain sensation to a specific area of the body.

Aricept – a medication used in mild to moderate Alzheimer's disease. Both my Mom and Dad were taking this drug. It had a great effect on Dad, but did not seem to help Mom's vascular dementia. We were advised, however, to continue Mom's Aricept, as discontinuing it might cause other problems.

Assisted Living – a type of retirement care facility in which the residents can receive additional daily assistance for the Activities of Daily Living (ADLs), such as bathing, dressing, or taking medication.

Ativan – a type of tranquilizer used to treat anxiety, tension, or insomnia; also called Lorazepam.

Background Checks – an investigation into a prospective employee's (such as a caregiver) background to ensure that this person does not have any criminal record or legal problems with finances (such as fraud). Background checks and past employment may be performed by private companies.

Cannula – a flexible, plastic tube; e.g., used in patients receiving oxygen to connect the source of the oxygen to a tubing that fits around the face and ears, with a small nose piece that inserts into the nose to receive the oxygen. Also, a term for tubing to drain fluids from the body or to insert medications into the body.

Capillary (ies) – tiny blood vessels running throughout the body connecting arteries and veins. Capillaries distribute oxygen and nutrients to the cells and remove waste products.

Cardiopulmonary Resuscitation (CPR) – a procedure that maintains breathing (oxygen) and blood circulation to a person who has stopped breathing and/or whose heart has stopped beating.

Chronic Obstructive Pulmonary Disease (COPD) – a chronic lung disease caused by bronchitis or emphysema, in which breathing becomes slow or forced.

Comfort Kit – a small box of medications used by Hospice personnel for treatment of pain, anxiety, or restlessness; eliminates a midnight trip to the pharmacy as medications are already in the home; administration of the medications are done by the family member or caregiver under the direction of the Hospice nurse on call.

Continuing Care – a type of retirement home that offers continuous care for seniors from independent living to full time nursing care; seniors are allowed to stay in the facility until death and do not have to move to any other facility for higher levels of care.

Continuum of Care – the full spectrum of facility type care from independent living to assisted living to nursing home, including rehabilitation care; care is provided from the time the senior enters the facility until they die; following an hospitalization, a senior would be able to return to the same facility for rehabilitative care until able to return to their prior room/level of care.

Do Not Resuscitate (DNR) - a legal form that is completed between the patient and the doctor, stating that the patient is not to be resuscitated should a cardiac or respiratory arrest occur.

Doppler Scan – an ultrasonic scan that measures blood flow via light or sound waves; particularly useful in detecting arterial disease and blood clots.

Draw Sheet – a draw sheet is folded and placed across the width of the bed, above the bottom sheet and under the patient. Caregivers can easily turn a bedridden patient by rolling up the sides of the draw sheet and lifting, turning, or sliding the patient in the bed. The sheets can be changed using this method, as well.

Docusate – an over-the-counter stool softener that retains water in the stool; can be used with Senna.

DynOmite – a mixture of prune juice and Milk of Magnesia used when constipation becomes a problem; we used it if a bowel movement had not occurred for three days. See Caregiving Chapter.

Durable Power of Attorney – a legal document in which a person can appoint another person to act for the 1st person with regards to any legal, financial, or any stipulated matter if the 1st person becomes unable to do so. The document can specify exact limits and may be conferred for one transaction or until the 1st person dies. The Durable Power of Attorney becomes invalid at death.

Emergency Medical Response (EMR) – the ambulance/fire teams that respond to a 911 or emergent call at any location.

Emphysema – a chronic long term respiratory disease in which the alveoli and capillaries supplying the lung tissue collapse and become destroyed over time. The outward manifestation of this disease is shortness of breath. In the United States, this disease is primarily due to long-term cigarette smoking.

Five Wishes – a national document that addresses how one wishes to be treated during the dying process; once signed meets the legal requirements for advanced directives; addresses comfort care, spirituality, forgiveness, and final wishes.

Gerontologist – a medical doctor trained in the scientific study of the biological, psychological, and sociological processes associated with old age and aging.

Haldol – known as haloperidol – a very strong tranquilizer generally used in the treatment of psychotic, schizophrenic, or Tourette's diseases; however, may be used under Hospice direction to calm anxious patients or to help them sleep.

Handicapped Placards – placards authorizing the use of handicapped parking spaces that may be obtained from the Department of Motor Vehicles (DMV); the state DMV form is obtained and signed by the patient's primary care physician; the form is taken back to DMV for the handicapped placard. Placards may be permanent or temporary and are dated or color-coded as such.

Health Care Power of Attorney – a legal document in which a person can appoint another person to act for the 1st person regarding healthcare decisions if the 1st person becomes unable to do so. Decisions include whether to use life support measures such as artificial breathing machines, feeding tubes, etc. May also be named Medical Power of Attorney (MPOA)

Health History – A summary of one's health including current health condition, current diagnoses (such as diabetes, heart disease, cancer), medications, past surgeries, pregnancies (if female), diet and exercise, alcohol consumption, primary care physician, medical record number, date of birth.

Hospice - a team based approach to patient care that offers support to both the patient and the family; generally used for patients with terminal illnesses. Hospice care is designed as comfort care or palliative care and does not provide proactive care. Palliative or comfort care includes pain management, depression care, weekly vital signs and nurse visit, aide for ADL assistance, and other assistance as required. See Types of Homes chapter.

Incontinence – loss of voluntary control over excretory functions, such as urine and bowel functions.

Independent Living – a type of retirement community that allows independent living such as an apartment or townhouse, but offers community living resources, such as dining hall, social activities, beauty/barber shop, library, etc.

Inhaler – a device containing medications to ease breathing difficulties; device is put in mouth and medication is dispensed upon inhalation.

International Institute for the Advancement of Medicine (IIAM) – a link between tissue/body parts donors and scientific research and education; http://www.iiam.org

Intensive Care Unit (ICU) – an advanced ward in a hospital that provides the highest level of medical care through life support, monitoring equipment, and specialized staff.

Intubation – the insertion of a tube into the body, e.g., a breathing or feeding tube into the lungs/stomach.

Letters Testamentary – a legal document issued by the court to appoint and empower the executor of an estate to carry out the appointed responsibility of fair and equitable dispersement of the estate. See Personal Representative

Licensed Home Care – home care provided by a licensed agency; caregivers operate under the rules of the agency; the patient pays the agency directly.

Life support – techniques and equipment used to maintain airway, breathing, and circulation following a cardiac arrest or respiratory failure.

Long term care insurance – an insurance that provides monetary assistance for assisted living or nursing home care; charges for long term care insurance are usually paid once per year and may vary widely depending on insurance company and state of residence.

Lorazepam – see Ativan

Magnetic Resonance Imaging (MRI) – a type of medical imaging technology used to see images of soft tissues and organs within the body; the equipment uses strong magnets and radio waves to create the images. Patients with artificial implants containing metal will not be able to have MRIs, e.g., pacemaker, knee or hip replacement, screws holding together bones, metal clips used in internal surgery, etc.

Medical Advocate – a family member or trusted person who accompanies a patient to doctor's appointments, is there during hospitalizations, whose purpose is to assist families and patient in understanding what care is being provided, for what reasons, what the prognosis (outcome) is, to watch medications given, to watch for changes in the patient's condition, and to report or question any concerns to/of the family.

Medical Alert – a bracelet identifying a health condition OR an alarm system in the home that signals a response team to call for emergency help; signal is triggered by pressing a button on a wrist band or pendant.

Medi-Gap – the health care insurance that assists in paying for health care expenses not paid for by Medicare; in New Mexico, the patient signs up with a local hospital for health care – their Medicare premium is paid directly to the hospital; the patient may also have to pay a premium to the hospital. This premium could be based upon the amount of prescriptions required.

Mini-Mental State Examination (MMSE) – a questionnaire administered by a licensed health care person or neurologist to assess the mental status of a patient; score of exam can be used to determine Alzheimer's Disease.

Namenda - a medication used to treat mental confusion, forgetfulness, and disturbance of short term memory in Alzheimer's disease and dementia.

Neurologist – a medical doctor skilled in the treatment of nerve and brain related diseases, including dementia type diseases.

Nursing Home Living – a health care facility that provides long term care for the elderly or chronically ill; the level of care is higher than other types of care and goes beyond that of assisting the patient in taking care of themselves.

Office of the Medical Examiner (OMI) – the Office of the Medical Examiner investigates any death that is sudden, violent, untimely, unexpected, or in which the cause of death in unknown.

Ombudsman – one who investigates complaints and mediates settlements between a consumer and the long term care institution that is involved; in long term care health care settings, the ombudsman provides advocacy and assistance to residents of these types health care facilities.

Palliative Care – care that is provided to terminally ill patients without providing a cure for the disease, e.g., pain management, medication, comfort care. See Hospice section of Types of Homes.

Patient Self-Determination Act (PSDA) – requires inpatient health care facilities to give the patient information about the right to participate in and direct their own health care decisions, the right to accept of refuse medical or surgical treatment, the right to prepare an advance directive; and information on the facility policies that govern these rights.

Personal Representative – an individual who has been entrusted to manage another's personal property and money; upon death, this person would be required to administer the contents of the estate, including settling of debts and the distribution of assets. See Letters Testamentary.

Primary Care Provider – a medical doctor specializing in family practice or internal medicine who has the primary responsibility for medical care of patients; the primary care provider will refer patients to specialists as needed.

Pulmonologist – a medical doctor specialist for the field of pulmonology – diseases of the respiratory system.

Rehabilitative Care – a care wing responsible for "rehabilitating" or returning a patient to independent care following a medical or surgical inpatient admission; treatment could assist with activities of daily living or physical therapy.

Respite Care – care given to a patient by a family member, volunteer, or hospice related facility for a period of hours, days, or 1-2 weeks to provide a break for the main caregiver.

Rhinocort – a nasal inhaler used to reduce inflammation and manage allergic rhinitis symptoms

Senna – a laxative medication used to relieve constipation. Senna may be used in combination with Docusate.

Serevent – a long-active beta-agonist, administered with an inhaler, that relieves bronchospasms; is also used as a maintenance treatment for asthma and exercise-induced bronchospasm.

Step-down unit – a term for a hospital wing that provides care at a level lower than an intensive care unit, but at a higher level than a normal level of care wing.

Stroke – the sudden death of brain cells in a localized area due to inadequate blood flow; the severity of the stroke will depend on how long the blood flow is interrupted and which part of the brain is affected.

Sundowner's Syndrome – Sundowner's Syndrome usually occurs in the late afternoon around dusk (hence the name) in patients with dementia; Sundowner's Syndrome may be detected by increased confusion, anxiety, agitation or disorientation. The patient may be tired or have a disturbed sleep cycle. Watch to see if a particular room in the house triggers the Sundowner's Syndrome; if so, try a new sleeping arrangement in a different room. Keep the patient active during the day so they are more likely to sleep better at night.

Transient Ischemic Attack (TIA) – typically known as mini-strokes; a blood clot or spasm of a blood vessel can interrupt blood flow to the brain for a few seconds or longer. However, damage does not usually occur and once the TIA is complete, the patient will again seem normal. During the TIA, stroke-like symptoms of weakness or garbled speech may occur, if the TIA lasts long enough. Any evidence of TIA should be a warning sign for the possibility of a larger stroke occurring in the future.

Vascular Dementia – also known as multi-infarct dementia, is a common form of dementia in older persons that is due to cerebrovascular disease, e.g., recurrent TIA's that may eventually cause enough damage to affect neurologic functions.

Ventilator – a breathing machine that automatically breathes for a patient, allowing oxygen in and releasing carbon dioxide. See Life Support.

Bibliography

1. American Medical Association. "Guide to Home Caregiving," Angella Perry, M.D., Editor. John Wiley & Sons, Inc., New York, NY, 2001.

2. Callanan, Maggie & Kelley, Patricia. "Final Gifts," Bantam Books, New York, NY, 1997.

3. Cherry, Reginald, M.D. "Healing Prayer," Thomson Nelson Publishers, Nashville, TN, 1999.

4. Cohen, Donna, Ph.D. and Eisdorfer, Carl, Ph.D., M.D. "The Loss of Self," W. W. Norton & Company, New York, NY, 2001.

5. Delehanty, Hugh and Ginzler, Elinor. "Caring for your Parents: The Complete Family Guide." Sterling Publishing Co., Inc. & AARP, New York, NY, 2005.

6. Grote, William J. "Helping Your Aging Parent: A Step-by-Step Guide." Boomer Books, Vista, CA., 2002.

7. Haley, James, Ed. "Death and Dying: Opposing Viewpoints," Greenhaven Press, Farmington Hills, MI, 2003.

8. Higley, Connie and Alan. "Reference Guide for Essential Oils," 9th Ed., Abundant Health, Spanish Fork, UT, 2005.

9. Kaplan, Karen Orloff, M.P.H., Sc.D. and Lukas, Christopher. "Staying in Charge: Practical Plans for the End of Your Life," John Wiley & Sons, Hoboken, NJ, 2004.

10. Kaufman, Sharon R. "…And A Time to Die: How American Hospitals Shape the End of Life," A Lisa Drew Book/Scribner, New York, NY, 2005.

11. Mace, Nancy L., M.A. and Rabins, Peter V., M.D. "The 36-Hour Day," 3rd Ed., The Johns Hopkins University Press, Baltimore and London, 1999.

12. Linda Rhodes, Ed.D. "Caregiving As Your Parents Age: The Complete guide to Helping Your Parents Age Gracefully, Happily, and Healthfully." New American Library, New York, NY, 2001. (Previously published as "The Complete Idiot's Guide© to Caring for Aging Parents)

13. Rhodes, Linda Colvin, Ed.D. "The Complete Idiot's Guide© to Caring for Aging Parents," Alpha Books, Indianapolis, IN, 2001.

14. Grant, Icor, Adler, Karen A., Patterson, Thomas L., et al. "Health Consequences of Alzheimer's Caregiving Transitions: Effects of Placement and Bereavement. Psychosomatic Medicine 64: 477-486. 2002.

Index

ABOUT THE AUTHOR

Janice Louise Long carried her forty year experience and knowledge of the health care arena home to care for her parents in their remaining years. She applied medical advocacy and systems concepts to the caregiving environment. The author has chaired performance improvement teams in small and large healthcare environments and is passionate about using updated knowledge to achieve improvement in any process.

Janice Louise Long began working in the health care field as a teenager and carried her love of medicine into her professional career, acquiring a Bachelors Degree in Nuclear Medicine. She later earned her Masters in Business Administration. Ms. Long has worked in clinical medicine, research and development, as a technical representative, in marketing, as a statistician, and in systems management for a worldwide health care system. Her most recent expertise was concentrated in performance improvement, disease management, establishment and monitoring of metrics, and metrics report card design.

Ms. Long lives in Albuquerque, New Mexico near her two daughters and three grandchildren. She participates in P.E.O., book clubs, bell and church choir, duplicate bridge, quilting, reading, and volunteers for Hospice and Albuquerque Reads.

DYING THE **RIGHT** WAY: A SYSTEM OF CAREGIVING
AND PLANNING FOR FAMILIES

www.dyingtherightway.com
www.dyingtherightway.blogspot.com
jllong@dyingtherightway.com

The caregiving forms are available individually as downloads on
the author's website, www.dyingtherightway.com. Laminated
copies of the Caregiving Maxims and the Grief poem are available
at a nominal cost, also on the website. Reference books and
articles will also appear on the website.

Please visit my blog site, www.dyingtherightway.blogspot.com, for
discussions and questions.

Personalized forms or new forms may be requested through my
email address: jllong@dyingtherightway.com.

Thank you so very much for your interest in DYING THE RIGHT
WAY: A SYSTEM OF CAREGIVING AND PLANNING FOR
FAMILIES. I wish each of you the very best in your caregiving
journey. I look forward to hearing from you.

Janice Louise Long

BUY A SHARE OF THE FUTURE IN YOUR COMMUNITY

These certificates make great holiday, graduation and birthday gifts that can be personalized with the recipient's name. The cost of one S.H.A.R.E. or one square foot is $54.17. The personalized certificate is suitable for framing and will state the number of shares purchased and the amount of each share, as well as the recipient's name. The home that you participate in "building" will last for many years and will continue to grow in value.

Here is a sample SHARE certificate:

THIS CERTIFIES THAT
YOUR NAME HERE
HAS INVESTED IN A HOME FOR A DESERVING FAMILY

1985-2005
TWENTY YEARS OF BUILDING FUTURES IN OUR
COMMUNITY ONE HOME AT A TIME

1200 SQUARE FOOT HOUSE @ $65,000 = $54.17 PER SQUARE FOOT
This certificate represents a tax deductible donation. It has no cash value.

YES, I WOULD LIKE TO HELP!

I support the work that Habitat for Humanity does and I want to be part of the excitement! As a donor, I will receive periodic updates on your construction activities but, more importantly, I know my gift will help a family in our community realize the dream of homeownership. **I would like to SHARE in your efforts against substandard housing in my community!** *(Please print below)*

PLEASE SEND ME _____ SHARES at $54.17 EACH = $ $_____

In Honor Of: _____

Occasion: *(Circle One)*   *HOLIDAY*   *BIRTHDAY*   *ANNIVERSARY*

     OTHER: _____

Address of Recipient: _____

Gift From: _____ *Donor Address:* _____

Donor Email: _____

I AM ENCLOSING A CHECK FOR $ $_____ PAYABLE TO HABITAT FOR HUMANITY <u>OR</u> PLEASE CHARGE MY VISA OR MASTERCARD *(CIRCLE ONE)*

Card Number _____ Expiration Date: _____

Name as it appears on Credit Card _____ Charge Amount $ _____

Signature _____

Billing Address _____

Telephone # Day _____ Eve _____

PLEASE NOTE: Your contribution is tax-deductible to the fullest extent allowed by law.
Habitat for Humanity • P.O. Box 1443 • Newport News, VA 23601 • 757-596-5553
www.HelpHabitatforHumanity.org

Printed in the USA
CPSIA information can be obtained
at www.ICGtesting.com
JSHW052015140824
68134JS00027B/2476